Creative New Employee Orientation Programs

Creative New Employee Orientation Programs

Best Practices, Creative Ideas, and Activities
for Energizing Your Orientation Program

Doris M. Sims

Boston, Massachusetts   Burr Ridge, Illinois
Dubuque, Iowa   Madison, Wisconsin   New York, New York
San Francisco, California   St. Louis, Missouri

Library of Congress Cataloging-in Publication Data

Creative new employee orientation programs : best practices, creative ideas, and activities for energizing your orientation program / [compiled by] Doris Sims.

    p. cm.

  Includes an index.

  ISBN 0-07-138184-8 (hc.)

  1. Employee orientation. I. Sims, Doris.

HF5549.5.I53 C74 2001

658.3'1242—dc21   2001051334

McGraw-Hill

*A Division of The **McGraw·Hill** Companies*

    5 6 7 8 9 0   BKM / BKM   0 7 6

ISBN-13: 978-0-07-138184-0

ISBN-10: 0-07-138184-8

The sponsoring editor for this book was Richard Narramore. The production supervisor was Elizabeth J. Shannon. It was set in New Baskerville by Inkwell Publishing.

Printed and bound by Bookmart.

This publication is designed to provide accurate and authoritative information in regard to the subject matter covered. It is sold with the understanding that neither the author nor the publisher is engaged in rendering legal, accounting, or other professional service. If legal advice or other expert assistance is required, the services of a competent professional person should be sought.

                                        —From a Declaration of Principles jointly adopted by a Committee of the American Bar Association and a Committee of Publishers

To order multiple copies of this book at a discount, please contact the McGraw-Hill Special Sales Department at 800-842-3075 or 212-904-5427 (2 Penn Plaza, New York, NY 10121-2298).

To ask a question about the book, contact the author, or report a mistake in the text, please write to Richard Narramore, Senior Editor, at richard_narramore@mcgraw-hill.com.

To my husband and best friend Hunter,
in the 20th year of our marriage

Contents in Brief

Complete Contents

PART 4—ORIENTATION FOR NEW MANAGERS

PART 6—ORIENTATION CHECKLISTS AND SURVEYS

PART 7—THE ORIENTATION ORACLE ANSWERS YOUR QUESTIONS

Preface

The new employees you bring into your organization will create, sell, and support your products and services. I see the orientation process as a chance to start employees off on the right track—to build a culture, attitudes, knowledge, and skill sets right from the beginning that will support and grow the company's business.

If you are responsible for orienting new employees, then you are also responsible for first impressions, as well as initial job satisfaction and accelerated new employee productivity. You represent the entire company to each new employee, so your job is critical. The organization has only one chance to create a first impression, and you have been chosen to deliver it.

Yet many companies have hundreds or even thousands of employees coming into their organizations every year without being properly oriented and trained. Many other companies have orientation processes that address the paperwork issues but do not include vital information about the company's products and services, culture, policies, customers, safety issues, and so forth. This book is designed to help those who are responsible for their organizations' orientation processes by providing unique and creative ways to make your own orientation special, memorable, and effective.

In every other aspect of life, we know that preparation increases success. Prospective parents attend childbirth classes, engaged couples go through prenuptial counseling, new college students first visit campuses and then attend orientation programs. Leading companies understand that this concept applies to starting a new job as well, and they capitalize upon the moment to fully prepare the employee to be successful—because successful employees lead to a successful organization.

New employee orientation is the most variable and customized program in the training and development industry. Orientations must be customized to the company's culture, processes, values, procedures, and policies, so most companies develop their own programs. But there aren't as many resources available to assist trainers and human resource employees in this development process as there are for other types of training and development needs. This book is a new resource for people who are creating orientation programs for the first time, and for people who want to enhance and energize existing orientation programs.

This book contains a wide variety of ideas for organizations of any size and shape. There are models and ideas from leading companies, as well as ideas from and for smaller companies, and ideas for companies that have small offices in remote locations. When I've given presentations on new employee orientation, I have noticed that people are interested in benchmarking what others are doing in their orientation programs, and this book allows the reader to do that. It is designed to be a "conference in a book."

People who teach new employee orientation have a special role in the organization. Yes, I know that teaching orientation over and over can sometimes seem tedious; but remember that you are the one person in the company who is creating the first impression for new employees, and you represent the entire organization. Everyone will know you and remember you from the orientation experience.

Work to keep your orientation material fresh by trying new activities, updating the presentations with current information, and remembering that even though you've presented the information many times, it is fresh information for the new employees. They are coming into the company with high hopes, and looking to you for assurance that they made a great decision!

I thank the many contributors who put their time, energy, ideas, and advice in this book. They have provided a wealth of diverse options, so that anyone can find ideas that will work for their organization. I also thank the contributors who connected me to other contributors. A special note of thanks goes to Susan Steinbrecher, whose vast network of friends and colleagues brought several new contributors to this book.

I thank my personal Chief Technology Officer (and husband), Hunter Sims. Hunter assisted many times with computer issues, and faithfully backed up these chapters so I could sleep at night without worrying that my computer would crash and the chapters would be lost.

I thank my son Jeremy, who gave the "Orientation Oracle" a wonderful face and body, and my son Spencer, who kept me going with his hugs and happy outlook on life.

Thanks also go to my parents, Eldon and Marilyn Rebhorn, who listened to me talk about this book weekend after weekend, and provided continuous encouragement and motivation.

Finally, thanks go to our faithful watchcat Meowmi, who kept my lap warm while I was writing, and kept the writing interesting as she occasionally walked on the computer keyboard.

This book is designed to provide ideas, handouts, and tools that you can use immediately on the job. I hope that you will find many uses for these resources, and I encourage you to keep trying new ideas on a frequent basis. While you want to cover consistent objectives in each orientation, you can still try different ways to deliver the message. This keeps the program fresh and interesting for you, the orientation facilitator, and it provides a forum to try new training methods to find those that best suit your style and your organization's needs.

Go forth and orient others!

Doris M. Sims

Creative New Employee Orientation Programs

Part 1
Introduction

Chapter 1

New Trends in Employee Orientation

"Fill Out Section B, Part 1 . . ."

> *New employee orientation is increasingly helping companies to motivate and retain productive, loyal employees.*

How many of us have attended employee orientation programs that consisted mainly of filling out confusing and lengthy forms? When I speak at conferences on the topic of new employee orientation, I pose this question to the group, and I have found that nearly every audience member has had this same type of orientation experience in one job or another. That suggests that this approach is still considered by many companies to be what new employee orientation is all about.

Certainly the accurate and timely completion of payroll and benefit paperwork is critical to ensure that employee needs are met, that employees all have an equal opportunity to select compensation package options, and that all paperwork is completed consistently to ensure compliance with employment law.

But if a company's orientation program stops at that point, tremendous opportunities are missed to build commitment, relationships, productivity, sales potential, and so much more. Rather than viewing new employee orientation as a paperwork session, more and more companies are learning about the power of a well-designed, comprehensive program that works to train and retain employees in a competitive economy.

THE TRADITIONAL PARADIGM—TEDIOUS DATA DUMP AND PAPERWORK

A traditional orientation program often takes place on the first day of employment, or within the first few days or weeks on the job. The traditional program consists of survival information—a virtual data dump (also known as the "fire-hose approach") of procedures and policies presented in a traditional setting, or possibly through a computer-based training (CBT) course.

The new paradigm of new employee orientation recognizes that the employee's support needs do not end as soon as the ink dries on the forms and the employee walks out of the orientation classroom or out of the human resource department door.

THE NEW PARADIGM—A TIMELINE OF TRAINING AND SUPPORT

The new paradigm for orientation programs includes a training and support system that extends beyond the employee's first-day jitters. When Jan Torrisi-Mokwa joined Arthur Andersen in 1997 as the director of human resources, she discovered (from data compiled from a Strategic People Audit) that new employees said they "felt invisible," and that the one-year retention rate of employees in consulting roles was only 40 percent.

Considering the high cost of recruiting and training consultant employees, Torrisi-Mokwa, who is now Global Leader of Career Management at Andersen, created a local employee "Transition Program" that ensures employees feel welcome. One of the components of the Transition Program is a quarterly Welcome Reception (current employees attend the reception as well to welcome the new employees).

Andersen's Transition Program also includes photographs and bios of new employees, which are circulated within the firm to stimulate employees to find common hobbies, restaurants, interests, etc. with their new Andersen peers, and to connect new faces with names. The program follows the employee through their first months on the job, including a 60-day follow-up with a Human Resources member, guided learning experiences, expectation agreements, sponsors, and mentors.

Companies that understand the importance of employee orientation also consider mentoring and formal on-the-job training to be important components of the process. These programs include the traditional paperwork and basic information, but they also include interactive training courses that alternate between presenting industry concepts and explaining company structure and strategy. This approach allows an employee to learn a concept, and then learn how that concept is applied within the company.

Technological advances allow the orientation timeline to start even before the employee's first day on the job. Some companies deliver benefits information and paperwork to the employee's residence prior to the starting date with the company. The information may be accompanied by a videotape or the company's Web address to assist employees in completing their paperwork at home, working with their family members to make benefit decisions prior to their first day of employment. Employees are encouraged to bring completed paperwork or questions with them to the orientation program, where questions are answered, paperwork is gathered, and benefits are highlighted as part of a motivational presentation rather than the traditional presentation. This approach reduces the time spent on paperwork activities during the orientation program.

Using a timeline orientation approach rather than a one-stop, one-time approach also helps employees build relationships with other new employees and with those who teach, coach, and mentor them during the orientation period.

THE NEW PARADIGM—ENERGIZE AND MOTIVATE

There is no reason for new employee orientation to be a series of boring lectures and tedious forms. This book is filled with orientation program designs, games, and activities that engage the employee in the orientation process. These ideas will increase learning as well as increasing the motivational and energy levels of the participants.

Most companies actually celebrate more when employees *leave* the company than when they *arrive*. When a valued employee leaves a company, often the work-group takes the departing employee to lunch or buys a gift to remember the workgroup by. This is certainly a nice way to tell employees how much you appreciate what they did for the company. But why not learn to celebrate and appreciate the value of employees from the start?

Dena Wilson, a member of Southwest Airline's University of People, refers to their program as their "New Hire Celebration," and jazzes the atmosphere with fun music, confetti, and inflatable airplanes![4] Rebecca Harmon of DeRoyal (a provider of medical supply products) offers more ideas in Chapter 9, Twenty Ways to Celebrate New Employees.

Some companies build their orientation programs around a theme, to keep the program interesting and cohesive. The theme can be related to the company's business or to the concept of a starting point, to represent the employee's starting point with the company. DeRoyal's orientation program uses a racehorse theme, adopting the concept of starting out of the gate. All of the program's games, visual aids, and training materials employ this theme.

Even if presentations are the mainstay of an orientation program, there are many creative ways to spice up any presentation. Look for ideas in Chapter 42, If They Snooze, You Lose.

THE NEW PARADIGM—ADDRESSING "NEW JOB REMORSE"

Everyone has experienced buyer's remorse—that worrying, nagging guilt or concern that can occur after making a very large purchase, such as a new car, a piece of furniture, or a house. Many employees experience the same type of emotion when they make the decision to leave one company and join another. We could call it "new job remorse."

An effective new employee orientation program recognizes this emotion and works to create a dynamic, motivational atmosphere that erases employees' doubts and concerns, leaving them confident that they made the right decision. The reality is that our customers are not the only population we must continually sell to; employees must also be initially and continually sold on the benefits of staying with and growing with the company, or they will be wooed elsewhere.

Based on data from fourteen manufacturing industries, researchers Lam and White[1] conclude, "Through a strong HR orientation, companies enjoy a more competent and committed workforce, thus creating a sustainable competitive advantage that rivals will find difficult to surpass."

THE NEW PARADIGM—CREATING A PLANNED CULTURE

Kahunaville Management, Inc., a tropically-infused restaurant chain, focuses its orientation on the culture of the company. Although important restaurant procedures and policies are included in the program, the company's number-one priority in the orientation process is to infuse its fun and customer-service-oriented culture into the mind and heart of every new employee.

Red Lobster includes sections in its orientation program called "Our Compass" (bringing the Red Lobster vision to life) and "Making Wraves" (*wraves* is part of the customer service and crew member vocabulary and philosophy at Red Lobster).

These companies understand that creating and maintaining a planned culture starts on the employee's first day. If this golden opportunity to make a distinct impression is missed, the employee starts to form his or her own impressions based on specific experiences, usually within one department. Every company has a culture and values. The question is, does the company have the culture and values it needs to be successful within its industry and market, or does the company have a culture that was created by accident?

If a company's orientation program does not include discussions and opportunities for employees to learn about the company culture, expectations, norms, and strategic plans, then a critical link in the process of creating a planned culture, with employees aligned with strategic goals, is lost.

New employees want to know what to do, what *not* to do, what to wear, and specific words or phrases that are valued either positively or negatively in the corporation. New employees desire to fit into the culture, avoid embarrassment, and be viewed as successful—and they want to know what is expected of them.

> *New employees are usually unaware of organizational expectations and social norms. Orientation should include information on these "soft skills."*

It is sometimes assumed that organizational expectations and social norms are consistent and universal in all companies, and that people should know them intuitively; but that is simply not the case. This can be verified by looking at even simple differences, such as the variety of dress codes throughout companies in the United States.

An effective orientation program helps new employees feel comfortable and confident by sharing this type of information and ensuring that employees know the strategic goals, and know how they can contribute to achieving those goals. In addition, orientation programs should include phone numbers, contact names, and titles of the company's human resource personnel, so employees know where they can go for help when they need it.

The orientation process should also include a discussion of the company's revenue sources. After all, if employees don't know how the company makes money, how can they help the company make more of it, to increase their own success and the overall success of the company? Some companies also include discussions of their products and services to help increase the size of the sales force by imparting to all employees the knowledge to help the company sell, no matter what position they may officially be in.

THE NEW PARADIGM—EMPLOYEE RETENTION

The jury is in, and the verdict is that an effective new employee orientation program is a measurable asset in the effort to retain talented employees. A study at Corning Glass concluded that employees were 69 percent more likely to remain with the company after three years if they completed a full orientation program.[2]

Troy Van Houten, coordinator of Micron Technology's corporate new employee training program, credits its employee orientation and training programs for the company's lower employee turnover rate. Like many other companies with superior orientation programs, Micron includes more than an initial first-day training. The program, called NET (New Employee Training), includes technical training, safety programs, reaching high performance, and an overview of the company's products and processes.

THE NEW PARADIGM—ACCELERATED PRODUCTIVITY

New employee orientation should be designed to help employees become productive more quickly on the job. A two-year study conducted at Texas Instruments demonstrated that a well-constructed orientation program can directly accelerate productivity in new employees. The results proved that employees who completed the company's comprehensive orientation were able to reach full productivity two months sooner than employees who did not complete the program.[3]

Champion Laboratories, Inc., one of the world's largest suppliers of filters, filtration products, and related services, saw an increase in both productivity and quality after its new orientation program, developed with INTECH Interactive Technologies, was implemented. New hires got up to speed more quickly and produced fewer rejected filters, resulting in lower costs.

THE NEW PARADIGM—SPECIALIZED ORIENTATION FOR SPECIAL EMPLOYEE GROUPS

Some companies provide a more extensive orientation process for recent graduates and college interns, noting that their assimilation into the corporate environment typically takes longer and that they need more support to be successful. Alcatel has a separate orientation training program for its Co-op (college intern) Program. New college graduates attend the general population orientation program, but they also attend additional training designed just for them after they complete the general program.

At Ford Motor Company, all new salaried employees attend REV, a one-week orientation program. REV focuses on developing inspired employees who will be tomorrow's business leaders. Recent graduates attend a multiweek program that includes experiential learning and team-building activities, technical training courses, a dealership assignment, a vehicle development project, and a community service project. The extended program is for technical employees who are primarily in the fields of engineering and manufacturing.

THE NEW PARADIGM—TEAMWORK

I've conducted informal surveys with my audiences during speaking engagements to determine how many people think (in retrospect) that they stayed with a company longer because of the strong friendships and relationships they have built with their coworkers. The large majority of people indicate that coworker relationships and friendships in the workplace have played a major part in their decision to stay with a company.

People spend a large amount of their lives at work, and forming strong and positive relationships with coworkers is critical not only for job satisfaction, retention, and effective teamwork, but also for one's personal happiness. Employers who understand this include activities in the orientation program to foster the forming of employee relationships on the new employees' first day. Many of the games in Part 5, Orientation Games and Activities, are designed to help new employees meet other new employees in the orientation program and to meet veteran employees in the workplace.

THE NEW PARADIGM—LEGAL AND COMPLIANCE ISSUES

Certain topics should be covered with all employees at some point during the orientation process to reduce potential lawsuits, to ensure the safety of employees, and to comply with employee law. It is impossible to provide an all-inclusive list here, because different industries and different geographic regions have different requirements. Topics to be covered include the following:

- Sexual harassment policies and reporting procedures
- Safety/OSHA topics
- Specific industry regulations
- Diversity topics
- Employee Complaint Process
- Actions resulting in immediate termination

The delivery method and timing for this type of information varies by company; some believe it is critical to address these issues up front; others believe these topics can have a "damper" effect on new employees and should be handled separately from the orientation program.

EXERCISE THE POWER OF EFFECTIVE ORIENTATION!

In the year 2000, companies that participated in the ASTD Benchmarking Service spent only 7 percent of their training dollars on new employee orientation—a training program that every employee in the company needs, a program that can provide all of the important values described this chapter.[4]

Fortunately, more companies are starting to recognize the importance and value of this first-impression program on many different levels. They are hiring full-time or part-time orientation facilitators, and even full staffs devoted entirely to the effort of orienting new employees. Watch for, and implement in your own company, the rising power of new employee orientation!

REFERENCES

[1]Lam, L., and White, L. "Human Resource Orientation and Corporate Performance." *Human Resource Development Quarterly* (Winter 1998). No. 4, vol. 9, pp. 351–364.

[2, 3]"Putting Out the Welcome Mat." *Training Magazine* (March 1998) pp. 54–62.

[4]"2000 ASTD State of the Industry Report." [Online] *www.astd.org.*

Chapter 2

A Six-Step Guide to Creating or Updating Your Orientation Program

If you are creating a new orientation program, use this step-by-step approach, with references to ideas in this book, during your program development process. If you are updating an orientation program, review each step here to ensure that each part of your program is running as smoothly as possible. Refer to the other chapters for ideas to enhance your program.

STEP ONE: DEFINING OR REFINING THE NEW EMPLOYEE NOTIFICATION AND SETUP PROCESS

First, you will need to determine if there is currently a process in the company for dealing with the arrival of a new employee—recording the new employee's name, expected work location, and so on. If you are working in a start-up company, for example, this process may not yet be in place.

If you are updating your new employee notification process, check the list presented here to ensure that each department that plays a part in the orientation process is notified of the new employee's arrival in a timely manner, and that each receives all the information needed to complete their task(s).

Schedule a meeting with a representative of each department that will need to know and act when a new employee enters the company. It is amazing how many people it can take to set up a new employee in the organization. Examples of personnel who are part of this process (in addition to the training department) include:

- Benefits personnel (insurance enrollment, 401(k) enrollment, etc.)
- Payroll personnel (payroll setup, direct deposit, W-2 forms, etc.)

- HR/Compliance personnel (I-9 forms and identification verification)

- Information Systems personnel (computers, identification codes, passwords, etc.)

- The intranet Webmaster (if the company keeps an employee phone and e-mail directory online)

- Receptionists (to update their phone listings)

- Administrative assistants (to order office supplies, prepare the workspace, order business cards, update organizational charts, etc.)

- Facilities personnel (to determine where the new employee will sit, to order office furniture if needed, obtain furniture keys, etc.)

- Accounting personnel (to keep head count accounts, payroll accounts, and cost center chargebacks accurate)

- Stock options personnel (to handle the administrative work associated with setting up stock options for new employees)

- Phone system personnel (to bring in a new phone if needed for the new employee, or to set up the phone number and voice mail system to reflect the new employee's name)

- Security personnel (to obtain a temporary or permanent badge, a parking sticker or card, building access keys or cards, etc.)

When you conduct this meeting, use the chart on the following page to determine the information each department needs and when they need it, to obtain feedback regarding how well the process is currently working, and to obtain ideas regarding how the process should work.

THE NEW EMPLOYEE NOTIFICATION PROCESS—A MEETING AID

Who needs to know when a new employee starts?	When do they need to know about the new employee?	What service(s) do/will they provide?	What do they need to know about the employee to provide this service?	Comments regarding how this information is currently obtained, suggestions for improvement.
SAMPLE	**SAMPLE**	**SAMPLE**	**SAMPLE**	**SAMPLE**
Payroll Personnel	When the employee accepts an offer of employment. If payroll doesn't receive notification on Friday before payday, a manual process is required to ensure the employee receives his or her first check on time.	Enter the employee's basic information and compensation data into the payroll system. Set up direct deposit for new employee. Obtain W-2 form information to keep on file and to record in the Enter automated payroll deductions.	1. Name 2. Job title 3. Department 4. Manager's name 5. Work location 6. Phone extensions 7. Home address 8. EEOC code 9. Compensation 10. W-2 Selections 11. Paycheck deductions	Currently, the payroll department receives the employee's basic information and compensation data from the new employee's recruiter, and this is working well. Currently, obtaining completed W-2 paperwork from employees is a manual process and payroll often must follow up with the employee to obtain the W-2, so this is an area that needs improvement.

STEP TWO: CONDUCT A NEEDS ASSESSMENT TO DETERMINE OR REVIEW THE TOPICS AND OBJECTIVES OF YOUR ORIENTATION PROGRAM

Whether you are creating or updating a new employee or management orientation program, it will need to be customized to your company's strategy, culture, values, policies, procedures, expectations, regulations, and processes.

To help you determine the content, delivery methods, timing of the program, and activities to use in your program, review the orientation designs of other companies in Part 3, Program Designs and Case Studies.

Use Chapter 13, The New Employee Orientation Shopping List, or Chapter 24, The Management Orientation Shopping List, to help you during the needs assessment process to determine which topics are applicable to your own company.

When conducting the needs assessment to finalize the content of your program, talk to:

■ Senior managers, to determine what they want new employees to know and to identify content regarding the company culture and strategy to be included in the orientation program.

■ Recently hired employees, to determine what they wish someone had told them when they were hired.

■ Experienced employees and department assistants, to determine the questions they are most frequently asked by new employees.

■ All personnel who are involved in the orientation process (see Step One), to determine what they want new employees to know and the most frequently asked questions from new employees.

■ Supervisors and middle managers, to determine what they want new employees to know.

STEP THREE: IDENTIFY YOUR AUDIENCE(S)

Depending on your company's needs, your budget, and your resources, you may want to develop one general orientation program, or you may want to have additional, specialized programs for:

■ Managers—Refer to Part 4, Orientation for New Managers, for program designs and activities.

■ New college graduates or interns—Refer to Chapter 7, Developing a College Intern Program.

■ Professional, salaried employees—Refer to Chapter 15, The REV Orientation Program.

■ Technical employees—Refer to Chapter 19, Orienting and Retaining a Technical Population.

STEP FOUR: DETERMINE THE DELIVERY METHOD(S) FOR YOUR PROGRAM

There are many different ways to deliver your orientation program, and many companies combine a variety of delivery methods. Some examples of delivery methods are listed here.

1. **Instructor-led, classroom delivery—Refer to these chapters for examples and ideas regarding this delivery option.**

   ■ Chapter 14—Tried-and-True Orientation Design

   ■ Chapter 15—The REV Orientation Program

   ■ Chapter 18—Orientation at Alcatel USA

   ■ Chapter 19—Orienting and Retaining a Technical Population

   ■ Chapter 23—Designing an Annual Residential Orientation Program

   ■ Chapter 20—Wyndham International Beginnings

   ■ Chapter 4—Orientation for a Global Population

   ■ Chapter 12—Using Icebreakers and Games

   ■ Chapter 9—Twenty Ways to Celebrate New Employees

   ■ Chapter 10—Subject Matter Experts As Orientation Speakers

   ■ Chapter 11—Designing Your Own Orientation Board Game

2. **Online or video delivery—Chapters to refer to for examples and ideas regarding this delivery option include:**

   ■ Chapter 17—Case Study: Champion Laboratories, Inc.

   ■ Chapter 3—Moving Your Orientation Program Online

   ■ Chapter 5—Creating a Customized Orientation Video

3. **On-site delivery by managers—Chapters to refer to for examples and ideas regarding this delivery option include:**

   ■ Chapter 21—New Crew Members "Take the Plunge!" at Red Lobster

   ■ Chapter 22—Self-Directed Orientation Modules

   ■ Chapter 6—Employee Orientation for Small Businesses

   ■ Chapter 56—New Employee Checklists—Before, During, and After!

   ■ Chapter 51—A Manager's Checklist: Helping New Employees Succeed

   ■ Chapter 54—New Employee Workstation Survey

4. **On-the-job training programs and buddy systems—Chapters to refer to for examples and ideas regarding this delivery option include:**

   ■ Chapter 8—Designing a Buddy Program

- Chapter—53 I'm New Here—What Should I Learn?
- Chapter—52 Before the Employee's First Day

5. **A train-the-trainer approach—Chapters to refer to for examples and ideas regarding this delivery option include:**
   - Chapter—16 Kahunaville's Pursuit of Wow—POW!
   - Chapter—57 Selecting On-the-Job Trainers

STEP FIVE: IDENTIFY ACTIVITIES AND GAMES, AND DEVELOP VISUAL AIDS FOR YOUR PROGRAM

Review Part 5, Orientation Games and Activities, to find new ways to make your orientation program active and fun as new employees learn.

STEP SIX: CONTINUOUSLY IMPROVE YOUR ORIENTATION PROGRAM

Use Chapter 55, A 90-Day New Employee Survey, to obtain feedback from employees about their orientation experience, now that they've been on the job for a while. Try different ideas from Part 5, Orientation Games and Activities, to add variety to the program. Keep the orientation materials current, and keep yourself energized about the important role you play in creating that crucial first impression with each new employee of your organization.

Read Part 7, The Orientation Oracle Answers Your Questions, to find answers to frequently asked questions about orientation programs. And refer to the appendix, Additional Orientation Resources, if you would like additional help, products, and services for your orientation program.

Part 2

Best Practices in Employee Orientation

Introduction

Would you like advice from the leading new employee orientation consultants? Would you like to hear from internal practitioners about the unique orientation methods they have implemented in their own companies? This chapter provides "best of class" advice and step-by-step instructions to implement the ideas in your own company.

Part 2 provides best-practice ideas and advice in these areas:

- Converting part or all of your orientation program to an online delivery platform
- Developing and delivering orientation programs in different countries and cultures
- Creating an orientation video
- Orientating employees in a small business
- Developing a college intern program
- Designing a buddy program to complement your orientation program
- Celebrating the arrival of new employees into your organization
- Helping subject matter experts deliver effective orientation presentations
- Designing your own orientation board game, customized to your company's culture, products, services, and customers
- Using icebreakers and games effectively in your orientation program

Chapter 3
Moving Your Orientation Program Online

Getting Out of the Classroom

Everyone wants an orientation program that doesn't involve classroom time. Trying to put new hires in one place for orientation is inconvenient and time-consuming, and it is sometimes hard to get buy-in from supervisors.

Everyone is looking for orientation training in which new hires can receive all the instruction they need on their own time, and at their own workstations, desks, or even homes. (Let's call this asynchronous training; it sounds good and impresses budget planners.)

Historically, asynchronous training has involved using videos, PowerPoint presentations, or CD-ROMs. Increasingly, companies are contemplating using intranets, extranets, or other Web-based alternatives.

However, in our experience, well over 90 percent of all attempts at designing and implementing an asynchronous orientation program fail.

Why is this? We receive calls on a daily basis asking for asynchronous orientation, and yet there are only a handful of companies actually doing it successfully.

Here are Seven Steps to successful asynchronous orientation.

1. FOCUS ON THE CONTENT FIRST

Don't start by deciding you "want a CD-ROM," or you "have to have an Intranet solution." Start by deciding on the orientation program *content*.

Get an absolutely clear idea of what you want to say to the new hires. Write it out (*all* of it!) in whatever form you prefer—by hand, word processed, in PowerPoint style, or in HTML format. Gather all the information you need from others, and finish the drafting process first.

This is important for four reasons:

a. Frankly, writing the program content is the hard part. It takes time, hard work, and basic instructional design skills. It's too easy to kid yourself that by opting for a specific delivery platform (such as an intranet), this hard work will somehow melt away and be automatically subsumed into the technical process of actually constructing the intranet. It won't. The folks constructing the intranet site (or producing the CD-ROM, or whatever) cannot write your orientation program for you—you still have to do it.

b. It's the content that counts, not the format. Few people these days are impressed by multimedia presentations of any sort, and they will see through bells and whistles to what's underneath. Make sure what your presentation *says* is great.

c. Sometimes, *what* you want to say dictates *how* it will be said. In my experience, writing the actual content usually gives me a feel for the best delivery platform (face-to-face, CD-ROM, intranet, Internet, video, etc.).

d. If you choose the delivery platform (face-to-face, CD-ROM, intranet, Internet, video, etc.) first, without having decided on the content, you will run up a big budget producing the product. Writing the content first makes the production process easier, and therefore cheaper.

2. CHOOSE A DELIVERY PLATFORM THAT WORKS FOR YOUR COMPANY

Once the content has been written, it's important to deliver the message in a way that's consistent with your company culture. A company with no computers using a Web-based training program is as silly as an Internet company using quill pens (though you'd be surprised to see what many companies do use).

What format are your people using? What tools are available to new hires? If you're going to produce a CD-ROM, does everyone have access to a computer? With a CD-ROM drive? If your chosen platform is an intranet, do 100 percent of your employees have access to the intranet?

If the answer to any of those questions is "No," you're back where you started, having to schedule new hires to be in one place at a particular time, to get access to the appropriate hardware and software.

Similarly, if your supervisors are not fully familiar and comfortable with the platform you choose, the first time a CD-ROM refuses to run or an intranet crashes, you can assume that your orientation program has crashed too. No one will fix it, it will fall into disuse, and all that hard work will be just one more great project listed on your resume.

3. WALK BEFORE YOU RUN

Test, test, test.

If you've got great content (see step 1), it will move easily from one format to another.

Test your program content on a simple, inexpensive platform—say PowerPoint—with one or two new-hire groups before trapping it on your intranet or other expensive platform. If the program doesn't work on this basis, putting it on an intranet won't make it a great program. If the content isn't good enough, you'll end up with an expensive white elephant.

4. USE A DELIVERY PLATFORM THAT'S EASILY UPDATED

I haven't met anyone who's really comfortable with a CD-ROM-based program; they are expensive and both costly and difficult to update (although this is changing with CD-Write technology). Additionally, everyone needs access to a CD-ROM drive on his or her computer to run it, or you need to load it onto a centrally available server.

On the other hand, if you have a centrally available server, a dedicated in-house intranet site can be set up easily and inexpensively, and all anyone needs is a browser. Changes can be made in a snap, and at no cost. This is the solution we most often recommend.

For examples of free intranets, check out this site: http://www.communityzero.com. There are a number of sites like this one, but to my mind this is the best. We use it all the time, and it's free.

5. THERE ISN'T ANY GOOD OFF-THE-SHELF STUFF

Save yourself a lot of time. Any off-the-shelf CD-ROMs and so on that I'm aware of are hokey or embarrassingly poor in quality. Don't bother with them. This isn't necessarily a reflection on the companies that produce them; it's just impossible to deliver a generalized but high-caliber orientation program that's not tailored to a specific company.

6. BUILD YOUR OWN IN THREE WEEKS

Here's a reasonable timeline, based on our experience. (This assumes that you want a program of around three hours length, that you're reasonably experienced at writing training programs, and that your content is already outlined.)

a. Write the materials. Realistically, this takes four days. (The four days include one day of fact-finding, two days for drafting materials, and one day for reviewing and re-editing.)

b. Explore alternative delivery platforms (face-to-face, CD-ROM, intranet, Internet, video, etc.). This takes three days (one day of detailed exploration of each of the three front-runner options—video plus PowerPoint, CD-ROM, and intranet—including costing).

c. Select and brief a production company for your chosen platform (this will take a minimum of one day). Finding the right person to convert the materials isn't too hard, but it's an important decision, and you will want to talk to more than one production company to comparison shop.

d. Wait for the final product. As you've already written great content and picked a cost-conscious provider, the product should be completed in five to seven working days (including a couple of review sessions with you).

7. CALCULATE THE COST

For a three-hour program, expect to spend from $8,500 to $35,000, depending on the complexity of the final product and on how much you're prepared to do in-house.

Good luck with your world-class "asynchronous" orientation!

J. Leslie McKeown is the president and CEO of Yellowbrick Consulting. Yellowbrick provides employee development solutions for organizations of all sizes, particularly in the areas of retention, orientation, and mentoring and coaching. Author of *The Complete Guide to Orientation and Re-Orientation*, *The Complete Guide to Mentoring and Coaching*, and the "Deliver the Promise" Retention Master Class, Les travels widely, speaking and consulting on issues of employee development and corporate strategy.

This article is based on material contained in *The Complete Guide to Orientation and Re-Orientation*: http://orientation.deliverthepromise.com/manual.htm.

Contact Information   *c/o Julie Wilson, Program Manager*
P.O. Box 954
Tiburon, CA 94920
800-446-9706
http://www.deliverthepromise.com
julie@deliverthepromise.com

Chapter 4

Orientation for a Global Population

Cross-Cultural and Global Orientation Programs

As employee populations become more diverse, one increasingly important component of orientation programs is the need for trainers to account for workers from different countries and cultural backgrounds. It may not always occur to a trainer, for example, that individuals who do not have an American cultural orientation may receive and process information differently, may be uncomfortable with our approach to training and group meetings, or may not understand the cultural importance of some topics that we take for granted.

These differences in values and behavior can be explained through the concept of *cultural dimensions*. For instance, some cultures tend to be more egalitarian, while others are more hierarchical; some are formal, while others are informal; some have a direct style of communication, while others are more indirect. In this chapter, we explain these and other cultural dimensions and the ways in which they affect people's work styles.

With that in mind, here are some things to consider in both the design and delivery of an orientation program to a culturally diverse group of employees.

STYLES OF LEARNING AND INTERACTION— CULTURAL EXPECTATIONS

In the United States, we tend to emphasize an interactive, participatory style of learning. The training leader is not just an instructor, but a facilitator. We design our orientations and other training programs with the expectation that there will be a give-and-take between the trainer and employees.

These are natural assumptions in our egalitarian culture. We expect that all individuals will be equally able to contribute to a discussion. Job title or status shouldn't prevent anyone from offering an opinion. Likewise, while we respect the position, knowledge, and achievements of the trainer, we still feel at liberty to question or challenge that individual, if necessary.

Closely related to these egalitarian values is an informal culture. We have a relative lack of protocol expectations. It is acceptable to address other people, including our superiors, by their first names. We are also comfortable in approaching and talking to individuals who are several levels higher than we are in the company hierarchy. These behaviors are also common in such other egalitarian cultures as Australia, Israel, and Sweden.

However, people from some countries would consider this behavior unusual. In China and other Asian countries, the education system stresses rote learning, or memorization by repetition. Because of their hierarchical culture, instructors are treated with esteem and there is little or no expectation of active participation by the group, unless expressly called upon by the instructor.

These cultures also tend toward a higher degree of formality. First names are used with family or friends, less commonly with business colleagues, and never by a student to an instructor. There are also social codes that dictate behavior, depending on one's status and position. In Korea this may involve a need to bow lower when greeting a superior. Even in some Western cultures, such as France, employees do not greet their superiors using first names, nor do they have much direct contact with managers above their immediate supervisors.

When dealing with employees from a more hierarchical or formal culture, a trainer may need to take additional steps to ensure the comfort level of employees in an orientation program, especially considering that new employees are already anxious about starting a new job and trying to fit into a new environment. If necessary, make it clear that you are a facilitator, not a lecturer. Emphasize the interactive or informal nature of the program. Don't assume that everyone shares the same cultural orientation or the same expectations for how a meeting will be run.

EXPECTATIONS ABOUT INDIVIDUAL INITIATIVE AND PARTICIPATION LEVEL

Not only do we expect participation in group or classroom activities in the United States, but we also expect that individuals will initiate their own involvement. In most training sessions, we want employees to volunteer, to be assertive, and to ask or answer questions. This extends to an individual's job performance. In many cases, we evaluate employees on their level of individual initiative. The cultural reasons for this go beyond our egalitarian values and touch upon our high regard for the individual, as well as our comfort level with risk.

In a group-oriented culture, however, individual initiative is not merely uncommon, but is often looked upon unfavorably. Japan is an example of a culture where employees work together in teams and don't usually expect individual recognition for their work. In fact, anyone who shows too much individual ambition may be regarded as less than a stellar employee. A well-known Japanese expression notes that "The nail that stands up will be pounded down." This aptly expresses the culture's preference for group effort over individual achievement.

Likewise, individuals from a low-risk culture may be hesitant about pursuing individual initiative. In these cultures, there is more of a stigma attached to failure and thus more of a fear of making mistakes. As Western companies have expanded into the former Communist states of Eastern Europe, such as Poland, they have discovered this lower comfort level with risk. This invariably means that employees are more tentative, because they are less accustomed to taking initiative or solving problems.

When orienting individuals from a group culture or those who tend to avoid risk, a good strategy is to move away from a focus on individuals and to utilize more group activities. Instead of expecting individuals to provide their own answers or opinions, a trainer might organize employees into small break-out sessions. There is more comfort in discussing a topic within a small group, and one representative of each group can then report the group's conclusions back to the larger gathering.

PRESENTING COMPANY POLICIES IN A CROSS-CULTURAL ORIENTATION

Although the presentation of company policies may seem a relatively benign part of employee orientation, there are instances when cultural differences should be taken into account. For instance, such programs as incentive pay or bonuses may seem odd to an employee from a group-oriented culture. If a person is not accustomed to working for individual gain, an incentive program may be less successful than we would normally expect.

The practice of shying away from incentive programs is often related to a reluctance to praise individuals. Any recognition that would set workers apart from their peers, such as an employee of the month program, could cause discomfort. In a culture such as China's, there is a strong emphasis on what is called "face." To criticize someone or point out an individual error in public would cause another person to lose face and would damage your relationship with that person. What Americans might not expect, however, is that to praise individuals may also cause them to lose face, because it makes them stand out from the group.

In addition, in some cultures it is common for job advancement to be based on age or status (which is the case in Asia), or on one's personal relationships and connections (which is more likely in a Latin country). In Mexico, for example, it is not uncommon for subordinates to be assigned to a new job along with their manager, in what is called the *patron* system. Individual skill is certainly not unimportant in these cultures, but it carries somewhat less weight than it does in the United States, where individual achievement and competition are rewarded.

This is not to suggest that company policies should be changed, but additional effort must sometimes be made to explain policies in light of U.S. business culture.

FEEDBACK AND PERFORMANCE REVIEWS

Many companies present their performance review policies during orientation, and sometimes even distribute blank copies of a performance review form, to set employees' expectations for how they will be evaluated by the company. The way in which this information is presented deserves special attention in a cross-cultural program. Also, when providing feedback to individuals, the orientation facilitator should consider the various cultural expectations already discussed so as to avoid any misunderstandings or unintentional insults.

Feedback is provided in many ways—not only during a formal evaluation, but also during one-on-one or group meetings, or even as a side comment during a training session. It is important to remember that Americans have a fairly direct style of communication. We are usually honest and don't "beat around the bush." Interestingly, though, we often use a "sandwich" style of providing feedback. That is, we sandwich a critique with a compliment, which serves to soften the blow.

Compare this to the feedback styles of a few other cultures:

- The British may be a bit more direct than Americans are, but they are also more subtle. They are likely to mask a direct statement with politeness or humor so that the point gets across in a nonconfrontational manner.

- The Israelis are blunt communicators. They rarely cushion a direct statement with a nicer phrase. This is not meant as an affront, but is a mere statement of the facts as they see them. The Israelis call this "dugri talk," which they see as a more realistic and sincere form of communication, stripped of the surface niceties that characterize the communication styles of other cultures.

- In a country such as Thailand, on the other hand, people are more focused on the ideal of *kreng cai,* as they try to maintain group harmony by not provoking an open disagreement or criticizing another person publicly. As in most Asian cultures, feedback is given indirectly. It is often done in private and is usually subtle. Sometimes, a criticism is delivered in the form of a suggestion or a question, because even a very subtle message will be received.

These differing cultural styles should be considered when interacting with employees during an orientation session or other training. Also, when presenting information about your company's system of performance review, remember that not all business cultures utilize formal evaluation systems as we do in the United States.

Formal performance reviews are less common in a hierarchical or centrally controlled culture in which there has been a tradition of lifetime employment. They may also be used less in relationship-oriented cultures. In many Arab companies, for example, not only are performance reviews less common, but so are written job descriptions. This is because less initiative is expected, while more tasks are accomplished through the daily interaction between managers and subordinates.

DISCUSSING SEXUAL HARASSMENT IN A CROSS-CULTURAL ORIENTATION

When designing a curriculum for an employee orientation program, it may help to consider which topics are culturally based, rather than universal areas of concern.

One topic that is currently popular in U.S. companies is sexual harassment. This is often an expressed concern of employees who come to the United States from other countries, where there is less emphasis placed on the issue. Thus, the topic of sexual harassment needs to be explained more carefully to non-U.S. employees. They need to understand not only the rules of workplace behavior, but also the reasons why they are important in American companies.

These reasons include the fact that the United States is an egalitarian culture that believes males and females should have equal rights, opportunities, and choices. In addition, we have a "low-context" culture, meaning we tend to have extensive verbal exchanges and to explain and write down our concepts of right and wrong. This leads to a strong emphasis on legal issues. Finally, some cultures are simply more male-dominant and are more accustomed to comments or behavior that would be unacceptable in a U.S. environment.

ORIENTATION SCHEDULES AND TIME MANAGEMENT

Another popular topic at training sessions in the United States is time management, and a common American practice is to provide the orientation agenda to the new employees to refer to throughout the program. American culture has a monochronic orientation to time, which means that we break our day into organized segments, accomplish tasks one at a time, and appreciate precise schedules. This is also common in countries such as Great Britain, Germany, and Denmark.

However, the whole issue of time management means a lot less to someone from Brazil or Turkey. In these and similar cultures, there is a polychronic orientation toward time, so that schedules and agendas are less regimented, individuals don't feel the need to be prompt, and interruptions are taken in stride. These cultures tend to be strongly relationship-oriented, so time is seen as more relative. Whoever you are with at the moment is considered more important than what may be on the schedule for the next hour or day.

IN CONCLUSION

These are some of the more obvious challenges you'll face when putting together an orientation program for a diverse employee population, although a variety of other topics could be considered. None of this requires wholesale changes in orientation programs; but it does require that trainers, managers, and human resource professionals be aware of these cultural differences. Small adjustments in design and delivery can go a long way toward ensuring that goals and outcomes are met for all employees, regardless of national or cultural background.

Dave Eaton is president and founder of Eaton Consulting Group, a cross-cultural training and consulting firm. As an international consultant, Dave has assisted many companies with complex issues surrounding the need for cross-cultural sensitivity in areas such as human resource policy development, multinational team building, joint venture management, corporate communications, and sales and marketing. Dave has a master's degree in Cross-Cultural Training and Consulting from Lesley Graduate School in Boston.

As manager of editorial services at Eaton Consulting Group, Bob Riel is responsible for all of the country-specific information in ECG's training materials. In this capacity, he has researched and written about the business cultures of more than 60 countries. Bob has a background in both intercultural education and journalism. He has a master's degree in Political Science, with a focus on international politics and comparative government, from Boston College.

Contact Information   *Eaton Consulting Group*
192 South St., Suite 300
Boston, MA 02111
617-338-8883
info@eatonconsultinggroup.com
www.eatonconsultinggroup.com
deaton@eatonconsultinggroup.com
briel@mediaone.net

Chapter 5

Creating a Customized Orientation Video

Internet Killed the Video Star?

When I was young (don't get me started...), there was a one-hit wonder band called Buggles. Their one hit was "Video Killed the Radio Star." (Ahhh, the memories. ...)

Recently, there has been such an emphasis on Web-based orientation that you might think that old favorite, the orientation video, is dead. Not so. We get about one inquiry a week asking how to produce a good orientation video.

The video format has gotten (deservedly) bad press. Most orientation videos are either incredibly cheesy (1970s hairstyles, kipper ties, flared trousers ... oops, there I go again) or fabulously expensive, corporate, "rooftops-filmed-from-a-helicopter" bloated irrelevancies.

However, video will have a long life ahead—not everyone is ready to plunge into Web-based interactivity—and it's still a great way to trap information for a canned presentation.

If you're planning to produce an orientation video soon, this chapter will tell you what you need to think about before getting started, how to plan your video production, and what to avoid.

First, note that some of the comments here may seem rather basic. I have made no presumptions about your understanding of the video process or industry.

One further aside: Video production companies are mostly made up of professionals, and most of them are great at what they do. Corporate communications employees in major companies similarly have talents I couldn't begin to comment on. The information in this chapter is not meant to be an assessment of either of those roles. My comments relate to the *orientation* video as a distinct animal. I include tips to help you create the best video product for your budget.

STEP 1. DEFINE THE NEED

This is where most orientation videos go wrong—right at the start! Here's a checklist of what to define up front:

❑ *Who is the video for?*

Is it just for new hires, or will it be used for wider corporate events? Will it be used only at your corporate office, or will your branch or field offices want to use if for their orientation programs as well?

❑ *Why is it being produced?*

If it's a corporate video for wider use, it's probably best to focus on mission, values, and a bit of history. If it will be solely for new hires, more specific information will be needed if it's not going to seem a bit cheesy. My advice is that you make the video specifically for new hires. It puts a clear edge on the final product and helps focus on the message you want to get across. Avoid the temptation to let the video become a catch-all corporate video.

If the video will be used in your branch or field offices in other parts of the country (or the world), be sure to exclude services that are offered only at the corporate office, or any other information that it is not applicable to other locations. You don't want to start off new employees in the branch offices already frustrated because they may not have access to some specific corporate services.

❑ *What is the message you want to get across?*

This is probably the hardest part to get right. Although it's connected to "why" the video is being produced, it's not the same issue. Decide the specific message you want to convey. For a corporate video, for example, this may be "We're Growing" or "We're Innovative."

For an orientation video, it's vital to decide the exact message that you want to convey. For example, "This is where we've come from" (i.e., Our History) is valid, but not vital. "Here is how you add value" is more so, or "Here's the sort of thing you can accomplish with us."

I suggest you use the video to accomplish three goals:

a. Concisely convey the history of the organization. That's an important part of what most new hires want to know about, and the story isn't going to change rapidly and outdate the video. This section might take approximately 3 to 5 minutes of the total video time.

b. Present the key aspects of your corporate culture (i.e., customer focus, innovation, or whatever is relevant to your company). This will take approximately 3 to 5 minutes of the total video time.

c. Show and tell how new employees can add value and discuss the availability of opportunity in the organization. Again, this will take approximately 3 to 5 minutes of the total video time.

❑ *How long should it be?*

Most organizations want a video that is 10 to 20 minutes in length. Any longer is a lot of time to expect new hires to remain alert in a darkened room. If cost and time are issues, you might even consider a 5- to 10-minute video of the CEO presenting the company's vision and mission, and relating how new employees can contribute to each of these. Of course, if your CEO leaves the company, your video will be invalid; but the vision and mission may very well change with new leadership anyway.

STEP 2. DEVELOP THE SCRIPT

Many organizations don't develop the script until after the video production company has been selected (see step 3), and some don't do it at all—they leave it to the production company. Without exception, any orientation video that I have seen that endures and adds value has been (at least initially) scripted by company personnel (that's *you!*) before the production company got their hands on it.

Production companies can help you decide what will and won't work, and how best to get your story across. But they don't know your business well enough to write the script initially, and few will take the trouble to try to do it well.

STEP 3. REQUEST A PROPOSAL FOR TREATMENT (SELECT YOUR PRODUCTION PARTNER)

After defining the need and writing a first draft of what you want, put the results into a three- to five-page document and send it to several production companies that have proven expertise in this field. Ask for a response to include at least two suggested treatments (just outline, "look and feel" suggestions; it isn't fair to ask them to project a full production schedule).

There are two main options: Look for a full-facility production house that will do everything (from initial script to a FedEx package on your desk with 20 copies of the final video); or hire a talented producer who will subcontract the rest. I've seen both work well; it depends on who you hire. Costs tend to be lower with the first method, because of economies of scale.

In any case, insist on meeting the actual director who will be working on your video. This is where the chemistry must work. You can meet an excellent producer (essentially a resource-juggler), but end up working with a director who just doesn't understand what result you want. Try to have the director involved as early as possible.

STEP 4. PREPRODUCTION

When you've selected your production company or producer from the short list, they'll produce the final treatment, a production schedule, details of the talent (who's appearing in the video), and, of course, the final script.

You will need to decide whether you want to use professional actors or actual employees of your company in the video. I believe that a mix is best. A professional announcer should be used (an employee probably wouldn't do a very good job lending this level of professionalism), while actual employees should represent themselves. (Actors posing as employees will drain the video of any credibility.)

Don't be concerned that the employees you include in the video will leave the company and then your video will be out of date. It doesn't really have much of an impact if the employees in the video leave the organization at a later date. It's unlikely that they would have met new recruits at the water cooler, anyway.

It's important to stay with the project. You may well find that your initial understanding of what you're getting is slowly lost in the mire of production planning.

At this stage, it's vital that your orientation video remains a two-way, instructional exercise. In planning for its production, thought needs to be given to interactivity, such as a participants' workbook and some exercises that can be undertaken after the video is completed. If these tasks are not planned at this stage, the video can easily become a monologue or a documentary, and exercises and interactivity never work if they are tacked on at the end. A good example of interactivity can be found at www.qmr.com/products/titles/adventure/. Although this is a canned (prepreared) orientation video (which I don't recommend), and although I find the format and space theme a bit cheesy, the idea of the associated workbooks and exercises worked out well here. You can view the workbooks and facilitator's guides online by clicking on the links. (As with any third-party resource we mention, we're not associated with QMR in any way.)

STEP 5. PRODUCTION

Time to say "Action!"

Let this phrase be spoken only when you're absolutely sure you're going to get what you want. It's too late (and too expensive) to fix it afterward. Your production company should have provided you with a concise, understandable, and realistic production schedule, which you should check on as time goes by. Having said all that, if steps 1 through 4 have gone okay, this should be (for you) the easiest bit.

STEP 6. POSTPRODUCTION

This is where the off-line or rough edit cut is subjected to graphics, music and other sounds, narration, and the other bits that make a rounded, finished product. Again, if the other steps have been planned well, this step is easier. It is also a good idea to ask to sit in with your production company to help with this editing step, and to help make decisions about what to leave in or take out to finalize the video.

Also, a decision will be made now as to the final media to be used—classic videotape, DVD, CD-ROM, or other multimedia format.

STEP 7. DUPLICATION AND PACKAGING

Make copies, dress 'em up in pretty boxes, and you're done!

STEP 8. SHOW TIME!

I think we all realize these days that it's just not good instructional technique to have people sit in darkness for 20 minutes and then move them quietly on to another topic.

We strongly favor the use of an interactive dialog—get the participants to *do something*. You may want to have them participate in a group activity or an individual exercise, and you will need to decide if they will do something during or after the video presentation.

At the outset, draft an interactive exercise that the new hires can be involved in to turn the video from a listening and viewing exercise to one with active participation.

And now, sit back and enjoy your new orientation video!

J. Leslie McKeown is the president and CEO of Yellowbrick Consulting. Yellowbrick provides employee development solutions for organizations of all sizes, particularly in the areas of retention, orientation, and mentoring and coaching.

Author of *The Complete Guide to Orientation and Re-Orientation*, *The Complete Guide to Mentoring and Coaching*, and the "Deliver the Promise" Retention Master Class, Les travels widely, speaking and consulting on issues of employee development and corporate strategy.

This article is based on material contained in *The Complete Guide to Orientation and Re-Orientation*: http://orientation.deliverthepromise.com/manual.htm.

Contact Information   *c/o Julie Wilson, Program Manager*
P.O. Box 954
Tiburon, CA 94920
800-446-9706
http://www.deliverthepromise.com
julie@deliverthepromise.com

Chapter 6

Employee Orientation for Small Businesses

While large companies can justify the time and expense necessary for providing an orientation to new employees that covers all the bases, small companies can't afford the luxury of allowing prolonged time away from work for an employee to go through an extensive orientation. It is also likely that most small companies do not have the promotional materials and formal work policies established that large companies do. So the challenge for a small company is to welcome new employees and explain the working policies and expectations in a way that takes a minimum amount of time, but lets the employees know they are valued as part of the team.

Large companies design their orientations to instill the culture of the workplace and what it takes to be a team player. Some spend a month or more, with one or two days each week devoted to a different facet of the company culture.

While culture and teamwork are important for a small company, the more significant concentration should be on the specific skills and knowledge the employees need to begin their jobs as quickly as possible. Therefore, on-the-job training becomes the focal point for small company orientations.

The approach a company will take depends a great deal on the type of organization: A retail company will tackle orienting its employees much differently from a software development company, a firm engaged primarily in office work, or a business doing automotive repairs. There is no one right way of doing it when it comes to orientation in a small company, but there are some wrong ways—and some basic concepts to consider.

SMALL BUSINESS ORIENTATION—HOW TO DO THE JOB

Before you start developing any orientation program, you should first have a firm idea of what you want it to accomplish. That will be different for each organization.

An example might be a small furniture store. It will want its new employees to know the kind of furniture it specializes in and the process they should use in dealing with customers. The employees will need to know how to handle a sale from beginning to end, and what kind of customers are most likely to come into the store. You want them to understand how they record the hours they work and when will they be paid. And, of course, they will have to learn how to use the technology associated with sales.

On the other end of the spectrum, take a look at an auto repair shop: No outright sales here, but new employees will need to know how to use all the equipment or, at least, learn how you want them to use the equipment. They also should know the quality of repair work you expect. And while there may not be the same level of customer contact, the new employees will need to understand how to deal with the types of customers the shop will draw.

Spend some time identifying just what new employees walking in the door should understand about the company and what skills and knowledge they should develop to successfully do their jobs and be productive members of the team.

Unfortunately, this initial process, more often than not, is never even considered. Too many small firms dump their new employees right into the job and expect them to pick up what they need to know as they go along. New employees often have to rely on other employees to show them the ropes. They can make mistakes that are costly, because they have never been shown the right way.

HOW MUCH TIME CAN THE COMPANY AFFORD?

On the surface, this appears to be a dollar and cents issue, but it goes beyond that in affordability. You may think that putting new salespersons right out there on the floor means they will start earning their keep in a very short time. In reality, it just is not true. All new employees need some time to get their bearings and learn how things are done. If a new employee gets information the right way in the beginning, there is less downtime spent correcting mistakes.

Remember the auto repair company. Let's use it as an example to illustrate the consequences associated with the amount of time allocated to new employee orientation. We will assume a new certified mechanic is reporting for his first day on the job. Let's assume he is shown around the shop by the lead mechanic, assigned a workstation, and told to pick up the next work order and get to work. So much for orientation!

Under this scenario, the employee knows nothing about what is expected of him. Even if he is an experienced mechanic, he will know nothing about any specific methods the company may have for handling work orders, the processes for ensuring quality work, and particular equipment he may not be familiar with. So, on the first day, he ends up making mistakes that cost the company a customer— all because no one took the time to explain how this company does things and how he is expected to perform.

While it may take time to orient a new employee—perhaps a day or two in the case of our new mechanic—the payoff in dollars and cents, as well as the benefit of having an employee who starts off on the right foot, will be more profitable in the long run. The company will benefit from fewer mistakes, more knowledgeable employees, and a team of employees who are able to contribute to a successful company.

WHAT TRAINING METHOD WILL FIT YOUR BUSINESS?

Now we know what information and skills new employees in the organization will need to begin their employment. We have made a commitment to allow time for them to absorb this information and understand the work methods and procedures. The next step in developing the orientation is to decide the best approach for communicating the information.

For every company, one element of a new employee's orientation is going to be the completion of necessary forms—general personnel data records, company benefit applications, and information required by state and federal governments. This takes place on the first day, before anything else, so we know what the first part of the orientation plan will be.

Most organizations, large and small, follow the paperwork with an introduction to the work environment: a tour of the facility, an introduction to the supervisor (if the supervisor is not already taking part), and meeting other employees. In a small company, this is generally an informal endeavor.

It has proven very useful to introduce new employees to a "buddy"—someone designated to help them through the first couple of days and be a resource for questions that might come up. Obviously, the buddy should be someone who is knowledgeable about company expectations and how things should be done. Buddies should also have friendly, open personalities. They are going to be helping to form the new employees' views of the company and the work environment.

Right about now is when small companies and even some of the larger ones make their biggest mistake: They hand new employees a two-inch binder with all the rules and regulations and procedures and such. The new employees are instructed to spend the rest of the day reading through the binder. Not only does this overwhelm the new employees, it is also pointless. They will not remember a tenth of what they read. It also sends the message that company management does not want to spend the time to ensure the new employees know they are appreciated. What it does do is satisfy the company's lawyers, so they can demonstrate that employees were informed of the rules.

If you must ensure that new employees are informed of specific laws or requirements such as OSHA safety rules or invention agreements, provide the information in increments and at appropriate times. In the auto repair shop of our earlier example, safety is of foremost importance. Give the new mechanic the safety material to read separately from the other orientation materials. Don't water down the significance of safety by lumping the material together with all the other information that is of lesser importance.

Each company must consider how it will customize the next step in the program, job training. The best approach a small company can take to instructing a new employee in the ways of the company and the necessary skills for the job is to use an incremental format. Begin with the fundamental information and build from there. Decide what is most important and make sure that information is passed on to the employee first. The remaining material is given out in order of greater to lesser importance. Remember, the importance of the information is determined from the perspective of the employee and his or her successful integration into the job.

A final caveat about the method of orienting a new employee: Do not do it all in one day. At the least, spread out the information in segments over a period of a week. Remember the old saw about how to eat an elephant—one bite at a time.

WHO SHOULD CONDUCT THE ORIENTATION TRAINING?

In a very small company, the most likely person to handle new employee orientation is probably the owner or manager. In a somewhat larger company, it might be a supervisor. However, there are other possibilities. If the firm has someone who does office administration, this might be the person to handle the initial paperwork, tour, and introductions. An employee who knows the job well and has a welcoming manner toward others might be given the responsibility of overseeing the training of the new employee.

Some organizations are trying out newer technology as a way to orient new employees. Providing information in a Web-based format, either on a computer or on a CD, is one approach that may save time and the cost of taking someone away from the job, whether a supervisor or another employee. Be aware, though, that this is much the same as giving out that two-inch binder, and can be seen as impersonal by the new employee.

Electronic presentations can be a real benefit to companies, large or small. However, there must be a balance, with the opportunity for live interaction and a chance to have questions answered and to clarify what is not understood.

No matter who is appointed to carry out the orientation, management must take an active part in some way. Do not shuffle a new employee off on someone else because you don't have time. *Take* the time to welcome new employees, at the very least. If new employees are recognized and acknowledged as important to the company, they are significantly more inclined to do their best.

Maureen A. Lansing, SPHR, is principal consultant at Lansing Consulting.

Contact Information   *Lansing Consulting—Aim for Success*
7942 W. Bell Rd., Suite C5 #455
Glendale, AZ 85308
623-214-1750
Fax 623-214-1700
business@lansingconsulting.com

Chapter 7

Developing a College Intern Program

Alcatel is a leader in end-to-end telecommunications solutions. We are part of an industry with leading-edge technology and a lot of competition for talented employees. The Alcatel Co-Op (College Intern) Program was developed and implemented in an effort to build one of several employee pools from which to hire. (The following information is based on Dallas area activity).

THE ADVANTAGES OF A CO-OP PROGRAM

The program enhances a college student's education by providing valuable hands-on work experience during the hours or days when the student is not in the classroom. As they learn about the industry and their field of study, students also learn about the company. If there is a mutual interest between Alcatel and the student upon graduation, a co-op may be hired as a full-time employee—one who has been trained to some extent and is already familiar with the company culture, philosophy, and goals.

Historically, about 45 percent of the Alcatel co-ops have taken a full-time position with Alcatel upon graduation. About 95 percent of those students have technical degrees, while the other 5 percent have business degrees. The more positive results and experiences managers have, and the more potential they see, the more motivated they are to participate.

This program essentially gives students a chance to "take a test drive" in our company, and it provides Alcatel with a chance to review the employees' initiative, skills, and drive extensively before making a hiring decision. It also provides various platforms from which to promote Alcatel. In addition, our business units are provided with fresh ideas and new perspectives.

Alcatel brings in approximately 150 co-ops each semester. The students are found via campus career fairs, employee referrals, and Internet submissions. The program works with about 25 schools through the campus co-op office and various student organizations, to increase awareness about the company and the program.

THE CO-OP IDENTIFICATION AND SELECTION PROCESS

In order to recruit co-ops, we must know who we are looking for. The first step in our process is to identify business needs for co-ops. We ask managers and supervisors to complete Co-Op Requisitions. (A sample of this form is included at the end of the chapter.)

Once the hiring manager completes and returns this form, we know what major or area of concentration the manager would like the co-op to have, the minimum grade level required of the co-op, and the basic skill sets required to complete the job functions. This requisition also serves as a tool to evaluate the position and verify that it would provide a valuable experience for college students, thus enhancing their education while they are working with us.

Once we have collected our request forms, we begin to match resumes to them, which we have collected from various campus career fairs across the country. We give the students as much company and community information as we can, because it can be difficult to sell students on the idea of moving away from school or home for a semester. But once they do, the majority seem to come back at least once more before graduating. We try to hire a balance of students from different schools across the country in order to provide a good mix of skill sets for our business units.

After we send managers our selection of resumes, it is their responsibility to interview (either by phone or in person) those candidates they think would be good fits for the positions. Once the manager or hiring supervisor has made a decision, we extend the student an offer of employment into our co-op program. Along with the job, we offer students a very competitive hourly rate, based on specific criteria.

THE CO-OP ORIENTATION PROGRAM

On the first day of employment at Alcatel, the employee attends a specific orientation program designed just for co-ops and attended only by co-ops. This special orientation program is held three times per year: at the beginning of the fall, spring, and summer terms. We provide general company information as well as information specific to each co-op's work location, to assure the student's transition into Alcatel will be as smooth as possible.

The co-op HR representative conducts orientation. This HR representative is also the primary contact for the co-ops to ask questions about any job issues, raises, transfers, activities, and so on during the term. Students begin work within their new departments the day following orientation.

THE ALCATEL CO-OP
ORIENTATION PROGRAM

Time	Activity or Topic
8:00–8:25	Building Access Badges/Photos
8:25–8:35	Icebreaker and Review of Agenda
8:35–8:45	Corporate Company Welcome
8:45–9:00	Company Video—Products and Organizational Structure
9:00–9:20	Quality at Alcatel
9:20–9:25	Education and Training Center
9:25–9:40	Break
9:40–10:15	Completion of HR Forms
10:15–10:45	Co-Op Benefits Presentation
10:45–11:00	E-Mail Video (Security, Appropriate Use)
11:00–11:20	Data Security at Alcatel
11:20–11:40	Safety and Security
11:40–1:00	Lunch and Company Store Visit
1:00–1:20	Sexual Harassment in the Workplace
1:20–1:30	The Alcatel Intranet Walkthrough

SPECIAL CO-OP ACTIVITIES AND PROGRAMS

During their semester at Alcatel, co-ops can participate in several activities to enhance their personal, professional, and community involvement. For example, their HR representative plans co-op lunches, which provide an opportunity for the students to get together and see what's going on in other groups.

There are also group outings that provide the co-ops with a chance to get together with other co-ops and have fun away from work. In addition, the program encourages students to get involved with charitable activities. The students enjoy these opportunities to get together, to go places, and to do things they normally would not have a chance to do.

In addition, there is usually a resume writing or interview skills luncheon, which is used to provide the students with some helpful ideas as they approach graduation and as they will be "shopping around" for their best opportunity—hopefully within an Alcatel business unit. These activities help students, many of whom have never been away from home, feel comfortable in unfamiliar surroundings. They meet several people they share common interests with, or people they might go to school with but never had the opportunity to meet before.

We spend a lot of time making sure that we have the right positions for students and that we are filling the positions with the right students. We put a lot of effort into making the co-ops' experience well-rounded, positive, and educationally enhancing. Not only do our co-ops provide us with a great amount of word-of-mouth promotion, but many of them are the future of our company. The program is a wonderful investment that can reap tremendous rewards as a win–win effort.

EVALUATION OF THE PROGRAM

Keeping the program valuable means constantly asking for and collecting feedback from our co-ops and from our managers and hiring supervisors. Halfway through the term, we ask managers of the co-ops to complete evaluations, to determine how well the co-ops are performing in their jobs.

In addition, we ask the co-ops to complete an evaluation. We want to know how our managers and supervisors are doing as coaches and as effective leaders for our co-ops. We want to know that our supervisors are providing a good working environment for our students. If there are any issues we need to address, we want to do so as soon as we can so both students and managers have good experiences with the program.

At the end of each semester, we ask for end-of-term evaluations from managers and supervisors. We want to know of any changes in the employees' quality of work or about increases in the co-ops' knowledge base. The co-ops also have exit interviews when their internship semesters are complete. The HR representative also schedules one-on-one time with the co-ops to get their final thoughts and feelings on the co-op program and on their positions.

It is very important that we get as much honest feedback as we can, so we can provide both students and managers with what they need. This is critical to the continuing success of the program. Questions such as, "Where do I get a co-op?" and comments that suggest misconceptions about the program lead to an informational session each semester to explain the program, in its proper form, to employees.

We often heard from managers, "[My co-op] has done an outstanding job all semester. What special recognition does the program have for outstanding co-ops?" This led us to develop a semester-end recognition program for both outstanding co-ops and outstanding supervisors.

We also received feedback such as, "It would be valuable to me to evaluate my co-op at the conclusion of the first month, and not wait until midsemester." So the co-op program recently began to send out evaluations earlier than midsemester. The co-op program typically rates a 4 on a scale of 5 (5 being excellent).

LESSONS LEARNED

Constant follow-up with students and supervisors is very important. Always take the opportunity to see how things are going on both sides, to make sure both parties have a good experience. It is important to keep abreast of changes in the industry, and to know how our company is different from our direct competitors. Finding the right person for the company is a very important step. The more you know about the company (not just the industry), and the more you can tell what is really important to the students, the more efficiently and effectively you will spend your time looking for the right people.

"Developing a College Intern Program" was written by Katherine M. Lunkes.

Contact Information   *Joyce Wood, Talent Resources Director*
1000 Coit Road, M/S CHB-1074
Plano, TX 75075
Joyce.Wood@alcatel.com

COLLEGE RELATIONS CO-OP REQUEST
JOB DESCRIPTION FORM

Co-op Req #: (office use) _____

Hiring Contact:_____

Hiring Supervisor: _____

Cost Center: _____

Building: _____

Mailstop:_____

Division: _____

Group: _____

Extension: _____

Fax: _____

Circle Your Organization: *Network Systems, Terrestrial Networks, Access, OPS, IT, Fin, HR, Sales, Marketing, Engineering Proc. and Svcs., Customer Network Svcs.*

(Circle Applicable) Position: *Alternating (Full Time) or Parallel (Part Time) Co-op*

(Circle Applicable) Start: *Fall, Spring*

Educational Requirements: College Undergraduate, Graduate Student, Major

Required Skills: (Include specific computer languages, computer skills, etc.)

Job Duties/Responsibilities:

This position is:

1. **An addition** ☐

    A replacement ☐ *(If replacement) Replacing whom:* _____

2. **For a new candidate** ☐

    For a returning candidate ☐ *Returning co-op's name:* _____

Hiring Supervisor: _____   **CC Manager:** _____

Director: _____   **Senior Director:** _____

COOPERATIVE EDUCATION
EXIT INTERVIEW

Name:_____   Date: _____

Permanent Address: _____

_____

Phone#: _____   Permanent E-mail:_____

Major:_____   Minor: _____

Supervisor's Name: _____

School: _____   Graduation Date: _____

Position: _____

Do you plan on returning to Alcatel for another co-op work term?

_____ Yes, I plan to return on _____(MM/YY)

_____ No, but I will seek full-time opportunities in _____(MM/YY)

_____ No, because: _____

Supervisor

Rate your supervisor on the following criteria: (1=Poor—5=Excellent)

■ Outlined clear job expectations	1	2	3	4	5
■ Set a good example for you	1	2	3	4	5
■ Was eager to help and answered questions	1	2	3	4	5
■ Gave you feedback in a positive manner	1	2	3	4	5
■ Made you feel important	1	2	3	4	5
■ Allowed you to participate in meetings, conferences, etc. pertaining to projects	1	2	3	4	5

Comments:

My overall rating of my Alcatel supervisor   1   2   3   4   5

Job and Work Environment

(1=Poor—5=Excellent)

Rate your job and work environment on the following criteria:

- Adequate training   1   2   3   4   5
- Challenging work/projects   1   2   3   4   5
- Group members accepted you as an equal   1   2   3   4   5
- Work was related to your degree plan   1   2   3   4   5

What did you like most about your position?

What did you like least about your position?

Co-Op Program

Rate the co-op program on the following criteria:

- Fulfilled my expectations   1   2   3   4   5
- Readily answered questions/assisted   1   2   3   4   5
- Good communication (E-mail/Phone)   1   2   3   4   5
- Social activities   1   2   3   4   5

Your suggestions for improving the Alcatel Co-Op Program:

Your overall co-op experience with Alcatel   1   2   3   4   5

Your overall *work* experience with Alcatel   1   2   3   4   5

May we give a copy of this evaluation to your supervisor?   Yes   No

Student Signature:_____ Date:_____

Co-Op Coordinator Signature:_____ Date:_____

ALCATEL CO-OP
STUDENT EVALUATION

Semester: _____

(Please return the completed evaluation to College Relations)

Supervisor's Name:_____   Co-Op's Name:_____

Rate on the following criteria. (1=Poor – 5=Awesome)

Skills:

Possesses necessary technical knowledge	1	2	3	4	5
Readily adapts to new situations	1	2	3	4	5
Cooperates and works well with others	1	2	3	4	5

Performance:

Listens well and follows directions	1	2	3	4	5
Works well without supervision	1	2	3	4	5
Meets deadlines and schedules	1	2	3	4	5
Produces acceptable quality work	1	2	3	4	5
Works productively	1	2	3	4	5
Demonstrates good judgement	1	2	3	4	5

Attitude:

Is a self-starter	1	2	3	4	5
Accepts responsibility for mistakes	1	2	3	4	5
Good attendance/Rarely tardy	1	2	3	4	5
Adheres to company policies	1	2	3	4	5
Is enthusiastic and a positive influence	1	2	3	4	5
Overall Rating of Co-Op's Performance	1	2	3	4	5

Please comment on your Co-Op's strengths and areas in need of improvement:

Do you recommend this student for another co-op term?   Yes   No

If no, please explain:

Supervisor Signature: _____   Date:_____

Co-Op Signature: _____   Date:_____

(Please share this evaluation with your co-op.)

Chapter 8
Designing a Buddy Program

Orientation and retention are all about making your new employees feel at home. Along the way, that also means helping them understand your organizational culture and politics. A buddy program is a great tool to assist in both of these objectives.

It's tough being a new employee. You're not too sure what lies behind each door, there are enough acronyms and buzzwords to fill a book, and somebody keeps moving the photocopier!

These concerns pale into insignificance, however, when compared with the sheer confusion of not knowing what's "normal" in the organization: What's right and wrong here? What's expected of me? What's the company's culture?

Not knowing the answers to these and similar questions makes every new employee feel like an outsider, at least for a while.

Consequently, the typical new employee is less confident and somewhat insecure when it comes to relating with colleagues—senior, peer, or junior. Not knowing what's right or what's accepted here can make the new employee hesitant and confused in interpreting the responses of others.

A buddy program is a great way to accelerate the new employees' abilities to deal with these early, disconcerting issues.

By matching your new employees with a buddy—someone who has been in the organization for a while—you will not only assist in cultural integration and orientation. If done properly, your managers and supervisors will find that their interaction with new employees is much less about low-level, operational issues, and much more about adding value.

What's the difference between a buddy, a coach, and a mentor?

- **A mentoring program** seeks to assist individuals with their development, both personally and professionally.

- **A coaching program** seeks to increase the individual's job-related skills.

- **A buddy program** is solely involved with providing a one-point access to operationally necessary information. In essence, **the development of the individual** is not an expected output.

What should the structure of a buddy program be?

We've designed the rest of this chapter as a briefing document that you might provide to prospective buddies. It explains how the structure of a buddy program works.

THE BUDDY PROGRAM—A BRIEFING DOCUMENT

Use this text template to create an introductory letter to the new Buddies.

1. Overview

[Company] has decided to implement a Buddy Program to assist new employees in the early months of their employment with us.

This document is primarily designed to brief those who will be the new employees' Buddies, but it will also help new employees and the managers of both to understand more fully what the Buddy Program is, and what is expected of each party involved in the Buddy relationship.

2. The Orientation Program

The Buddy Program is an integral part of the company's orientation program for new employees. It is strongly recommended that you read this document in that context. Please refer to:

- [List other available materials here that will give an understanding of the wider context of the orientation program.]

Buddies will be expected to occasionally attend the company's other orientation activities, including the associated classroom training, to give an overview of the program to new employees. You will be contacted by [coordinator's name] regarding this in due course.

3. Outline of the Buddy Program

The Buddy Program matches new employees with employees who have been with the company for some time (typically 6 to 12 months), for a period of six months, with two goals:

- To provide the new employee with a point of contact for general queries regarding day-to-day operational issues [such as the location of facilities, information processing requirements, and relevant company policies].

- To help the new employee integrate with the company by providing access to someone who is familiar with our culture, attitude, and expectations.

The program is coordinated by [name of coordinator] and supported by the line managers.

4. Goals and Objectives of the Buddy Program

By providing such a relationship, it is intended that:

- The new employee will feel more at home with the company, in a shorter period of time.

- Relatively straightforward queries regarding basic operational issues will be dealt with in a timely and nonbureaucratic manner.

- The initial confusion and uncertainty faced by all new employees will be lessened.

- Other orientation activities, such as classroom and on-the-job training, can be related to real-world activities, and the resulting basic queries can be resolved.

- Our new employees find out how best to manage us, the company, in a supportive and risk-reduced environment.

- Manager and supervisor time with new employees is freed up to deal with added-value issues.

- The new employee begins to add value more quickly, leading to increased confidence and self-esteem.

- You, the Buddy, are actively involved in making this a better place to work and making our new employees more productive.

5. Selection and Pairing of Buddies

Employees are nominated as Buddies by departmental managers on the basis of two criteria:

- the employee's interpersonal skills, and

- the employee's understanding of and commitment to the company's vision and values.

Additionally, at the end of the Buddy relationship, you will have the opportunity to nominate as a Buddy the new employee with whom you have been working, if you feel he or she fulfills these criteria.

The Program Coordinator will allocate nominated Buddies to new employees. When possible, Buddies will be matched with new employees in their own departments.

6. The Role and Responsibilities of the Buddy

The primary aspects of the Buddy's role and responsibilities are detailed in number 4. Please review that section now. Then continue on to read about the role of a Buddy versus that of a manager, coach, or mentor.

The role of a buddy must be distinguished from that of a *manager, mentor,* or *coach:*

A *mentor* is someone who is typically a more experienced employee or manager, and is involved with the all-around development of an individual.

You are *not* being asked to act as your new employee's mentor. You are not responsible for his or her growth or development as an individual, and it is not part of the role of a Buddy to take on such a responsibility. You will not be assessed on your success as a Buddy by whether or not the new employee you work with develops as an individual during the six-month period.

A *coach* is someone tasked with developing an individual's job-specific skills. You are *not* being asked to act as your new employee's coach. Although your role as Buddy may involve explaining some simple job-related issues or straightforward procedures, it is not your job to replace formal training processes. If you feel your new employee's queries are too detailed or specialized for you to answer, direct them to the supervisor or manager.

You are not the new employee's *manager* or supervisor. Your role as buddy does not mean you will be held responsible for your new employee's performance. If queries arise regarding performance, disciplinary, or policy matters, while you are free to give your opinion and advice on how to approach the matter, you are *not* in a position to adjudicate or resolve the matter. The new employee must be directed to the manager or supervisor for resolution of the relevant issue(s).

7. Meeting with Your Buddy

After you have been notified of the name and other relevant information regarding the new employee you will be working with, it is up to you to make contact at the earliest available opportunity. This may be on the employee's first day on site; or if orientation training occurs on day one, you may wish to arrange to meet the employee for lunch or otherwise on that day.

CONTENT OF MEETINGS AND DISCUSSIONS

Your first meeting with your new employee should be introductory in nature. Show the person around your department, make introductions to their colleagues, and provide directions as to where the employee will be working. Explain the operation of any equipment or systems needed in order to commence work. Be familiar with the content of the orientation training so you do not duplicate any training being provided there.

Explain how the new employee can contact you during the day, and make it clear that you are available as needed, but that the employee should use discretion at all times. Explain that you will be meeting regularly and that non-urgent issues should be left until those times, but emphasize that anything that is materially hindering work or performance can be discussed with you immediately.

Explain the difference between a mentor, coach, and manager to the new employee to set clear expectations, and clear any ground rules regarding contact outside working hours. Ask if he or she has any initial queries or issues, and deal with them. Then leave the new employee to get on with the assignment! Remember, your role is to help new employees get on with the task at hand—not to prevent them from doing so!

FREQUENCY AND TIMING OF MEETINGS

You should aim to meet regularly for at least 30 minutes, once a week during their first month and at least once a month thereafter. This meeting (often best held over lunch or in an informal setting) should be used to discuss any non-urgent issues the new employee may have.

During the working day, it may be reasonable to expect as many as four or five brief queries a day from the new employee in the first few days, tapering down to one or two a day thereafter. Although all new employees are different, after two to three months, you may hear little or nothing on a daily basis. *This is a good sign.* If you are still getting a large number of urgent queries after the first month, then the Buddy program is not working, and you should speak to the Program Coordinator for advice.

Within the parameters above, it is expected that you and the new employee meet within working hours. (Your manager will let you know if you are spending too much time on this.) Some Buddies and new employees agree to meet on a social basis, outside working hours. This is an entirely discretionary matter between you and the new employee. It is up to you to indicate to the new employee how you feel about being contacted regarding work-related issues outside of working hours.

The company has no policy on this. Many Buddies have felt happy being contacted when necessary outside working hours, up to about 9 p.m. on weeknights, but not on weekends. This is entirely up to you.

8. Expectations of the Relationship

Your relationship with the new employee should be open, confidential, positive, and supportive.

Discussions between you and the new employee should be confidential. The company has no interest in knowing the details of any discussions between you and the new employee, and we are not involved in monitoring Buddy relationships. We simply ask that you be supportive of the company and your coworkers. We discourage gossip and speculation within a Buddy relationship, particularly as many new employees are not in a position to form opinions on most issues during their early months with us.

9. Available Support

If you are having any trouble with the interpretation of these guidelines, or with any aspect of the Buddy relationship, contact [name of Program Coordinator], who will be happy to give you guidance.

MAKING YOUR BUDDY A BUDDY

We would like to see the new employee you are working with become a Buddy in turn after being with the company for a while. If you feel he or she could fulfill such a role, find time in the last two months of the relationship to share with the employee any tips or techniques you think would help in performing such a role.

Give the name to your manager, and suggest the employee be considered as a Buddy.

10. Termination of the Relationship

The Buddy relationship between you and the new employee will be terminated if either:

- six months pass, or

- either party requests it.

The Buddy relationship operates under a no-fault termination mechanism. This means that if either the Buddy or the new employee so requests, the Buddy relationship immediately ends. The new employee is allocated another Buddy, and the Buddy is allocated to a different new employee.

No reasons will be sought or proferred, no discussion will ensue, no blame will be apportioned.

Contact the Program Coordinator if you wish to trigger the Buddy relationship.

Note: Many buddies form separate, social relationships with new employees that continue beyond the formal Buddy program. This is entirely a matter for the employees.

11. Review of the Relationship

At the termination of the Buddy relationship, the Program Coordinator will ask you to fill in a brief questionnaire aimed at improving the Buddy program. It does not involve the issues discussed between you and the new employee.

Other Topics You May Include in Your Buddy Introduction Document

- FAQ—containing frequently asked questions regarding the Buddy Program

- FAQ—containing questions frequently asked by new employees

- An intranet site address containing discussion group used by Buddies

---

J. Leslie McKeown is the president and CEO of Yellowbrick Consulting. Yellowbrick provides employee development solutions for organizations of all sizes, particularly in the areas of retention, orientation, and mentoring and coaching. In addition to being the author of *The Complete Guide to Orientation and Re-Orientation, The Complete Guide to Mentoring and Coaching,* and the "Deliver the Promise" Retention Master Class, Les travels widely, speaking and consulting on issues of employee development and corporate strategy.

This article is based on material contained in *The Complete Guide to Orientation and Re-Orientation:* http://orientation.deliverthepromise.com/manual.htm.

Contact Information   *Julie Wilson, Program Manager*
P.O. Box 954
Tiburon, CA 94920
800-446-9706
http://www.deliverthepromise.com
julie@deliverthepromise.com

BUDDY THANK-YOU LETTER AND EVALUATION

Dear   ,

Thank you so much for participating in our Buddy program. I sincerely hope you got a lot out of it personally, and that you will consider acting as a Buddy again.

This brief questionnaire is intended solely to help us in the review and redesign of the Buddy Program, to continuously improve the program to best meet every-one's needs.

Your responses and comments on the questionnaire are confidential, and are not used for any other purpose.

Please return this questionnaire to _____
by_____ (date).

Sincerely,

[Program Coordinator's Name and Personal Signature Here]

BUDDY QUESTIONNAIRE

Please indicate which of the following apply to your Buddy Program experience, by circling the relevant number.

Use the following rating scale in this evaluation:
1 = Strongly disagree
2 = Disagree
3 = Neither agree not disagree
4 = Agree
5 = Strongly agree

1. I was satisfactorily briefed regarding my role and responsibilities as a Buddy.

   1   2   3   4   5

2. I was happy with the way in which I was allocated to my Buddy.

   1   2   3   4   5

3. My Buddy seemed satisfactorily briefed regarding his or her role and responsibilities.

   1   2   3   4   5

4. I was happy with the support provided by the Program Coordinator.

   1   2   3   4   5

5. The frequency of our Buddy meetings was adequate.

   1   2   3   4   5

6. The content of our Buddy discussions was appropriate.

   1   2   3   4   5

7. The goals and objectives of the Buddy relationship, as explained to me by the Program Coordinator, were met.

   1   2   3   4   5

8. The program was well organized, and the Program Coordinator managed the program appropriately.

   1   2   3   4   5

9. The time I spent as a Buddy was time well spent. I see it as an investment in our new employees and in our company's future.

   1   2   3   4   5

10. Overall, I feel this program is a valuable service for new employees and it should be continued within the company.

    1   2   3   4   5

Use the section below to add any comments regarding the Buddy Program:

_____

_____

_____

_____

NEW EMPLOYEE THANK-YOU
LETTER AND EVALUATION

Dear   ,

Thank you so much for participating in our Buddy program. I sincerely hope you got a lot out of it personally, and that you will consider acting as a Buddy to a new employee yourself in the future. We hope this program helped you feel welcome and comfortable in our company very quickly.

This brief questionnaire is intended solely to help us in the review and redesign of the Buddy Program, to continuously improve the program to best meet everyone's needs.

Your responses and comments on the questionnaire are confidential, and are not used for any other purpose.

Please return this questionnaire to _____
by_____(date).

Sincerely,

[Program Coordinator's Name and Personal Signature Here]

NEW EMPLOYEE QUESTIONNAIRE

Please indicate which of the following apply to your Buddy Program experience, by circling the relevant number:

Use the following rating scale in this evaluation:
1 = Strongly disagree
2 = Disagree
3 = Neither agree not disagree
4 = Agree
5 = Strongly agree

1. I was satisfactorily briefed regarding my role and accountabilities as a Buddy.

   1   2   3   4   5

2. I was happy with the way in which I was allocated to my Buddy.

   1   2   3   4   5

3. My Buddy seemed satisfactorily briefed regarding his or her role.

   1   2   3   4   5

4. I was happy with the support provided by the Program Coordinator.

   1   2   3   4   5

5. The frequency of our Buddy meetings was adequate.

   1   2   3   4   5

6. The content of our Buddy discussions was appropriate.

   1   2   3   4   5

7. The goals and objectives of the Buddy relationship, as explained to me by the Program Coordinator, were met.

   1   2   3   4   5

8. This program helped me to feel welcome, valued, and comfortable in the company.

   1   2   3   4   5

9. The program was well organized, and the Program Coordinator managed the program appropriately.

   1   2   3   4   5

10. Overall, I feel this program is a valuable service for new employees.

   1   2   3   4   5

Use the section below to add any comments regarding the Buddy Program:

_____

_____

_____

_____

Chapter 9

Twenty Ways to Celebrate New Employees

When valued employees leave a company, often their peer group and managers take them out to a nice lunch, or they may have a get-together after work, or they may buy the departing employees gifts. We "celebrate" when an employee leaves the company. Doesn't it make even more sense to celebrate when a new employee arrives on the first day with the company? New employees want to feel included and valued when they start a new job. This chapter provides twenty great ideas to help you celebrate the arrival of your new employees and to help them feel like a part of the organization right away.

Appropriate Group Size: There are ideas in this section to fit any size orientation group. If you like one of the ideas but you have only a few new employees each week or month, consider having a quarterly New Employee Celebration, and use the ideas in this section to make all of the new employees for the quarter the guests of honor. The ideas listed vary in cost (some are no-cost ideas) to fit any company's budget.

NEW EMPLOYEE CELEBRATION IDEAS

1. Bring a cake with candles (one for each new employee) to the orientation program to celebrate the employees' "birthday" with the company.

2. Ask the CEO or division or department manager to call new employees on the phone to welcome them to the company.

3. Obtain a volume discount with a local florist and have a small plant or flower arrangement sent to the new employee's home.

4. Create a welcome banner for an employee's new office or cubicle that is signed by everyone in the department.

5. Give the new employee a restaurant gift certificate to celebrate the new job with a spouse or friend.

6. Send the new employee and his or her family a welcoming greeting card at their home.

7. Have a new employee lunch for spouses or friends during the first month or first quarter.

8. Give the new employee a blank greeting card to take around the department and obtain the signatures of all their department coworkers. A completed card can be rewarded with a small gift.

9. Schedule a donuts and coffee welcome breakfast for current employees to attend and meet the new employees.

10. Take a team picture of the group on the first day. Have this enlarged and signed by everyone in the photo.

11. Place notices about the new employees (individuals or groups, depending upon the number of new employees) in your company newsletter.

12. Give the new employee a pre-dated 5-year pin or certificate to show your desire and expectation that the employee will be part of the "family" for a long time.

13. Give employees license plate covers with the company's name and logo for their cars.

14. Give new employees "lunch for two" certificates to treat the person who has been the best mentor for them within the first 90 days to lunch.

15. Schedule a quarterly Appetizers and Applause event for current and new employees in the company or in each division to enjoy finger foods and applaud the new employees.

16. Provide party horns and plastic champagne glasses filled with white grape juice in the orientation program to create a party atmosphere. Place party confetti on the tables, crepe paper on the ceiling, and so on to achieve a celebration look in the room.

17. Give each new employee a white cap or an autograph bear (autograph bears are available through *www.orientaltrading.com* for only $4.80 each) to obtain the autographs of department coworkers.

18. Place photographs and brief bios of your new employees in a special place on your intranet Web site.

19. Send a welcoming e-mail message to the new employee's department that describes the new employee's past work experience and the new position to be held in the department.

20. Give each new employee a "Welcome Basket" of new office supplies, candies or other goodies, special crackers, a soda, and so on.

Rebecca Harmon is director of corporate human resources at DeRoyal. Rebecca received her bachelor's degree in Psychology with an emphasis in Industrial Organizational Psychology from the University of Tennessee. Rebecca joined DeRoyal in 1997, where she is responsible for all hiring practices, for ensuring compliance with all federal contract guidelines, and for facilitating employee relations. Rebecca served as a presenter at the 2000 International ASTD Conference.

Contact Information   *200 DeBusk Lane*
Powell, TN 37849
865-362-2341
rharmon@deroyal.com

Chapter 10

Subject Matter Experts As Orientation Speakers

Help Subject Matter Experts Deliver Effective Presentations

When designing a New Employee Orientation Program, one of the most frequently asked questions has to do with subject matter experts (SMEs)—those individuals who deliver orientation sessions on very specific topics, such as the use of particular computer software, benefits and compensation issues, or health and safety matters.

While these individuals can often do a superlative job, bringing enlightenment to otherwise arcane issues, sometimes they can put a wet blanket on an otherwise excellent learning experience. There's nothing worse than someone pulling on the handbrake right in the middle of your well-planned, world-class orientation program.

Even senior executives, who should be excellent presenters, have been known to speak too softly to be heard, or jingle the coins in their pockets, or drone on and on, or comment that they hoped the participants were still awake. Unfortunately, you can't assume that anyone is a good presenter until you've seen him or her in action.

Here are some actions plans to help make the most of your subject matter experts.

1. MAKE SURE YOU NEED THEM

Sometimes SMEs are used for historical reasons—lack of alternative resources, complexity of the subject—that have since been invalidated.

For example, maybe four years ago using Lotus Notes was a horrendously complex issue for your company, so you brought in someone from IT to deliver a session on it. Nowadays, there are enough prepackaged, asynchronous, Web-based training modules available for Lotus Notes that your IT person can be doing something she'd prefer doing, and you can reschedule Web-based learning sessions for times that suit the employees, rather than after lunch on your orientation day.

It's also important to choose your presenters very carefully. It's awkward and difficult to have to ask someone *not* to continue presenting at new employee orientation, so make good SME selections in the first place, to the best of your ability.

2. CONSIDER TRAPPING THE PRESENTATION

If you must use SMEs, why have them do it "live" every time?

Let's say you have a benefits presentation that is substantially the same each time it is made. Why not trap a PowerPoint presentation and add an audio commentary and a handout FAQ? Give out the SME's e-mail address and let him handle individual queries as necessary. Your SME can update the PowerPoint presentation as needed, and his appearance can be dispensed with or reduced to a 15-minute Q&A at the end of the orientation.

If you want to experiment with trapped presentations, start at: http://www.astound.com/ (free trial download of excellent software tool for multimedia presentations), or http://www.webex.com/ (Web-based system; good for interactive presentations).

3. SEND A BRIEFING NOTE

Perhaps for some reason, you must have SMEs there, delivering their spiels in person, every time. In that case, produce a clear, concise briefing note, clearly stating:

a. Who the audience will be and how large the audience is expected to be on average. Also, remind them that their audience will be new employees, and that they cannot make any assumptions that the participants will understand company-specific acronyms or other shorthand.

b. What, specifically, you want covered. (If necessary, specify what you *don't* want them to cover, or what they need to drop from their presentation.)

c. How long their sessions should last.

d. Whether you want them to take questions, and if so, for how long.

e. Whether they should have visual aid or slides (with text at least 24-point size), or handouts.

f. The time they should arrive to give their presentations, and how important it is to arrive a little early so there is no dead-air time in the program.

Send the note with a full agenda for the day and a copy of the other materials the participants will be receiving.

4. ASK FOR A RUN-THROUGH

Invite the SMEs to give you a run-through of what they propose to say. It's really too late to wait until they're in front of a live audience. Some SMEs believe they know their subject so well that they don't actually need to prepare; they'll want to just "wing it." Having a practice session usually convinces them otherwise.

5. INCLUDE OTHER SMEs

Not convinced your SMEs will turn up to give you a run-through? Ask *all* the SMEs to come to a practice run-through at the same time, and make the session interactive (i.e., have the SMEs give each other feedback). You'll find peer and competitive pressures will work for you and will push up the numbers (and the standard of delivery).

6. USE VIDEOTAPES

People who don't deliver training regularly (and most of your SMEs won't) often do not realize just how poor their delivery skills can be. Use a video replay to illustrate this. This should not be done from a negative standpoint; you don't want your SMEs to think you're just taking a pop at them.

Instead, brief the group gently on what to look for in a good presentation (eye contact, lucidity, summarizing, use of visual aids, etc.), and give them a checklist to mark each presentation *positively*—giving marks for each good point demonstrated by the SME. This will throw shortcomings into focus without seeming negative.

7. INSERT EXERCISES

The single greatest weakness inherent in most SME presentations is that they tend to become lectures rather than learning experiences.

People with exceptional functional knowledge (SMEs by another name) are not necessarily good trainers (though some of them are), and during an SME presentation you will often be faced with a group of new employees who are simply drowning in a sea of facts and statistics.

Break the SME's presentation down into modules of about 5 to 7 minutes in length. For each module, gently suggest an exercise of some sort that will give program participants an opportunity to test their understanding of what they've just been told. (Be careful that this doesn't become overcomplex in itself. If you're dealing with engineers or, God forbid, CPAs like myself, you might find that they'll take the idea of an exercise and run with it so far that you will end up with a three-day case study, examining every known variable.)

8. GIVE FEEDBACK

Make sure every SME-delivered session is scored separately and commented on by the participants, by you, and *by the SME.*

SMEs are rather contradictory in this regard. If you never bring up the subject of self-assessment, they'll happily deliver one presentation, wander out of the training room, go about their business for a month, and wander back in to take another session, all without giving the efficacy of their presentation a moment's thought.

On the other hand, ask an SME to analyze how he or she did, and the SME will often go into paroxysms of self-analysis.

You'll often find that the simple act of consistently asking SMEs to fill in a one-page assessment of how they thought the session went will in itself produce substantial improvements in later presentations.

IN SUMMARY

Not all SMEs are as bad as they've been painted here; but I was an SME for many years when I was a practicing CPA and, gosh, I know how bad we can be.

Don't let an unprepared subject matter expert drain the life from your orientation training. Take time to quietly implement these eight suggestions, maybe one by one, and in six months you'll have removed that SME "kiss of death."

J. Leslie McKeown is the president and CEO of Yellowbrick Consulting. Yellowbrick provides employee development solutions for organizations of all sizes, particularly in the areas of retention, orientation, and mentoring and coaching.

Author of *The Complete Guide to Orientation and Re-Orientation*, *The Complete Guide to Mentoring and Coaching*, and the "Deliver the Promise" Retention Master Class, Les travels widely, speaking and consulting on issues of employee development and corporate strategy.

This article is based on material contained in *The Complete Guide to Orientation and Re-Orientation*: http://orientation.deliverthepromise.com/manual.htm.

Contact Information　　　*Julie Wilson, Program Manager*
P.O. Box 954
Tiburon, CA 94920
800-446-9706
http://www.deliverthepromise.com
julie@deliverthepromise.com

Chapter 11

Designing Your Own Orientation Board Game

PIONEER'S CUSTOMIZED BOARD GAME: THE SEEDSMAN

As an educational consultant at Pioneer, I developed an in-house, customized, advanced orientation board game called The Seedsman, to match Pioneer's product line, industry, and organizational structure.

The Seedsman board game and simulation replaced a program that was the second step after the NEO program in which departmental guest speakers paraded in front of the group, talking about their respective departments. As each of them talked, they showed department budgets, organizational charts (typically of positions and people no longer in them!), departmental goals, and what they might be working on today. Does this sound familiar? Statistics and facts, goals and budgets, plus organizational charts of people and positions, when combined together, create a l-o-n-g day, and deaden the brightest of minds!

What would happen if you could combine several of these components and tell what the departments do and how they do it together, and have fun doing it at the same time? Using a game board platform for the industry simulation and teaming it up with a themed lecture format, you too can create a true learning experience in a fun environment.

A lot of people were skeptical at first about what I was trying to do. The terms board game, fun, business environment, and learning just don't seem to go together. But if you stick with it, you can create a fun learning platform that will help you to achieve your targeted outcome.

In the case of The Seedsman game, the primary outcome was to have our employees understand the complexities of the seed industry and how we launch products into the market. The game simulation and lecture format also allowed employees access to key departmental managers, networking beyond their traditional groups, presentation skills, and last but not least, team-building skills.

This chapter describes how we conduct The Seedsman program, and a step-by-step process is provided to help you create your own customized orientation board game.

CREATING THE GAME BOARD

How do you build the components to make your own game board simulation? In today's market, everyone is on the computer. If your simulation is computer-based, it can replicate everything you can do on a board-based game. I chose the manual approach for my first outing, as I wanted to take away the "black box" effect that most simulations have. (For example, I made this move and this is the outcome but I do not know why, since the cause and effect are performed by some algorithm.)

No matter what format is chosen, it is important that it represents what is happening and could happen in your industry, and represents how your company does business. If you can create a fantasy industry that is tied to specific business realities, you will add credibility to your program. As you lay out your theme or desired outcomes of the program, you need to identify specific groups within your organization. I chose the product launch of a new technology of genetically modified corn as my targeted theme.

Next you need to identify which departments contribute to make a product launch successful. In my industry group, several major departments are involved in launching a product: marketing, research, production, regulatory and government affairs, sales, and finance (administration). This fact-finding portion of the work has to be done to lay the foundation of your program.

You need to get a consensus on your theme and then layer in how each of these departments contributed to your desired outcome. In my case, I wanted to identify how each of these departments had affected the product launching process. For each major group, you will need to understand what fundamental components need to be in place (this would be matched to the concept or theme you have chosen). Then, identify the tools, technologies, and systems that should be in place in order to make your game or simulation reality-based. The information gathered in this process will determine the game cards and the industry impact cards used in the playing of your business simulation.

While you are gathering the information for the tools of your game, start laying out your board. In years of playing various board games, I had never paid attention to the number of spaces on a game board or how they were laid out—until I started laying out mine. I used a sheet of flip chart paper to give me enough room to lay out the board.

Draw out a rectangle within a larger rectangle. Give yourself enough space between the rectangles so that you can draw lines to create the spaces on your game board. After playing around to determine how many spaces should be on the board, I found that the range is somewhere between 20 and 28 spaces. Too few, and the game moves too fast; too many, and the game moves too slowly. I ended up using 24 spaces on my board and laid it out using Post-It notes. This gave me the flexibility to lay out action squares on the board without having to erase everything each time I made a change.

The game board also has several free spaces, such as the four seasons: Spring, Summer, Fall, and Winter. The board also has spaces that help move the game along, such as "Fall back one space," "Spring forward two spaces," and my favorite, "Fall back the number on a single die roll." People always question why the last one should be on the board. In everyone's markets, some companies seem to keep moving forward while others are slowed down for whatever reasons. Falling back the number of a single die roll seems to capture what goes on in the markets.

There are two other special spaces on the board that allow teams to build facilities for research and production and to determine where they want to source their products or research—overseas or domestically. There is one penalty space on the board, labeled: "Summertime blues—Pay the tax man 10% of all fixed assets." You can name your own penalty, based on what might occur in your industry.

A graphic of the layout of The Seedsman game is included later in this chapter. The actual game layout was designed in-house by our graphic artists. I gave them the number of squares and contents for each one, and I let their imaginations build the rest. The board was then overlaid on an illustration by a contracted outside artist. The end product resulted in a game board that's appealing, functional, and professional-looking. (Parker Brothers, watch out!)

CREATING ACTIVITY CARDS FOR THE GAME BOARD

In order to fill out the squares on the board, you will need to identify and categorize the information you have been collecting from the various departments within your organization. I chose some generic titles for my cards: Options, Technology, Disaster, and Workforce Needs.

For each deck of cards, identify key items and concepts that represent outcomes or tools needed to build a successful company. An Option card might read: "You have an option to upgrade your sales forecasting system to improve your delivery time and decrease excess inventory carryover. Cost is $3,000." Options represent ways to improve your company by giving it a competitive advantage over your competitors. Options could range from public awareness programs to ISO 9000 certifications or whatever is relevant to your industry group.

The next cards in The Seedsman game are Technology cards. These include technologies we currently have and those we could have or that will soon be on the market. The companies that have the new technologies will be better positioned for the future. A Technology card might read: "Your company has the option to buy access to a new gene-splicing technique that will allow for putting switches on genes. Cost is $6,000." Technology and access to it differentiates companies within each industry group. You could tie some technologies together to amplify ending outcomes of the game.

Disaster cards are special to the game of business, as some disasters affect only the company drawing the card. For example, "A tornado has partially destroyed your production facility, causing setbacks in supply; you have the option to repair the plant for $xxxxx and get back on line as soon as possible, or collect from insurance $xxxxx and lower your supply capabilities." Another Disaster card might read: "Your company has just been awarded a patent on a technique used by all of the other companies in your industry; collect $xxxxx from each competitor."

Workforce Needs cards were introduced in the game later in order to show the complexity of today's employment markets. These cards represent various jobs and careers within the company that add value. A Workforce Needs card might read: "Your company has been recognized nationally as being one of the best to work for in the industry. Because of this recognition, your recruiting costs have dropped by 20%; collect from the bank $xxxx."

Utilizing card decks to represent key components of your industry allows you to change, add, modify, or delete themes for your simulation. Since the beginning of The Seedsman game, the cards have been modified at least six times. This has kept the game as close to reality as possible and has allowed the outcomes to be tailored to the specific themes that departments would like highlighted during the simulation. Flexibility is key when you start thinking about putting the cards together, and it allows the session to stay current with what is going on in the industry.

Now that you have developed a master set of cards (options, disasters, technologies, and workforce needs) that shape outcomes for your industry, you need to put some values on what these companies have purchased or acquired during the session. I put three unique spaces on my board that I label "Industry Impact Card." These are written out on 3- by 5-inch index cards with outcomes for specific milestones or problems faced by your industry. When a team lands on one of these spaces, the game presenter pulls out a numerically sequenced card and reads out it out loud to all of the teams.

For example, if you operate a company in the agricultural sector, a drought would be disastrous to your bottom line; however, some companies would fare better than others if they had off-season production capabilities or irrigation systems in place. The impact card would indicate those that benefit and penalize those that did not put in backup systems.

Another Industry Impact card might read: "For those companies that invested in technologies X, Y, or Z, your market shares have gone up X%; collect $xxxx from the bank and $xxx from each competitor that does not own these technologies, as their respective market shares have dropped." The Industry Impact card rewards and penalizes teams, sometimes equally, but in most cases rewards those teams that have the tools, systems, and products in place, at the expense of the other teams.

One of the tricks I learned when setting up the game was to synchronize all of the card sets so that when an Industry Impact card is read out loud, there will be some teams with technologies or systems in place to benefit or be penalized. Some of the cards also have to be in place and coordinated with guest speakers' topics if they are used in conjunction with the simulation. The game or simulation can be played with or without guest departmental speakers, but I have found it works better with speakers than without.

THE PEOPLE AND RESOURCES YOU'LL NEED TO CREATE YOUR GAME

I approached the building of The Seedsman board game blind, not knowing what it took to build or lay out a project like this. I had played many different types of games in my youth, so from a player standpoint I had some expectations. I also had an understanding of how the industry and our company worked. Combining this background helped me to build The Seedsman board game.

To create your own game, you need to know where to look for the information to create the outcome you desire. Once I had the framework in place, I went out into the field and talked with folks about the base material I had in place. Was it accurate? What would happen if...? What should be added to make it more realistic? The questions just seemed to flow, and this resulted in a dynamic representation of what could happen in the agriculture sector that we do business in today. (Fact-finding and storytelling are important to the creation of a reality-based fantasy world.) Several months were spent (whenever there was free time available) creating the backdrop for the game.

In my group, we had some talented artists who shaped the board and brought a working model to life. Rich Azinger (*azingerrj@phibred.com* or *azingerrj@qwest.net*) and Jan Crouse (*scrouse@ruraltel.net*) both have extensive commercial art backgrounds, so ideas took form rather quickly. They identified an outside artist to draw the background illustration that the actual game is layered over. Using a professional illustrator to do the background and key pieces of the game cost around $1,500. We used a sticker format to create the team playing chips. These were then overlaid over common poker chips.

Small game boards were created so each team could track its respective movements. The small boards were glued over poster board stock. The master board is a piece of common steel that measures 30" by 36" (and cost under $20). The game board was glued over this and the edges of the steel were taped in order make the game safe to move and handle.

I used steel because I wanted to be able to create a vertical playing surface so that all of the teams could clearly see from a distance where they were as well as where the competition were. Using poker chips with team labels on them, I attached magnetic tape to the back of the chips (simple but effective). Now I can move team markers around the vertical metal-backed game board.

I used red poker chips with magnetic tape as markers for the Industry Impact spaces. As teams landed on these spaces, I could slide their markers down from the space. This helps me to identify which of these spaces is active or free while the game is in progress.

Cost for the chips, magnetic tape, and logo stickers was around $30. The game illustrations used to create the small boards and the larger master board were printed in-house, but this could be done at your local print shop. Cost for this would vary by area.

I also had the group create a currency we could use to play the game. The money used is in denominations ranging from $500 to $50,000, and on each bill is a VP or the CEO of the company. This adds a lot of flavor to the game, and in addition, gives recognition to the people who run the business. Instead of "In God We Trust," we inserted "In Corn We Trust," since corn is our biggest product line. Have fun and use your imagination to add a personal touch to your end product at very little if any incremental cost.

The card decks used in the game are printed on both sides on heavy paper stock. The thickness used is similar to what is used for common playing cards. For each of the decks created (Disaster, Technology, Options, and Workforce Needs), the front portion of each card has a specific color and graphic to depict the category, and the reverse side contains the action that is associated with the category. I made several copies (ranging from 2 to 4) of each incident that could occur, so in any given deck of 50 or 60 cards, you could have 15 to 30 individual outcomes replicated 2 to 4 times.

You can shuffle the cards to make actions happen at random, or stage them prior to the class to match lectures or Industry Impact outcomes. Being able to change the game by changing the cards gives you flexibility, and this also allows you to link all aspects of the game together.

THE LOGISTICS OF THE PIONEER ORIENTATION PROGRAM

Advanced employee orientation (The Seedsman game that is described in this chapter) is given once every three months and as needed for special occasions or seminars.

The average orientation group size ranges from 18 to 27 participants; the smallest size was 14, and we have had up to 165 participants at a time (in one large lecture format and in five simultaneous, independent games).

Depending upon your group size, the entire program can be held in a single conference room, or you could use an auditorium for the lecture piece and utilize multiple classrooms for the individual games. The game can be taken on the road with the use of taped guest lectures or done with just the game format.

To run the program, you will need a presenter and a banker. The presenter is in charge of the game and leads the participants through the program. The banker is the assistant and handles all the transactions that occur while the game is going on. I have led the game without a banker, and found that can take away the momentum of the game if you are not careful.

Most companies have very large departmental groups such as Production, Sales, Research, and Administration that work independently, yet are closely linked. Typically, everyone gets caught up in their respective departments and rarely has a chance to interact cross-departmentally.

In order to break down these artificial barriers, each team of four or five players is preselected and assigned to include as many different groups or functions of the company as possible. The goal is to have folks who don't already know each other work together on each game board, to create a chance for networking and for the interaction of different viewpoints. The tip is to take control of your participant list and not to let chance control your desired outcome.

Depending upon your target audience, you may decide to split up your players differently. In my application, I might have a wide range folks who are new to the company, or people who have been with the company for many years. The program not only acquaints new employees to the industry, but also fine-tunes the big picture for employees who have been around awhile.

During a full-day session, we typically play seven to eight game-playing rounds of 15 minutes each, with lectures between each round. During the course of a day, teams can circle several times around the game board. In any given trip around the board, there are only three Industry Impact cards per round; if a fourth team lands on the space it becomes a free space. Once a team has passed the starting position, the spots are reactivated as they move around the board. Multiple teams can land on all of the other card spots (Option, Technology, Disaster, and Workforce Needs) and pick up their respective cards, with no limit to the cards given out in a single round.

GAME TIME!

To conduct the game, each team is given its own board to play on and each team is responsible for tracking its individual progress. I also use a larger master board up front to track all of the teams. Having a master control board allows you to control the flow of the game and keeps everyone on the same page. Each team role its die, and then calls out the die results in sequence for each team, to be tracked on the master board. All transactions must occur before teams roll again. The design of the game is to make it as interactive as possible, so specific roles are assigned to the team members (Accountant, Runner, and Spokesperson).

Each game has a life of its own; how you manage it is key to its success. I start the program with lively music playing to set the mood for the game, and to help get the competitive juices flowing.

Set the scene by going over the rules (the participants should have been sent a copy of the rules and an agenda prior to the class) and explaining how the day is laid out. On the teams' respective tables are envelopes that contain documents giving the teams their starting points, cash or assets, and technologies, as well as team lists and additional background information they may or may not need to play the simulation. The information that is not needed to play the game still helps to set the stage and gets the players in the right frame of mind.

Note that the team's starting points are different in terms of how they are balanced. You will need to decide how you want to do this in your game. The team starting points vary quite a bit to represent what is going on in our market. Each time we have run The Seedsman game, the outcomes have been different. The strongest team at the start has not always finished on top, so we have had some interesting debriefings.

Game play is kept between 15 and 20 minutes at a time and is used to split up the lecture portion of the program. The lecture time per speaker is kept to between 30 and 45 minutes, including Q&A time. If the speaker and the audience are deeply into the topic, I will allow some slippage of time, as the learning piece of the program is more important than the gaming piece. The gaming piece is the platform for learning and keeps the fun element alive, and it adds life to what has been given in the lecture portion of the program. It is important to get the key personnel from each department to present their sections of the program, as this allows employees to meet and have a discussion with key influencers within the company.

Sequence the speakers' topics in the order of how they would impact the process you are trying to impart to your audience. It is important to have a common thread that pulls the day together, and to make sure there is a tie between the speakers and the game simulation. In the case of The Seedsman game, the product launch process is that common thread.

The cards should also be sequenced in the decks so they coincide with the presentations and with the Industry Impact cards that are read. The game/lecture format puts the day into high gear, and time moves fast. The game adds excitement to the learning process, a fact that comes out in every survey we have done on the program.

We do two other things to spice up the day and add some color to the program. One of the lectures has to do with regulatory affairs. Toward the end of this lecture, I have someone pound on one of the doors and I burst in through another entrance overdressed as a protester, carrying protest signs. The protester confronts the speaker with current issues regarding food safety, GMOs, monarch butterflies, and the science behind the industry.

If your company makes a product, you might have an irate customer crash your meeting and then have the presenter address and handle the complaints. Use your imagination—the more outrageous the skit is, the more active the class discussion becomes (and the more they will remember it!). After the skit, we debrief the situation.

One employee told me: "I went home for the holidays and while I was eating my dinner, my aunt asked me the same questions that were in your protester skit, and I actually had the answers. If I hadn't been in the program, I'm not sure what my response would have been. Thanks." What is it worth to have an informed employee with the ability to represent your company properly?

The second thing I add is that at the end of the session, I have a wrap-up exercise that helps pull the session together. Remember that each team has a spokesperson. The teams are given about 10 minutes to prepare to sell their companies to the shareholders in the room. Each player is given two voting shares to select which company and management he or she would invest in. They may vote for themselves individually only once; therefore, they must also select at least one other team. The teams consult among themselves and put together a prospectus to the investment community, explaining why they should invest in their company.

This is my favorite part of the program, because the participants actually have to tell you what they did, why they did it, and what their company is worth. Several skill sets come into play: team interaction and communication, creative thinking by individuals and groups, public speaking and presentation skills, and the fun of doing it! The class picks the winners and the losers.

I always have some gimmick prizes for the winning team and losing team (the team with the least votes). When the winners are announced, I call out the losing team first. At first, they think they have won. That is when I say that they hit hard times and the prize I have for them is a rain gauge, so that they can find better places to plant their businesses.

The actual winning team is then announced and the group is told that this team is so hot that we have selected a special prize for them—a thermometer to measure just how hot they are. Everyone laughs and has fun. The point is that they all won; we just found a different way of getting everyone up to speed on how the company and the industry do business, with a better understanding of how they fit into the big picture and how they contribute to make it happen.

LESSONS LEARNED ALONG THE WAY

When we did our first pilot program with speakers, we asked them to talk about their departments and how they were part of the product launch. During the first session, I found that even though I gave them a specific area of focus to talk about, the process flow from one speaker to the next was not there. Time was spent with each speaker and we customized the presentations so there would be a good overlap and a uniform message. The modifications made to each presentation were minor, but they had a major impact on the quality of the end product.

Make sure you conduct a program survey and share those results directly with all of the presenters. I had one presenter consistently score poorly in the surveys. I then spent time coaching him and helped him make some adjustments in his program. The result was higher survey scores and a manager who felt better about public speaking and now uses improved presentation materials. The outcome improved, the program got better, and so did the manager's presentation skills.

There is pride of ownership when creating a board game simulation, but it is important to listen to what your peers and participants have to say and to make modifications as you go. This makes for a more dynamic and realistic learning environment. Making changes to keep the game current in today's business climate adds credibility to your program. The design of the game allows for easy updating by changing playing cards and Industry Impact cards. The platform remains the same, but you can change the targeted outcomes.

RESULTS, FEEDBACK, AND MEASUREMENTS

The purpose of The Seedsman game simulation is to impart knowledge of how Pioneer does business and to introduce some of the quirks that face and shape industry outcomes. The goal then is to immerse the participants in this industry knowledge by showing how the company takes a product to market. We sprinkle in multiple scenarios for them to react to, and we reward them or penalize them based on the outcomes of the game.

A survey was designed to measure the program's effectiveness in generating knowledge of what is going on in the industry, and to measure the participants' understanding of how all the major departments work together.

We use a survey format that includes a rating system of 1 to 5 (with 5 being the highest rating), and we also ask for written comments when appropriate. Reviews are done for each presenter or lecturer, and the survey includes general questions about the game. We try to summarize results soon after the session and send the feedback to all the presenters. Our speakers have average scores in the low 4's (ranges between 3.2 and 4.4), and the game simulation's average score is in the low to mid 4's.

FEEDBACK FROM PARTICIPANTS ON THE LECTURE PORTION OF OUR ORIENTATION

The following are exerpts from last year's surveys regarding the lecture portion of the program:

"Speaker did an excellent job in intercepting the GreenPeace protester."

"The skit was a fun way to put it all into perspective."

"[The] interactive nature of presentation and discussion was refreshing and enjoyable."

"The mock activist crash really livened up the session."

"[The presenter] did a great job handling the questions."

"Lots of information in a short period of time—very beneficial—good presentation."

"I would have liked more time for marketing."

"Excellent—made it understandable and I loved the examples and stories used to fully explain the process."

"The speaker gave examples that were easy to understand and relate to."

"The speaker was very knowledgeable and fielded the questions quite well."

"The speaker was interesting and I could tell that [the speaker] knew and cared about what he was talking about."

However, presenter feedback is not always favorable. Examples of less favorable feedback include the following:

"[There is] room to increase presentation dynamics."

"The presenter spoke too fast."

"I did not grasp a lot of the concepts."

"Too much detail."

"Organization of marketing department could be shortened and spend more time on how to determine what products to launch."

"Nice casual pace—maybe too detailed."

FEEDBACK FROM PARTICIPANTS ON THE GAME PORTION OF OUR ORIENTATION

Here are exerpts taken from the last year's surveys regarding the lecture portion of the program:

"The Seedsman game was very good as it helped me understand Pioneer."

"The game was very interesting as it covered the most important aspects of a competitive company. It helped me make some decisions more easily."

"It gave me a better understanding of the industry."

"It was nice to have real-world issues in the format of a game."

"It made me think about some of the market effects that one does not tend to think about."

"I liked the gaming challenge."

"I liked how it integrated everything and allowed us to meet people and see how things are done in other countries."

"[I liked the] interaction between teammates and trying to pull everything together and market what we had."

"I enjoyed the breakup of the lectures and game play."

"Time flew by and I learned a lot."

"Great correlation to real life, as the Industry Impact cards dealt with real examples."

"I was overwhelmed with just how much I was able to absorb...Fun, fun, fun, and still able to learn!"

"It was a really exciting and instructive day."

Some of the negative feedback on the game and program is presented to help you consider these potential issues as you are developing your own games:

"I sometimes got more wrapped up in the game and not as wrapped up in the speakers."

"[There] didn't seem to be a penalty for growth."

"Decisions sometimes were all guesswork."

"There were several Workforce Needs spaces on the board; however, none of the Industry Impact cards concerned this area."

"Sometimes the game was too general and the speakers were too detailed."

"Some of the option cards need a more elaborate explanation to better understand their effect on the company."

"I could not always apply what the speakers talked about to what was happening in the game."

Overall, the format of using the game simulation and speakers has generated positive responses from both the participants and the speakers themselves. The lecture/game format works as long as the game is reality-based and you have identified a targeted theme or outcome. Good luck to you as you develop your own board game!

Tim A. Little is Educational Consultant at Pioneer Hi-Bred International, Inc. (a DuPont Company).

Contact Information   *7000 NW 62nd Ave.*
PO Box 1000
Johnston, IA 50131-1000
515-270-3154
Tim.Little@pioneer.com

PIONEER HI-BRED'S SEEDSMAN BOARD GAME

Here is a picture of The Seedsman game board. The actual game layout was layered over a professionally drawn illustration. It is important that the game board look and play like any other game that you might purchase on the market. The backdrop of the game is based on the agricultural sector and city of Des Moines, Iowa, reflecting the industry we are in and our company's location.

Chapter 12
Using Icebreakers and Games

Five Ways to Make Your Orientation Games and Icebreakers More Successful

Icebreakers and games have an important role to play in employee orientation—if they are used correctly. If used poorly, they can actually ruin a complete orientation process.

Here are our top tips for using icebreakers and games correctly in employee orientation.

1. MAKE SURE YOU KNOW THE ICEBREAKER OR GAME INSIDE OUT

Don't go into a session unsure of how a particular icebreaker or game is set up, how it plays out, and how to end it in a timely fashion.

Some games can appear reasonably simple when you read through the instructions, and there is always a temptation to "wing it" on the first day. This can be a recipe for disaster when, five minutes into the game, you find that there are unexpected wrinkles that are leading you down paths you never anticipated ... .

Always try out *any* games or icebreakers, however simple they may seem, *before* your program begins. It doesn't exactly instill confidence in new hires if one of the first things they do in the new job turns out poorly.

2. PERFORM WITH CONFIDENCE

If you cannot conduct the game with confidence, get someone else to do it.

If you are not relaxed about directing an icebreaker or game, you will make the participants nervous, and they will freeze. If you don't feel you can carry it off, get a colleague to present this part of the program, or drop the idea altogether.

3. BE CAREFUL WITH ENTRY-LEVEL NEW HIRES

In our work with new hires, we've discovered a very surprising, seemingly counter-intuitive fact: The closer the new employees are to their first job, the less they want (and the less they enjoy getting involved in) so-called fun and light activities.

Think about it. A bright young person straight out of college who wants to come join your organization, *doesn't* want to arrive on the first day and be treated as if he or she is back in college again. These new hires have enormous expectations for what is, to some extent, a rite of passage. It's their first job; they want to come in, wear whatever the appropriate dress is, and feel that they're being taken seriously as businesspeople and will be treated as such by others.

That's not to say you can't have icebreakers and games in an entry-level orientation program. Just make sure they are in context and are balanced with equally relevant, serious content.

Interestingly, in orientation activities for middle managers, you can have a lot more fun. Middle managers don't have the same expectations that entry-level hires do. They've had their ponderous "9 to 5 moments" and are quite happy to kick back, loosen up a bit, and have some fun.

4. AND WATCH REORIENTATION PROGRAMS TOO

When undertaking reorientation, perhaps after a merger or a major change in the organization's business plan, be careful again with icebreakers and games.

The atmosphere in a reorientation session can be very different from that in orientation. There can be fear, concern, and uncertainty. Coupled with this fact is the fact that the participants know the organization, and possibly you, very well. This can engender cynicism and create a difficult environment in which to carry off an icebreaker or game successfully.

5. FIND GOOD ICEBREAKERS AND GAMES

Given the caveats, a great icebreaker or game can help significantly in the difficult process of building rapport with new hires. The issue is, where can you find good ones? Here are a couple of sources.

1. First, refer to Part 5, Orientation Games and Activities (in this book) for tried-and-true games that are designed for use specifically in orientation programs.

2. *The Big Book of Business Games: Icebreakers, Creativity Exercises, and Meeting Energizers*

   (Games Trainers Play Series)

   Edited by Edward Scannell (Contributor) and John W. Newstrom

   Paperback; 170 pages. (January 1996) McGraw-Hill; ISBN: 0070464766

3. *The Complete Games Trainers Play*

   Experiential Learning Exercises

   Edited by Edward E. Scannell and John W. Newstrom (Contributor)

   Hardcover ringbound edition. (April 1995) McGraw-Hill; ISBN: 0070464324

Note: Items 2 and 3 are popular books on icebreakers and games. The danger is that, because they are so popular, everybody seems to have played every game in these books!

4. *Active Training*

   A Handbook of Techniques, Designs, Case Examples, and Tips

   Edited by Mel Silberman and Carol Auerbach

   Hardcover, 304 pages, 2nd edition. (June 1998) Pfeiffer & Co; ISBN: 0787939897

In addition to presenting icebreakers and games, this book is also a great resource for adding participant interaction in your training sessions in lots of other ways.

5. http://www.thiagi.com/

   Thiagi (Dr. Sivasailam Thiagarajan) is a genius, nothing less. If you like games, you'll love this site.

Finally, here are a few Web sites where various individuals have gathered together lists of icebreakers:

   http://www.du.edu/~citin/activitypage.html

   http://adulted.about.com/library/blicebreakers.htm

   http://www.hcc.hawaii.edu/intranet/committees/FacDevCom/guidebk/teachtip/101thing.htm

These sites contain lots of additional activities as well as icebreakers.

Enjoy! And remember, you don't have to use the exact same icebreakers and games in every orientation. Especially if the same person facilitates the orientation program each time, he or she can alternate games (that fulfill the same purpose or objective) to keep the program fresh and interesting.

J. Leslie McKeown is the president and CEO of Yellowbrick Consulting. Yellowbrick provides employee development solutions for organizations of all sizes, particularly in the areas of retention, orientation, and mentoring and coaching.

Author of *The Complete Guide to Orientation and Re-Orientation, The Complete Guide to Mentoring and Coaching,* and the "Deliver the Promise" Retention Master Class, Les travels widely, speaking and consulting on issues of employee development and corporate strategy.

This article is based on material contained in *The Complete Guide to Orientation and Re-Orientation:* http://orientation.deliverthepromise.com/manual.htm.

Contact Information   *Julie Wilson, Program Manager*
P.O. Box 954
Tiburon, CA 94920
800-446 9706
http://www.deliverthepromise.com
julie@deliverthepromise.com

Part 3

Program Designs and Case Studies

Benchmark Your Company's New Employee Orientation Program against These Industry Leaders

INTRODUCTION

Whether you are creating a new employee orientation program for the first time or updating your current program, one of the first things you will need to do is determine the topics to be covered in (or added to) your program. It is often difficult for a seasoned employee to think of all the things new employees need to know when they come into the company. Therefore, this section can be used, in addition to your internal needs assessment, to shape the outline and performance objectives of your own program.

This section provides the following tools:

- The New Employee Orientation Shopping List—This is a comprehensive checklist of potential topics for a new employee orientation program. Simply review the list and check the topics that pertain to your company. Then use the customized list to form the basic outline for your program.

- Program Designs—Several companies have contributed outlines and topics used in their own new employee orientation programs. Review these sample curriculums to help you to determine:

  - The timing of the orientation program

❑   The content of the orientation program

❑   How to intersperse activities, games, and videos into your program

❑   The sequence of topics covered in the program

❑   How other companies use guest speakers in their programs to cover specific topics

It is also a good idea to review feedback from new employees to determine topics that need to be added. It is best to obtain this feedback after employees have been with the company a few weeks but not more than one to two months. It is during this period that employees are still "learning the ropes" and can clearly tell you which ropes they are having the most trouble navigating. Those are the areas you need to add or enhance in your program. Refer to Part 6, Orientation Checklists and Surveys, for surveys that can be used for this purpose.

Chapter 13

The New Employee Orientation Shopping List

New Employee Orientation is often the most customized training program in any corporation; it must be geared to your company's specific culture, policies, procedures, and values, so it is very important to conduct a thorough needs assessment process to determine the objectives of your own program.

This New Employee Orientation "Shopping List" can help accelerate your orientation needs assessment process by providing a checklist of potential topics that have been used in the orientation programs of other companies. Use the checklist in needs assessment interviews, focus groups, or surveys. If you are in the process of updating your orientation program, use the shopping list to identify any potential objectives that should be added to your course.

THE NEW EMPLOYEE ORIENTATION
SHOPPING LIST

Check the topics that are appropriate to include in your company's orientation program, orientation materials, and/or employee handbook:

Company Culture/Integration Topics

❑ The Company's Mission Statement

❑ The Company's Vision Statement

❑ Company Strategy/Goals

❑ The Company's History

❑ Company Leaders/Executives

❑ A Facility Tour

❑ Organizational Chart(s)

❑ The Company's Quality Program(s)

❑ Group/Individual Photographs

❑ Lunch with Company Leaders

❑ Parent Company Information

❑ Company Subsidiary Information

❑ Industry Awards/Recognition

❑ Top Market Niches

❑ Company Values

❑ The Company's Products/Services

❑ The Company's Customers

❑ Company Logo(s), Marketing Plans

❑ The Company's Competitors

❑ Diversity Training/Cultural Awareness

❑ Customer Service Training

❑ NYSE Symbol/Information

❑ Company Locations/Size(s)

❑ Executive Presentations

❑ Company Growth—Past and Future

❑ Business Partners of the Company

❑ Press Releases

❑ Company Stories/Case Studies

Company Benefits

❑ Medical Insurance Benefits

❑ Vision Insurance

❑ Short-Term Disability

❑ Life Insurance

❑ Flexible Spending Accounts

❑ Stock Option Programs

❑ Free or Discounted Meals

❑ Tuition Reimbursement

❑ Dental Insurance Benefits

❑ Vacation Benefits

❑ Personal Accident Insurance

❑ Concierge Services

❑ Cafeteria Location

❑ Directory of Local Restaurants

❑ Compensation/Bonus Policies

❑ Profit Sharing Benefits

❑ On-Site or Near-Site Day Care

❑ The Holiday Schedule

❑ Long-Term Disability

❑ Floating Holidays

❑ Pension/Retirement Programs

❑ Child Care Assistance

- ❏ Paid Volunteer/Charity Time
- ❏ 401(k) Programs/Investment Options
- ❏ Employee Discounts
- ❏ Child Care Assistance
- ❏ Sick Child Assistance
- ❏ Employee Assistance Program

- ❏ Accidental Death/Dismemberment Insurance
- ❏ Business Travel Accident Insurance
- ❏ On-Site Health Services
- ❏ Workout Facilities
- ❏ New Hire Referral Bonus Program

Company Policies and Procedures

- ❏ Work Hours/Work Schedules
- ❏ Telephone Procedures
- ❏ Telephone Directory
- ❏ Emergency Procedures
- ❏ Computer/Internet Usage Policies
- ❏ The Payroll Schedule
- ❏ Inclement Weather Policy
- ❏ Travel Policies/Procedures
- ❏ Sick Time Policies/Procedures
- ❏ Performance Appraisal Periods
- ❏ Corporate Credit Card Policies
- ❏ Ethics Policies
- ❏ Code of Conduct Policies
- ❏ Emergency Procedures
- ❏ Locations of Fire Extinguishers
- ❏ Environmental Issues
- ❏ Purchasing Forms/Procedures
- ❏ Breaks and Meal Periods
- ❏ Weapons Policy
- ❏ Alcohol/Drug Abuse Policies
- ❏ Insider Trading Policies
- ❏ Family Leave Policies/Procedures
- ❏ Smoking Areas/Policies
- ❏ Sending Interoffice/U.S. Mail
- ❏ Visitor Policies

- ❏ Company Courier Services
- ❏ Worker's Compensation
- ❏ Conflict of Interest Policy
- ❏ Ergonomics
- ❏ Performance Appraisal Policies
- ❏ Jury Duty
- ❏ Gum Chewing Policy
- ❏ Uniforms
- ❏ Employee Suggestion Box/Policy
- ❏ Appropriate Grooming Guidelines
- ❏ The Dress Code
- ❏ Parking Policies
- ❏ Purchasing Policies/Procedures
- ❏ E-Mail Policies
- ❏ Timesheet Procedures
- ❏ Sexual Harassment Policies
- ❏ Harassment Reporting Procedure
- ❏ Recycling
- ❏ Bereavement Policy
- ❏ Overtime Policies
- ❏ Expense Report Procedures
- ❏ Reserving a Conference Room
- ❏ Break Room Locations/Policies
- ❏ Union Policies
- ❏ Attendance/Tardiness Policies

❏ Flextime Policies

❏ Serving Customers with Disabilities

❏ Risk Management Policies/Procedures

❏ Gross Misconduct

❏ Confidentiality Policies

❏ Solicitation Policies

❏ Policy on Radios in the Workplace

❏ Copier Locations, User Codes

❏ Office Furniture Requests and/or Keys

❏ Voice Mail Procedures

❏ Company Property Policies

❏ Proprietary Information Policy

❏ Security Services/Contact Information

❏ Handling Customer Complaints

❏ Equal Employment Opportunity Policy

❏ Visitor Policies

❏ Solicitation Policies

❏ Employee Complaint Resolution

Company Programs and Services

❏ Safety Programs/Sanitation

❏ The ATM Location

❏ Security Services and Policies

❏ Training Programs

❏ The Company's IT Help Desk

❏ Charitable Initiatives

❏ Volunteer Opportunities

❏ Corporate Travel Services

❏ Employee Suggestion Box/System

❏ On-Site College Courses

❏ Wellness Programs

❏ Internal Job Transfer Program

❏ Employee Programs

❏ Technical/Computer Training

❏ Sick Bay Area/First Aid Supplies

❏ Employee Sports Teams

❏ Ergonomics Products/Services

❏ Company Toastmaster's Club

❏ Company Weight Watcher's Club

❏ Family Services/Events

❏ Career Planning Services

❏ Company Newsletter

❏ Prenatal Programs

❏ Company Store—Physical or Virtual

Other Activities or Topics

❏ Have employees sign I-9 forms and provide appropriate identification.

❏ Take photos of employees for security badges.

❏ Conduct tours of laboratories, assembly lines, manufacturing areas.

❏ Plan team-building and icebreaker exercises.

❏ Demonstrate the company's intranet site.

❏ Hold breakfast or lunch for new employees.

❏ Prepare taped or live CEO presentation.

❏ Explain mentor or buddy programs.

❏ Provide a package of basic office supplies.

❏ Obtain information for business cards.

❏ Obtain a completed nameplate order form.

❏ Have employees complete an Emergency Contact form.

❏ Issue vehicle identification or parking stickers.

❏ Have employees complete automatic paycheck deposit forms and obtain sample canceled checks.

❏ Provide a basic office supply package.

Chapter 14

Tried-and-True Orientation Design

A Step-by-Step Guide to Orientation Planning, Delivery, and Evaluation

This new employee orientation case study began when a bank opened several new branches. Although orientations had previously been developed for various departments and branches within the bank, none was comprehensive enough to meet the current need. Further, the bank wanted to ensure that new employees acquired consistent knowledge and skills during their orientations. The bank contracted Alamar Performance Learning, Inc. to lead the development of an orientation program for the new branches.

Although the program Alamar ultimately designed for the bank continues to be updated and enhanced over the years since its initial implementation, the program design is solid and effective and is still used today.

STEP 1: IDENTIFY TRAINING NEEDS AND SKILL GAPS

Initial information was collected for the needs analysis through a printed questionnaire sent to a sampling of current branch employees, including recent hires, branch managers, tellers, and people who had developed their own orientation programs for their areas of the bank. The questionnaire covered demographics, skill and knowledge gaps, prior training experiences, attitudes, expectations, and resource availability. Using that information as a foundation, we conducted a focus group to get more specific information in certain areas, and to obtain reactions to possible instructional strategies.

STEP 2: CREATE AN ORIENTATION PROGRAM DEVELOPMENT TEAM

The program development team for the project was composed of cross-departmental bank employees, two computer system vendors, and Alamar. The Project Manager was a bank employee. Other bank employees helped design the program, developed training materials, installed hardware and software, facilitated the classroom-based sessions, and provided administrative support. Alamar consulted with the Project Manager about the organization of the team and the management of the project. We also developed the instructional strategy and program design, identified existing materials that could be used, developed new materials, and managed the control and production of materials.

STEP 3: IDENTIFY THE TARGET AUDIENCE

The audience for the orientation program included personal bankers, tellers, and branch customer service representatives. Some had prior banking experience. Surprisingly, all were computer literate. Although there was some overlap in the knowledge and skills required of the three audience groups, the technical skills related to each job differed.

STEP 4: INVOLVE THE NEW EMPLOYEES' MANAGERS

Bank managers attended a two-hour workshop to prepare for the orientation their new employees were about to attend. At this workshop, they discussed the orientation's performance objectives and structure and the roles and responsibilities of everyone involved. There was considerable discussion in the workshop about logistics and potential issues. The branch managers received a Branch Managers' Guide containing a schedule for each of their new employees, performance objectives, descriptions of all activities, a list of people to call for help, instructions for preparing their designated coach, and coaching guidelines.

Each branch manager was responsible for designating one or more coaches for his or her branch. The coaches were briefed by the branch managers on-site and were given a Coaches' Guide. Similar to the Branch Managers' Guide, the Coaches' Guide described the orientation and the various activities designed to enable the new employees to apply and reinforce what they learned during the workshops. It listed the performance objectives for each day and guidelines for helping the new employees achieve those objectives. It also included a "Who to Call" section and coaching tips.

Orientation program staff visited the branches throughout the orientation to answer questions and to provide support to the branch managers, coaches, and new employees.

STEP 5: DESIGN AND IMPLEMENT THE ORIENTATION PROGRAM

Alamar designed a two-week orientation program and divided the time between workshops designed for learners to acquire new skills and knowledge, and on-the-job application and reinforcement. The schedule was staggered, so an employee spent one or two days in class followed by one or two days on the job.

Two weeks before the orientation, each new employee received a Welcome Kit containing a welcome letter from the president of the bank, information about the orientation, benefits information and forms, a map, and a small gift bearing the bank's logo. The learners were expected to review these materials and complete their benefits forms before their first day of work.

To kick off the orientation, a breakfast was held on the first morning. Senior executives and everyone who had planned or developed the orientation joined the new employees for breakfast. The president spoke briefly, welcoming the new employees and reinforcing their decision to join the bank. The bank's orientation project manager explained the format and goals of the orientation, and showed a marketing video previously prepared by the bank. Following those presentations, the new employees had a chance to meet other employees and put faces to some of the names they had seen in their orientation packages.

The first two workshops included topics relevant to everyone, such as:

- An overview of the financial services industry

- The position of the bank within the industry

- The bank's competition

- A review of key banking concepts

- Specific bank terminology

- Benefits

- Employee development

Because the topics were universal, the entire group of new employees attended and had another opportunity to meet other new employees.

The remainder of the curriculum was segmented, so the learners attended only the workshops relevant to their jobs. For example, while Tellers reviewed debits and credits and handling the cash drawer, Loan Officers reviewed the terms of various loan products and the procedures for gaining approval for a loan. Subsequent workshops covered key bank directives, processes and procedures, product knowledge, and computer systems training. These workshops were highly interactive, incorporating small group activities, role plays, and brief lectures.

During the orientation curriculum, employees attended the computer system classes for the systems they would use on the job. These classes were hands-on and incorporated realistic bank examples to support the transfer of learning to the job. The new employees completed practice exercises using a training database and were expected to be able to perform all key systems operations. The instructors observed the learners and worked with any who were struggling. They also encouraged the learners to work through complex exercises in pairs.

In addition, the new employees took a tour to give them a more complete picture of the bank. They saw how checks were processed, where Help Desk calls were answered, and where other activities affecting them took place.

During the days when they were in their branches, the new employees split their time between reading product information, shadowing branch staff, and working through practice exercises focused on their responsibilities. Their New Employee Workbooks contained their schedule for the orientation, learning objectives for each day, reading assignments, a list of people to call for help on various topics, and practice activities. Each new employee also received job aids relevant to his or her position.

After a day or two on the job, the first 30 to 60 minutes of the following workshop was allocated to feedback about their on-the-job experiences and questions. Toward the end of the orientation, two half-days were unscheduled, and the new employees used this time to complete assignments and work on any areas in which they were having difficulty. They could sign up for review sessions, work with other new employees, or work alone, depending upon their needs.

STEP 6: EVALUATE THE PROGRAM: LEVEL ONE—CUSTOMER SATISFACTION

Performance-based evaluation forms were developed for each day of the program for new employee feedback. The branch managers, coaches, instructors, and Help Desk also completed evaluations so problem areas could be identified. The results of these evaluations were used to refine the program. The program has been updated and is still being used, although several years have passed since its introduction at the bank.

STEP 7: EVALUATE THE PROGRAM: LEVELS TWO AND THREE—TESTING FOR NEW SKILLS

The last two workshops were dedicated to testing. The new employees completed paper-based quizzes and demonstrated skills encompassed by the orientation (level-two evaluation). Other tests included on-the-job application skills (level-three evaluation).

For example, each teller was given a drawer and was expected to perform some of the transactions that would be performed on the job. The instructors and coaches worked with employees who had difficulties. Although two people dropped out of the program, everyone else passed the tests and received Certificates of Achievement.

STEP 8: REVIEW LESSONS LEARNED FOR CONTINUOUS IMPROVEMENT

In the spirit of continuous improvement, we present lessons learned during the development and implementation stages of the program, along with feedback from participants and managers. Enhancements and changes were made as appropriate to manage these issues and to further increase the high level of program success.

a. Although the new employees appreciated being able to learn a new area and then apply that knowledge on the job, many were overwhelmed at times during the program because of its scope. One suggestion was to cover all subjects except the computer systems during the first two weeks, and to provide computer system training during the following week or two. This suggestion was not feasible, however, because the ability to operate the computer systems was essential to all new employee jobs.

b. The quality of the coach had a significant impact on the learning experience. Initially, some coaches followed the program as it was designed, while others treated the new employees as extra pairs of hands, giving them tasks that were not necessarily those identified in the program. Until this situation was corrected, the new employees at these branches struggled. If time had permitted, holding a planning session with the coaches would have increased their commitment to the program and better prepared the coaches to perform their roles.

c. The branch managers agreed that the program was comprehensive and prepared the new employees for their jobs. Some branch managers said that they would have preferred to have the new employees complete the program offsite so that they would be fully trained when they started work at the branch.

d. Each workbook or guide was made up of many individual documents, so there were dozens, perhaps more than one hundred, separate documents. Although we used as many existing documents as possible, most documents were not available in electronic form. Additionally, we created new documents, so nearly all materials went through several stages of development and review. It became apparent very quickly that document control was going to be a challenge.

A week or two into development, this issue was addressed by bringing in a consultant who took responsibility for organizing the documents, tracking their status, and producing them. The consultant trained a bank employee to maintain the documents once the orientation was launched. Having a highly organized person design the document control system proved to be essential.

e. Including both experienced bank staff and consultants on the project team was effective. The bank staff brought subject matter expertise, an understanding of the bank's culture, and access to people who had useful materials. The consultants contributed strong project management experience, instructional design skills, and a fresh perspective on the previously developed orientation programs.

Kathy Kelso cofounded Alamar Performance Learning, Inc. She has extensive experience in the design of instructional strategies, management of training projects, and development of training materials. Kathy's work has earned her an Excellence in Practice Citation from the American Society of Training Development (ASTD) in its 1999 ASTD Excellence in Practice Awards in the Technical Training category.

Contact Information   *9055 Admirals Pointe Drive*
Indianapolis, IN 46236
317-823-9307
kkelso@alamar.com

Chapter 15

The REV Orientation Program

A Ford Motor Company Orientation for Salaried Employees

REV, Ford Motor Company's new employee orientation program for salaried employees, focuses on developing inspired employees who will be tomorrow's business leaders. New salaried employees from all functions of the company work together to build their understanding of the philosophy that they each "own" a piece of the business as their own personal responsibility.

Since the early 1990s, Ford Motor Company had a very strong new employee orientation that focused on employee assimilation, with an emphasis on understanding company processes and functions. In early 1999, Ford began a major transformation, moving from a manufacturing company to a consumer-focused company. It was decided that the new employee orientation program should also be developed to reflect this transformation, and REV was created.

WHAT DID FORD DO?

REV was developed to communicate a fast start to understanding and contributing to Ford's vision for the future. REV is what the new employee wants the future to be. REV means "revitalize" or "revolutionary," but it can also mean "revving an overall company engine."

THE DESIGN PROCESS

A design team was formed that included executive leadership from a business operation, two recent hires to the company, and the global director of education, training, and development. Lengthy team discussions, focus groups, and other research were used to determine the needs of both the company's business and the new employees.

The key concepts that emerged relate to new employees needing to be quickly exposed to an in-depth understanding of:

- brand and customer satisfaction, including their operational impact,

- flawless execution,

- Ford's transformation to a consumer company, and

- leadership and its evolving role for new employees.

New employees needed this information to be anchored in the context of the company's business strategy, including its designated leadership behaviors and "strategy pyramid," which is displayed throughout the company and reinforces the key concepts covered in the new employee orientation.

The team then developed a curriculum for a five-day event, linking the program and its content with other curricula in the company's executive leadership development center. This content was reviewed in one-on-one interviews with 35 of the company's top leaders.

Keeping the key concepts in mind as the overarching context of the entire new employee orientation experience, themes were assigned to each day:

- Monday—Ford heritage, vision, and business strategy

- Tuesday—Consumer connection and brand

- Wednesday—product creation and building for the consumer

- Thursday—Product, people, and careers

- Friday—Leaders at all levels, topical issues, and challenge for the future

USING SUBJECT MATTER EXPERTS

Since the company has a strong culture of leaders as teachers, a decision was made that company subject matter experts (SMEs) would be the developers and teachers of the course content. These SMEs link consumer concepts to the actual job processes in the organization. This provides high impact and transformational information with the immediacy of what is needed on the job. It also builds in an update capability to the course. These people are working directly with consumer concepts every day, and they can communicate that urgency to the group, with current implications and adjustments that the company is making to be responsive.

In REV, employee participation is important. This is not a comfortable, relaxing program in which participants sit in a chair, sip coffee, and nod as information is passed to them. There is a strong emphasis on interactivity. Speakers expect it and exercises are designed around it.

Speakers, for instance, do not simply show a picture of a truck coming up three model years from now. Instead, they show the picture of the truck and then ask, "How many of you like trucks?" Watching for a show of hands, the speaker then asks, "How many of you drive a truck?" Some hands stay up in the air. The speaker then follows with, "Here is a truck for XX model year. What do you like about it? What don't you like about it? Would you buy it? Would your friends buy it?" The leader then facilitates a lively discussion about the characteristics of the truck, how it is targeted to meet consumer demands, and what will surprise and delight the consumer. He also listens for new ideas coming out, which he then takes back to his group to share. It is a highly interactive dialogue.

Ford expects that new employees come to the company with good ideas. We want them to discuss and test those ideas during REV. Leaders have been coached on how to create interactive exercises that are structured for maximum discussion.

REV is a transformational program in which new employees are challenged to see their new roles as not just understanding where Ford is going with its vision, but recognizing that the company expects the new employee to pull the company in that direction as an owner of a piece of the business.

The speakers' material is presented via PowerPoint slides. This format allows for immediate and significant revision for each session. Subject matter experts are responsible for their content, and they take this assignment seriously. They freshen sales figures, industry trends, consumer reports, and so on constantly, sometimes as often as every session. Speed and flexibility are key assets of the program.

REV MATERIALS

REV participants do not get the typical thick three-ring binder. Rather, they receive a packet of worksheets, charts, and exercises. This, too, is printed in a just-in-time method so that charts and graphs can be updated as appropriate.

Each session features discussions of current issues. These discussions focus on current, topical issues that are incorporated into three major places in the program: the welcome, the special session on Friday, and the close. This is vital to the inclusion of new employees in current issues, trends, and tough issues facing the company. They are asked to be a part of the solution.

As part of the company's linkage, recruiters have been invited to attend the program so they can gain an understanding of the process.

An intranet site was created to convey logistical details, as well as concepts, topics, and descriptions of the program. The purpose of the site is also to provide employees with a glimpse of the program prior to their attendance, so they come expecting to participate fully in a highly intense, targeted program. They can read previous participants' comments, and they can see what each day has scheduled.

RESULTS AND EVALUATION

A pilot session was held in March 2000; thirteen subsequent sessions were held in the balance of that year. Sessions are presently continuing. Typically sessions are attended by 140 to 150 people.

Senior management recognized the importance of REV and decided it should be a mandatory program for all new salaried employees. The communication sent out to company management provided a background for managers, so they would understand the consumer mind-set REV provides for the new employee and for the company itself. Supervisors and managers of new employees were also invited to attend the program, as well as to participate as teachers. More importantly, the management team was encouraged to support the new employees when they returned to the workplace.

From the beginning, it was agreed that evaluation and continuous improvement would be cornerstones of the program. Each day, at the session conclusion, participants turn in a daily evaluation. These results are reviewed and discussed with the participants the next morning.

Whenever possible, suggestions given on the daily evaluations are immediately incorporated into the program for the next day. Other corrective actions are taken whenever possible. This adds to the participants' comfort, and it confirms to them in a positive way that their suggestions are being listened to and implemented when feasible. Overall satisfaction rates sustain consistently high results.

Participant comments have included:

> "Appreciate the goals of this program and hope that people really do understand the power we have to change the organization. That realization is the most important step."

> "I wholeheartedly endorse the concept of individual leadership roles and its place in changing an enormous organization."

> "REV is about vision and leadership. Thank you for making me part of this."

> "The REV program gave me a sense of pride to be a Ford employee."

> "I thought it was good that you stretched us."

> "We are a company in transition. It is difficult to know where you are in that evolution. A clearer picture of the end points is emerging, and I'm piecing together at what stage in the evolution different organizations are."

> "Entire group needs to be commended for maintaining an open, frank dialogue. This should be an important part of future training. It was fresh compared to other courses."

A supervisor commented, "Since my new employee attended REV, he is very excited about the company. He understands the underlying strategy. He is exceptionally positive about the company and has a clear grasp of the big picture and systemic thinking. When he does his job, he exhibits a strong connection between the company's mission and goals and how they relate specifically to his job."

Note: Although this case study referred to REV, the consumer-focused new employee orientation, Ford also has new employee orientations with a function focus. For instance, there is an extended technical new employee orientation (referred to as NEO) that typically includes engineering and manufacturing employees. This extended program is five weeks long and concentrates on automotive engineering and design concepts, lean manufacturing, computer tools, planning, problem solving, and community service. Special activities in this program include plant assignments, dealership activities, and a team project whereby participants simulate developing a vehicle to gain a crucial understanding of vehicle program management.

LESSONS LEARNED WITH REV

- Work closely with sending managers so that they review the spirit of REV with the employee prior to attendance, and so that participants are more productive the first day rather than being confused that this is not a "sit and listen" class.

- Work closely with second-generation speakers as leaders transition from original speaker to another. People change jobs or begin work on new projects, which results in new speakers coming to our program. We want to make sure that this new SME is familiar with the concepts behind REV and is prepared to maintain the spirit of free dialogue with participants.

THE REV CURRICULUM

Day One—Ford Heritage, Vision, and Business Strategy

- Introduction—objectives, purpose, material
- Welcome keynote speaker
- Ford heritage
- Competitive environment
- Transformation to a consumer company
- Shareholder value
- Your leadership role

Day Two—Consumer Connection and Brand

- Ford Research Library
- Brand fundamentals
- Consumer insight
- Personalized marketing
- Vehicle ergonomics
- Quality builds brands
- Marketing communication strategy
- e-Business paradigm
- Leadership role

Day Three—Product Creation and Build for the Consumer

- Order-to-delivery activity
- Creation, build, and delivery
- Plant video
- Henry's truck simulations
- Plant tour
- Your leadership role

Day Four—Product, People, and Careers

- Ford products
- Labor relations
- Safety leadership

- Environment and vehicle safety
- Environmental impact
- Ergonomics group
- Corporate citizenship
- Help a customer
- Diversity and work life
- Personal development (career information)
- Your leadership role

Day Five—Leaders at All Levels, Topical Issues, and Challenge for the Future

- Topical issue
- Unwritten rules
- Leaders at all levels
- Leadership enablers
- Your leadership role
- Closing keynote speaker

Christine R. Day is a human resource business solutions partner at Ford Motor Company's Fairlane Training and Development Center in Dearborn, Michigan. As a manager, she supports global learning and performance deployment initiatives, performance management, transformation and growth, benchmarking, and new employee assimilation strategy.

Christine has traveled extensively, taught classes, and managed programs internationally. She served as a project leader for the team that was awarded the American Society for Training and Development Automotive Industries Program of the Year. She also teaches part-time in the MBA program at Eastern Michigan University. Author of *Discovering Connections*, Christine holds a Ph.D. in organizational communications.

Contact Information   *19000 Hubbard Drive*
Dearborn, MI 48121
313-390-5052
cday4@ford.com
Fax: 313-390-4666

Chapter 16

Kahunaville's Pursuit of Wow—POW!

Award-Winning Service Excellence Orientation for Cast Members

Although every organization has an orientation, Kahunaville takes this a step further, developing an orientation that is informative, friendly, and most of all *fun*! Kahunaville created and maintains our version of new Cast Member orientation—Pursuit of Wow! (POW!). This first day of work for all new Cast Members presents the fundamentals for the quest to Wow! our Guests. Generating an effective way to take new, eager, and sometimes nervous people and transform them into productive members of a cohesive team starts by taking training seriously and giving a clear understanding of the organization and how they play a role in it.

Kahunaville is in the business of creating fun, not only for its guests, but also for each of its Cast Members and managers. Rapid growth, a strong culture, diverse trainees, changing markets, and increased competition inspired the new hire orientation program for our frontline Cast Members at Kahunaville. Our hiring philosophy, "Hire the Smile, Train the Skill," emphasized our commitment to hiring based on common core beliefs. A culture-based orientation program is the beginning of our commitment to continuous learning at all levels within the organization.

This chapter includes both the POW! Curriculum and the POW! Train-the-Trainer Curriculum.

THE PURSUIT OF WOW!

The Pursuit of Wow! means culture first! Our whole concept and work ethic revolves around a good corporate culture. Our version of new Cast Member orientation—the Pursuit of Wow! (POW!)—is the first day of work for all new Cast

Members. A "Kahunafied" welcome and Dynamics Practice (part of our entertainment package, a performing Cast) ensure pleasant memories of this potentially uncomfortable experience. Storytelling highlights the afternoon and sharing Wow! stories drives home our mission to exceed guest expectations.

We continually measure how well we are exceeding Guest expectations by reviewing comments and ratings from customer electronic "black box" surveys, comments and ratings from secret shopper visits, and e-mails we receive from our customers. See the Measuring Our Success section of this chapter for specific measurement data.

THE KAHUNAVILLE POW! ORIENTATION (FIRST DAY) PROGRAM

Time	Topic or Activity	Comments
2 Minutes	Welcome to the Pursuit of WOW!— Your Kahunaville Orientation	The group discusses the meaning of "pursuit" and why Kahunaville calls the orientation the Pursuit of WOW!
2 Minutes	Welcome to Kahunaville	Read welcome letter from David Tuttleman, Mayor (Chairman) of Kahunaville.
3 Minutes	The Kahunaville Training Model	A review of the training process and components of initial training at Kahunaville.
1 Minute	The Vision Statement	Service, Entertainment, and Fun!
8 Minutes	Kahunaville Terminology	Review terms (and the "why" behind them) used in the company, such as Cast Members, Backstage, Good Show, etc.
2 Minutes	The Kahunaville Success Formula	Review the success formula and the philosophies behind it.
3 Minutes	How We Chart a Quality Cast Experience	This section reviews all the training the employee will receive during the first week on the job.
1 Minute	Teamwork!	We cannot make our team work without teamwork!
6 Minutes	Cast Member Information	Cover the realities of the job, the inside scoop, "What's in it for me?", and most frequently asked questions.
5 Minutes	Quality Guest Experience	Guest Recovery and the WOW! Experience
4 Minutes	The Fab Four of Service Excellence	Safety, Courtesy, Show, and Efficiency
1 Minute	The Kahunaville Organizational Structure	The Cast Members are at the top of the chart, rather than the CEO as in most companies.
3 Minutes	Analyzing Kahunaville's Growth	Reviewing the Past, Looking at the Present, and Looking Ahead to the Future.
2 Minutes	Corporate Culture	Discuss the nine words that define the Kahunaville culture.
2 Minutes	The Kahunaville Mission Statement	A review of the Kahunaville Success Formula and how it ties into the company's mission statement.

Time	Topic or Activity	Comments
15 Minutes	Distribute training material and complete new hire paperwork.	New employees receive their training materials (specific to their own job functions in the restaurant), their training schedules, and the names of their on-the-job trainers for the rest of the week. In addition, new hire paperwork and required identification for the I-9 forms are collected.
30 Minutes	Kahunaville Policies and Procedures	New employees sign an acknowledgment receipt to confirm that they received the Policies and Procedures manual.
5–10 Minutes	Tour of the Restaurant	The trainer points out the unique things that make the restaurant different from others.
25 Minutes	Dynamics Lesson	The trainer teaches the group some dancing steps that are part of the entertainment in the Kahunaville restaurants.
5 Minutes	Farewell!	The group has now finished the WOW! training, and will be trained on their specific job functions during the remainder of the week.

THE POW! TRAINING SPECIALIST (TRAIN-THE-TRAINER) PROGRAM

Knowing the Training Department can't be in every restaurant unit all of the time, we recently introduced a POW! Guide Book, which is used to certify POW! Specialists in each unit. The POW! Specialist Program is designed to ensure that each unit is delivering the same message and following the same systems 100 percent of the time.

Specialists use the book as a tool to help gain the knowledge and skills necessary to instruct Pursuit of WOW! successfully, while renewing their own understanding and commitment of Kahunaville's Culture and Policies and Procedures. This POW! Guide Book is also a self-help instructor manual designed to assist the specialists throughout the class, as they lead our newest Cast Members on the first day of their Kahunaville journey.

Prior to becoming a POW! specialist, each trainer assists and practices in POW! classes with a manager or with a previously certified POW! specialist in the unit. Upon feeling confident of taking on the POW! responsibility, the management team will invite the training manager to the unit to observe the star trainer in action. Upon completion of the observed POW!, the training manager will review how the class went with the trainer.

The training department will then do quarterly follow-up POW! visits to ensure the specialist is receiving feedback and to ensure that critical areas such as company culture and consistency are being addressed and followed up on. The training department and managers are always supporting our specialists' efforts, just as they support the efforts of our new Cast Members!

Topics included in the POW! Train-the-Trainer Program include:

- Welcome

- Why POW?

- Who Is the Trainee?

- The Role of the POW! Trainer

- Skills of a Great Trainer

- Organizing a POW!

- Room Setup

- Administration

- Key Definitions

- The POW! Lesson Plan (Each unit has a printed flip chart distributed by the home office to go along with this.)

- Training Material Distribution

- The Policies and Procedures Lesson Plan (Each new Cast Member receives training material, including a copy of the Policies and Procedures.)

- The Tour Lesson Plan

- The Dynamics Lesson Plan

- Farewell

MATERIALS AND HUMAN RESOURCES NEEDED

Kahunaville is able to keep the costs of the training program low by using internally certified training specialists and internally developed materials. The materials and costs required for the program are listed here.

- The POW! Guide Book—one per unit = $52

- The POW! Flip Chart—one per unit = $450

- Training Materials/Guide—one per new Cast Member = $6

- Pens/Pencils/Candy/Material for Icebreakers—Variable Costs

LESSONS LEARNED ALONG THE WAY

Communicating effectively and frequently is unfortunately often a lesson learned the hard way, but it is key to the success of any organization. Communication from the training department to the managers is used in the form of guidance and must remain constant. It is a bit of a challenge to continuously stay aware of everything that is happening companywide. It is critical to keep our managers up to date on new paperwork systems, informed on changes in policies and procedures, and up on feedback regarding how well each team is meeting our expectations. (This information is gathered from the results of phone interviews with the new Cast.)

Manager involvement with the POW! programs is a must. It is necessary to take the feedback from the training department and relay the company changes and new Cast interview feedback to the specialists. Manager involvement doesn't stop there, though. Managers must constantly be aware that the specialists are upholding the standards of a POW! specialist. The qualities the managers expect the specialists to excel in include all of the following: Kahunaville Attitude, Knowledge, Skill, Pride in Appearance, Communication Skills, Flexibility, Patience, Integrity, Desire, and Energy and Enthusiasm.

Our biggest lesson companywide is the understanding that the success (or lack of success) of our orientation program can directly affect the bottom line and Cast Member retention. Not only do our guests feel good about dining with us when they encounter a well-informed Cast Member, but more importantly, our Cast Members and our internal guests want to continue to do business with us! If our Cast doesn't feel appreciated or well trained, they very easily could choose to work with a different company.

OBTAINING FEEDBACK FOR CONTINUOUS IMPROVEMENT

Kahunaville prides itself on seeking needed feedback directly from the Cast Members and managers themselves. Weekly, Kahunaville's training manager conducts phone interviews with new Cast Members, congratulating them on their certification while also receiving feedback to be shared with the managers.

Topics broached during the phone interviews include feeling ready to perform the job, feeling comfortable in the work environment, the quality of trainers, and the quality of materials. Because Kahunaville encourages feedback at any level of communication, Cast Members feel comfortable using open and honest communication, ensuring the improvement of the training process as a whole and validating a great Kahunaville experience. Because of the Kahunaville culture, our Cast will come for a job and stay for the *fun*!

MEASURING OUR SUCCESS

Participant certification within our programs is confirmed by the completion of the required materials, demonstrating that the participant developed relevant competencies and applied them to workplace challenges. For Kahunaville, Cast morale and retention will continue to be further indicators of our ability to meet the needs of today's diverse labor pool.

Guest survey results are perhaps the most obvious measurement of the success of Kahunaville's training programs. Increased "black box" (Electronic Guest Surveys) scores, increased scores on Secret Shopper Reports, and a trend in positive e-mails from guests have proven that Kahunaville's training programs are successful.

Kahunaville measurement methods and results are shown in the accompanying chart.

KAHUNAVILLE MEASURABLE RESULTS

Kahunaville	Time Frame	December 1999	July 2000	An Increase of...
Black Box Survey Scores	Weekly	8.148%	8.597%	.44%
Secret Shopper Reports	Monthly	79.0%	91.9%	12.9%
Positive Guest E-Mails	Weekly	63%	86%	23%

Number of New Cast Members per Month at Kahunaville: An average of 15 new Cast Members are hired per month in each unit. Each unit has approximately 170 Cast Members on its schedule. At any given time, Kahunaville has roughly 1,200 active Cast Members across all of its restaurants.

Frequency of the Pow! Orientation Program: Weekly or bimonthly as appropriate.

Average Orientation Group Size: 6 to 8 Cast Members.

Basic Orientation Logistics: The Pow! Program is conducted either in a community room in a mall, a training room in the unit, or the dining room when the restaurant is closed.

Company Size: 10 units...and growing! Future locations are destined for Treasure Island Casino, Las Vegas in July 2001; Tampa, Florida in September 2001; and Orlando, Florida in March 2002.

Shawna McNamee is a graduate of the University of Delaware; she has worked in the restaurant business for 12 years and has been an integral member of the Kahunaville management team. Shawna has been with Kahunaville for six years and serves as a training manager. She plans, coordinates, and directs training and cast/management development programs, prepares budgets, formulates training policies, selects appropriate training methods, organizes and develops training manuals, trains instructors and supervisory personnel, and plans and organizes training for all new restaurant openings.

Shawna began working at The Big Kahuna Nite Club & Deck as a server and has opened all ten Kahunaville locations. She is a certified National Restaurant Association Foundation ServSafe Instructor and a member of the American Society for Training and Development, the Society for Human Resource Management, and the Council of Hotel and Restaurant Trainers.

Shawna has received numerous awards, including the first annual Industry of Choice Award 2000 for Training and Education and the International Association of Amusement Parks and Attractions 2000 Spirit of Excellence Award for Supervisory Training.

Contact Information   *500 South Madison St.*
Wilmington, DE 19801
302-571-6200, x16
smcnamee@Kahunaville.com

Chapter 17

Case Study: Champion Laboratories, Inc.

Combining Online and Personal Touch Orientation Components

One of the challenges facing Champion is that it typically hires only one to five people at a time. In the past, each person was oriented individually. Prior to instituting online orientations, Champion's on-boarding process was very time-intensive for the human resource staff, for supervisors, and for the experienced workers charged with training the new hire.

In the old configuration, a human resource person would spend two or more hours talking with the new hire and filling out paperwork. Then the supervisor picked up from there, giving a plant tour each time a new employee was assigned to his or her area. After the tour, the new hire read the Standard Operating Procedure for his or her job, and was placed with an experienced person at the station.

The experienced employee was then responsible for facilitating on-the-job training (OJT) for the new employee. Since so little prior orientation had taken place and the new hire arrived unaware of how the production line worked overall, the OJT placed a heavy burden on the experienced worker because so much more had to be shown or explained.

Therefore, Champion was looking for a way to lessen the amount of time expended by the HR staff, the supervisors, and the senior workers, while still providing clear, consistent information that would help new hires feel both welcomed and well-informed about their new positions.

AN ONLINE SOLUTION FOR PORTIONS OF THE ORIENTATION PROGRAM

Champion selected INTECH Interactive Technologies to help them move factual portions of their orientation online. By moving portions of the orientation online, Champion would be able to consistently and conveniently:

- Provide the new hire with the big picture of the company and his or her place in that picture.

- Communicate the company culture and values and encourage a sense of community in the new hire.

- Help employees feel part of the team more quickly, resulting in lower turnover.

- Illustrate the company's commitment to quality and the employee's role in producing top-quality products, resulting in better quality products and therefore lower costs.

- Emphasize the company's commitment to the safety of its employees and their role in achieving a safe workplace, resulting in fewer insurance claims.

- Train the employee in best practices, resulting in increased employee productivity.

- Illustrate the company's commitment to training and to the development of its employees, resulting in lower turnover.

- Allow the human resources staff to interact personally with the worker but save the time used for routine passing of information, thus increasing productivity while reducing costs.

Another business case for this project was that it would be a substantial boost to Champion's ISO-9001 and QS-9000 certification efforts, because the company could document consistent efforts to:

- Focus on quality, its importance at Champion, and the new hire's role in producing a quality product.

- Focus on safety, its importance at Champion, and the new hire's role in being part of and promoting a safe working environment.

TOOLS AND VENDORS CHAMPION USED

Champion chose to contract out the redesign of the new employee orientation to INTECH because their already overworked staff didn't have the time to devote to a complete redesign. An outside contractor with proven skills in online design and development would bring fresh eyes to an orientation that had grown, a little at a time, over a number of years.

INTECH used Macromedia's Authorware for course development, which can be migrated to an intranet or to the Internet in the future with minimal additional programming. The source code was provided to Champion for making updates, if they care to do that internally.

WHAT INTECH DID

After defining the goals of the business discussed earlier, all materials currently in use were reviewed. Various people were interviewed to determine what should be added or discarded. Additions included:

- A history from the founder and current plant manager, Henry Jumper. The South Carolina plant had originally started as a small, independently owned company that was later bought by Champion Laboratories. Mr. Jumper's story, told in his own words, about how he and a few others built filters in his garage at night and sold them during the day, has become legendary in the plant and has fostered a sense of carrying on the tradition of hardworking individuals who take personal pride in the company's success.

- A welcome from the president of the company, whom many of these people will not get to meet in person because he works out of the corporate headquarters in Illinois.

- An overview of the types of products Champion produces and a walk-through of each line to give the employees the big picture of what Champion does and how their individual jobs fit into that picture.

- Information about ISO 9001 and QS-9000 certification and what that means as a way of doing business.

THE COMPONENTS OF CHAMPION'S NEW ORIENTATION

The layout of the program began to take shape with the following components:

- First, the employee is personally welcomed by an HR staff member.

- Next, the employee completes the Online New Employee Orientation (see the handout for the objectives covered in this online portion of the orientation program).

- Then, the individual participates in a follow-up question-and-answer time with an HR representative.

- The new employee then takes a personal tour with his or her supervisor.

- Next, the employee completes Online Production Line Training for:
  - the workstation to which the employee is assigned; and
  - the workstations preceding and following that workstation so the employee understands:
    - what quality to expect in assemblies as they arrive, and
    - what quality issues to be aware of at his or her own station and the impact on others down the line.

- Finally, the new employee is paired with a mentor who is experienced at that workstation.

MAIN MENU—CHAMPION LABORATORIES NEW ONLINE
EMPLOYEE ORIENTATION COURSE OBJECTIVES

What We Do	Quality	Safety	Attendance	New Employee	Benefits	Plant Map
History	Quality policy	Lifting	Absences	Initial evaluation period	Insurance	
Product description	Employee's role	Fire safety	Tardiness	Pay period	Holidays	
Locations	Standard operating procedures	Substance abuse	Overtime	Communications	Vacation	
Customers	QS-9000	Housekeeping	Job openings			
Importance of quality		Equipment	Badge system			
Overview of production lines		Injuries				
		OSHA				
		General rules				

A STORYBOARD PLAN FOR THE ONLINE ORIENTATION PROGRAM

When the general outline had been approved, paper storyboards were developed for the online portion of the orientation. Much of the material for the overview of the production lines was available from the individual modules of production line training already produced. The remainder of the material was gathered through interviews with HR staff, as well as a review of existing forms and documentation. There was minimal impact on HR staff time.

Upon review and acceptance of the storyboards, pictures were taken of various production line workers and processes, and of HR staff and various management staff. Throughout the development process, keeping the line moving was a top priority. As INTECH worked on-site to gather both photos and audio recordings, production was never impacted and the line was never stopped. Programming and narration were accomplished off-site.

Once the online program was complete, careful testing by both INTECH and Champion assured that the content was accurate and that the program worked correctly. The system was implemented within six months of the first site visit.

Implementation was approached in a low-key manner: Once the new employee orientation program was ready, the next employee hired used it!

The training is now delivered on stand-alone PCs in a training room right off the production floor. It has been developed for use over a network, but can move to an intranet or to the Internet if and when Champion chooses. This is possible because the development tool, Macromedia's Authorware, allows virtually the same code to be implemented on PCs or on the Web with little additional work.

MEASURABLE RESULTS

Managers and supervisors had a unique opportunity to observe the positive impact of the new online program when a third shift was added to the production line shortly after the new orientation debuted. Management observed a number of improvements among the new line workers, including:

- a clear commitment to the quality of the work,

- fewer rejected filters coming off the line and consistently good filters being produced more quickly than with other new lines, resulting in lower costs,

- a sense on the part of the new workers of being a part of the team, and

- a perception that Champion valued them as trained employees, resulting in less turnover.

Beyond these improvements, it was also obvious to all at Champion Laboratories that Human Resources could never have individually serviced an entire new shift coming on board at once with the old-style orientation program. Having significant portions of the orientation ready for online delivery freed the HR staff to address individual needs as they occurred, while keeping the entire orientation process moving to bring the new hires to the line in a timely fashion.

In addition, during Champion's ISO-9001 certification audits, they received only two minor training findings. They attribute this to the fact that the workers were more confident when speaking with auditors and had fewer problems answering questions, in part because they had consistent training and easy access to refresher training. Also, the fact that all training was recorded to a database as it was taken and thus was readily documented was a plus for the auditors.

LESSONS LEARNED

While much of what we learned was as we expected, there were a few unexpected advantages, too.

As we expected:

- A blended approach is best. While online materials are consistent, effective, and time-efficient, nothing can replace a personal welcome from several people in the company.

- Careful choices must be made about what goes online (including visuals and voices). There should also be a plan for how updates will be handled.

- If planning for immediate delivery on the desktop rather than over an intranet or the Internet, the development platform should be chosen with an eye to migrating to the Web. Our choice of development platform (Authorware) allows us to upgrade to delivery via the company intranet or the Internet with little additional work.

Unexpected advantage:

- Since the implementation of this orientation, Mr. Jumper has retired, but we continue to hear the story of the founding of the York division of the company in his voice and words. Because the online portion was carefully designed to accommodate personnel changes, it was a simple matter of changing his title on-screen from General Manager to Founder. Mr. Jumper always maintained a personal relationship with his employees so, if anything, this is an even more popular feature than before.

Keep in mind:

- Your work can serve several purposes. For example, much of what you would tell a new employee would be useful in recruitment of new employees, so once your orientation is complete, you can re-purpose much of your work to use for recruiting.

- If you use a development platform that can migrate to an intranet or the Internet, design accordingly. For example, be sure any graphics and interactivity will work well and not bog down if they might be used in a low-bandwidth situation, such as over a modem.

ANALYZING YOUR DELIVERY OPTIONS

Use this chart to determine the media option that will fit your needs.

If . . .	Then consider using . . .
■ You want the online orientation delivered in a specific location ■ You want to schedule specific times for employees to complete the online portion of your orientation	. . . Dedicated PC(s)
■ All new employees have access to a networked PC ■ Your orientation doesn't require video ■ Your orientation does require video and your IT department indicates that delivering video over your network is not a problem ■ You want to be able to track employee usage online ■ Not everyone has access to the Internet or your company intranet ■ You want to be able to update the orientation easily in one place	. . . Your company LAN
■ You want people to be able to use the program off-site as well as on-site, whether they have Internet access or not ■ You want to allow people access to the orientation pre-employment (Be careful, though; make sure all employees will have computer access at home.) ■ The content will not change frequently ■ You want to use video, audio, and high-end graphics ■ It is not critical to record employee usage of the program online	. . . CD-ROM
■ All new employees have access to your company intranet ■ Your orientation doesn't require video ■ Your orientation does require video and your IT department indicates that delivering video over your network is not a problem ■ You want to be able to track employee usage online ■ You want to be able to update the orientation easily in one place	. . . Your company intranet
■ You want to allow people access to the orientation pre-employment (Again, be careful about assuming all employees have Internet access at home.) ■ Your orientation doesn't require video ■ You want to be able to track employee usage online ■ You want to be able to update the orientation easily in one place	. . . Internet / extranet

SELECTING ONLINE ORIENTATION TOPICS

Use this chart to determine the topics that will best transfer to an online orientation format, as part of your overall orientation program.

	Possible Online Orientation Content
1	**Each organization's needs will dictate the final shape of the list, but these are big-picture topics that are usually safest to put online. These topics are the least likely to change frequently.** ❑ Official welcome(s) ❑ Corporate/organizational/enterprise structure ❑ History of organization ❑ Mission statement ❑ Safety overview ❑ Quality statement ❑ Ethics statement ❑ Policies and procedures ❑ Sexual harassment—policy statement and grievance procedures ❑ Dating/marriage within the company ❑ E-mail and other online policies ❑ Vacation/sick/personal leave policies
2	**This tier represents other likely possibilities for the online portion of an orientation that may need more updating or maintenance than those above. You can save these topics for a revision of the initial orientation, adding to a well-designed program as your skills, needs, or budget increases.** ❑ Position within the industry ❑ Benefits ❑ Types available ❑ Forms ❑ Key initiatives

Possible Online Orientation Content

3

This tier may or may not be work-unit–specific. If the item is applicable companywide or can logically be grouped into branches for delivery to selected subsets of employees, you may want to consider adding these topics to your online program.

❏ Working hours

❏ Dress code

❏ Reporting structure

❏ Employee ID, accounts, badges, parking stickers, etc.

❏ Telephone system and etiquette

❏ Performance measurements

❏ Probationary period

❏ Tools or forms needed on the job (expense and travel reports, mail system, computer systems, computer software)

❏ Training offered or required

❏ Building or plant map

Carrie Eaton is principal at INTECH Interactive Technologies.

Contact Information   *309 College Street*
Maryville, TN 37804
865-984-0200
tischlerbe@intechinc.com

Chapter 18

Orientation at Alcatel USA

A Comprehensive Program with Subject Matter Expert Speakers

Orientation at Alcatel USA is a team effort. All of the following people play a part in the preparation and delivery of the orientation program:

- The new employee orientation training specialist

- One or more orientation coordinators and administrative assistants

- Multiple subject matter experts, including several Human Resource employees

- A senior executive welcome speaker

- Testing laboratory tour facilitators

The detailed curriculum provided in this chapter also indicates which team member conducts each portion of the program. In addition to using a variety of speakers, the program also uses a variety of delivery methods, including games, videos, a laboratory tour, and a visit to the company store.

ORIENTATION LENGTH AND DELIVERY DETAILS

The overall length of the foundational orientation program is 12 hours for most new employees. Specific employees also take additional safety and hazard training that applies to their positions, which has recently become available online. Some employees also attend mini-orientations specific to their departments. In addition, new graduates and co-ops (college interns) attend programs designed specifically for them.

The foundational orientation program is instructor-led, but mostly in the sense that an instructor presides over the whole day to ensure that everything runs smoothly. The orientation instructor presents a few parts of the program, but subject matter experts, such as the director of benefits, the senior data security analyst, and so on, present the majority of the program.

Employees are in orientation from 8 a.m. to 3 p.m. on their first day of employment; all employees are required to start employment on a Monday. Employees begin the day with a continental breakfast, and photos are taken for their security badges, which are processed and delivered to each employee before the end of the orientation program. During the first day, information about the company is presented, company programs and benefits are discussed, and employees learn about additional company programs such as recycling at Alcatel and sexual harassment policy.

The second day of orientation begins again with a continental breakfast. The employees learn about more company programs, and benefits personnel attend the program to review and pick up completed benefit and tax forms. The second day of the foundational program is completed by noon. Employees then go to their jobs, or they attend specific orientation programs in the afternoon as applicable to their positions.

SPECIAL ORIENTATION PROGRAMS FOR SPECIAL GROUPS

All employees complete the general orientation, which is broad enough to cover all types of employees. Some are required to attend additional training (operations, manufacturing, safety) and some are required to attend a mini-orientation (customer service) to cover information that is more job-specific.

New college graduates have a special program tailored to their needs. They attend a mini-orientation at 12 p.m. on day two (15 minutes) to learn about the program, and are taken to lunch as a group. Exempt and nonexempt employees and managers attend the same orientation.

In addition, co-ops (college interns) and contractors attend separate programs. The Alcatel co-op program and orientation design are described in detail in Chapter 7 of this book.

Employees who will be working in manufacturing or operations are also required to take a Basic 4 training course as part of their orientation training, for safety and product-handling knowledge, which is also tracked through the Education and Training Center.

Frequency and Audience Size: Orientation is held once a week. The program is held all day on Monday and finishes by 12:30 p.m. on Tuesday.

Results and Evaluation: An evaluation form is distributed to obtain feedback on all aspects of the program. New employees are encouraged to give feedback using a scale from 1 to 5, with each presenter and subject being covered. Space is also provided for comments to be written out (most useful and least useful parts, what would you change, additional comments).

Testing: No tests are required in the foundational orientation program. Some job-specific or departmental new employee training programs have requirements to complete or skills to master to continue employment in the position.

"Orientation at Alcatel USA" was written by Adam Haddad.

Contact Information   *Joicelyn Fields*
Alcatel USA
1000 Coit Road, M/S HRD7
Plano, TX 75075
972-477-4366
Joicelyn.Fields@Alcatel.com

THE ALCATEL ORIENTATION CURRICULUM

Time	Topic or Activity	Facilitator	Comments
Day One 8:00–8:25	Badge pictures are taken. (All facilitators and managers present are encouraged to meet the new employees. Breakfast is provided, and employees meet each other.)	NEO Trainer Badging and Security Staff	Security staff prepares the badges for security access as the orientation continues. Temporary badges are given to new employees to assist current employees in greeting them.
8:25–8:35	Icebreaker (Autograph Bingo—see Chapter 34 for instructions) and a review of the agenda	NEO Trainer Everyone in the room participates in Autograph Bingo.	Autograph Bingo is a signature activity that is designed to get people out of their chairs to meet others.
8:35–8:45	Corporate company welcome	Senior VP or executive	The purpose of this presentation is to give new employees a welcome from the executive leader level, and to emphasize the importance and value placed on new employees.
8:45–9:00	Company products and organizational structure Company video	NEO Trainer	This section briefly explains the company at all levels. The Company/Press video is 4 minutes in length.
9:00–9:20	Quality presentation	Quality Leadership Council Member	The focus of this presentation is that quality begins with each individual Alcatel employee.
9:20–9:25	Vision Statement Game (see Chapter 33)	NEO Trainer A second Alcatel facilitator leads this game.	The purpose of this activity is to reenergize the participants, and to help new employees learn the Alcatel vision.
9:25–10:15	HR forms completion	Staffing Group	New employees complete necessary forms and provide two required forms of identification for the I-9 requirements. These are copied by orientation assistants and returned to the participants the same day.
10:15–10:25	Break	N/A	Coffee and breakfast selections are available.

Time	Topic or Activity	Facilitator	Comments
10:25–12:15	Benefits explanation	Compensation and Benefits Representative	All benefit plans are reviewed in detail and forms are passed out.
12:15–1:00	Lunch and company store visit	NEO Trainer	Employees can visit the company store at this point, or retake badge pictures if desired.
1:00–1:15	E-mail video	NEO Trainer	This video covers e-mail etiquette, e-mail security, and e-mail policies. The video is 12 minutes long.
1:15–1:35	Data security	Senior Analyst, Data Security	Data security is critical to Alcatel's success. Employees learn their role in protecting data and company information.
1:35–2:05	Safety and security	Security Advisor	Security programs and health programs available to employees are discussed.
2:05–2:15	Break	N/A	N/A
2:15–2:20	Alcatel Leadership Association (ALA) of the National Management Association (NMA)	President of ALA	ALA is an Alcatel division of NMA. ALA membership and programs are offered to all employees.
2:20–2:35	Bring in Talent (BIT) referral program	Senior Manager of Corporate Employee Initiatives	The BIT Referral Program rewards employees (monetarily) for referring other employees who are hired for Alcatel positions. Of all new Alcatel employees, 35 percent are referred by current Alcatel employees.
2:35–2:55	Sexual harassment in the workplace Initiatives	Senior Manager of Corporate Employee	This section includes the Alcatel sexual harassment reporting procedure and a sexual harassment video. The video is 15 minutes in length.
2:55–3:00	Recycle video	NEO Trainer	Alcatel has an award-winning recycle program. The recycle video raises awareness of the recyclable items and the company's philosophy on recycling. The video is 8 minutes in length.

Time	Topic or Activity	Facilitator	Comments
Day Two 8:00–10:00	Benefits explanation and benefit forms completion	Compensation and Benefits Representative	Forms are completed and other benefits are discussed (401k matching, insurance, stock options). Forms are gathered and reviewed for any blank spaces or other concerns before the benefits personnel leave the room, so that questions and issues can be address immediately.
10:00–10:15	Break	N/A	Breakfast is provided for participants.
10:15–11:00	Tour of the Alcatel Network Simulation Laboratory (NSC)	Lab Engineers	The NSC lab is used to present demonstrations of Alcatel products to potential customers. Some employees do not know what Alcatel's products look like without this tour.
11:00–11:25	HR forms completion	Staffing Group	Forms are filled out and information not collected the first day is now collected.
11:25–11:30	Education and Training Center (the ETC)	NEO Trainer	The Alcatel ETC is presented to new employees and class registration is demonstrated. Course catalogs have already been distributed in canvas bags supplied to new employees.
11:30–11:45	Completion of the evaluation form and a chance for final questions	NEO Trainer	This evaluation form captures feedback on employees' impression of the process. Changes are made based on this feedback. In addition, new employees are asked to complete a postorientation survey within their first 90 days (see Chapter 55).
11:45–12:00	New College Graduate Orientation	College Relations Specialist	New graduates have a special program within the company, so they are asked to stay for this presentation after the foundational orientation is complete. The components of the new graduate program are discussed in Chapter 7.
12:00–12:30	The Alcatel Fast Facts Review Game	NEO Trainer	This game uses a combined Jeopardy and Who Wants to Be a Millionaire? approach. A question is displayed on a PowerPoint slide, and the first person to ring a bell gains control. That person can answer the question or use a lifeline for help.

Chapter 19

Orienting and Retaining a Technical Population

The Micron Technology, Inc. NEO and NET Orientation Training Programs

Micron Technology, Inc. has established itself as one of the leading worldwide providers of semiconductor memory solutions. Micron has approximately 10,000 employees at its main location in Boise, Idaho and approximately 18,000 employees worldwide.

One of Micron's challenges is to orient as many as 100 to 200 new employees per month due to rapid company growth. Many of these new employees are in technical positions. Another challenge, which is a challenge for any organization with a high number of technical employees, is to retain employees with highly desired technical skills. Micron credits its orientation program with helping to keep its employee turnover rate low. *Micron's turnover rates are below both state and industry averages.*

Micron Technology has divided its new employee program into two parts. Each new employee hired into the Micron team attends a one-day New Employee Orientation (NEO) and a one-day New Employee Training session (NET). These are back-to-back agendas on Mondays and Tuesdays of each week. The outline on the accompanying handout gives an overview of each day.

HUMAN OR MATERIAL RESOURCES USED

Micron internal resources have been used for the development, implementation, and maintenance of its programs.

MICRON TECHNOLOGY, INC.
ORIENTATION AGENDA

DAY ONE—NEO

8:00–8:30   **Security Registration**

✓ Employee identification badge preparation

✓ Vehicle parking decal registration for Micron on-site parking

✓ Verification of employment form (I-9 Form)

✓ Personal files distributed to be taken back to area supervisor

✓ Coffee, tea, and water available

8:30–8:45   **Welcome to Micron and introductions**

8:45–9:00   **Introduction to Micron video**

9:00–9:15   **Training & Education department presentation**

✓ Map of Micron training facilities

✓ Training resources at Micron

✓ Core required classes

✓ Micron education assistance program

9:15–9:30   **Security**

✓ Vehicle tracking

✓ Employee tracking

✓ Property tracking

✓ Workplace violence prevention and reporting

9:30–9:45   **Health Services**

✓ Location of Health Services

✓ Health Services coverage, hours of operation, and cost

✓ Ergonomics, injury prevention, and health/wellness

9:45–10:00   **Break** (A Micron product table is available to review)

10:00–10:30   **Micron Officer Presentation**

✓ Micron company history

✓ Company core values and philosophy

10:30–10:45   **Micron Officer Questions and Answers**

10:45–11:00   **Stock Overview**

✓ Employee stock purchase plan

11:00–12:15   **Micron Benefits**

✓ Insurance

	✓ Time-off plan
	✓ Retirement at Micron plan
12:15–1:00	**Lunch (Provided by Micron)**
1:00–1:15	**Afternoon Facilitator Introduction (different from the morning facilitator) & Basic PC Preassessment**
	(The PC assessment is designed to identify basic PC skill competencies for all new team members. Employees who fail to meet assessment expectations will attend a basic PC class the morning of NET.)
1:15–1:30	**Micron Workforce/Equal Employment Opportunities**
	✓ EEO policies
	✓ Harassment policies
1:30–1:50	**Payroll**
	✓ Direct deposit
	✓ W-4 information
1:50–2:00	**Department-Specific Training Schedule**
2:00–2:15	**Break**
2:15–2:45	**Personnel Paperwork Wrap-Up**
2:45–3:45	**Plant Tour**
3:45–4:00	**Q & A and Closing**

DAY TWO—NET

7:30–8:00	**Basic PC Training**
	(This class is only for new team members who failed to meet expectations on the assessment during NEO. The audience size is typically about 10 percent of our total group size, or about 3 to 5 team members a week.)
	Supporting Objectives:
	✓ Define the PC and its common uses at Micron
	✓ Practice using the mouse to left/right click, double-click
	✓ Practice opening, closing, moving, and resizing a window
	✓ Discuss the most commonly used keyboard keys
8:00–10:00	**Harassment-Free Workplace**
	(Separate groups of no more than 30 employees)
	Supporting Objectives:
	✓ Define what harassment and discrimination are
	✓ Recognize behaviors that may be perceived as illegal harassment
	✓ Understand Micron's harassment policy

	✓ Understand the complaint process for reporting
	✓ Identify additional resources to help prevent harassment
10:00–10:15	**Break**
10:15–12:45	**PC/VAX for New Hires**
	(Separate groups, with no more than 16 employees per group)
	Supporting Objectives:
	✓ Log onto the Micron network
	✓ Discuss and identify desktop terminology
	✓ Discuss Window buttons using the Internet Explorer (I.E.) browser window
	✓ Change passwords using password maintenance
	✓ Log onto H.R. Online and enter personal data
	✓ Practice using Timesheet in H.R. Online
	✓ Discuss and identify basic I.E. features and links
	✓ Log onto Outlook and practice using e-mail and calendar
	✓ Log onto the VAX and use Phone and the TRAIN program
12:45–1:45	**Lunch**
1:45–2:15	**Information Security**
	(All new team members, large-group setting)
	Supporting Objective:
	✓ Identify how you can protect Micron information to maintain our competitive position in the semiconductor industry
2:15–3:00	**Safe Work Practices**
	(All new team members, large-group setting)
	Supporting Objectives:
	✓ Reduce injuries and claims related to work injuries
3:00–4:00	**Electrostatic Discharge—ESD**
	(All new team members, large-group setting)
	Supporting Objectives:
	✓ Define electrostatic discharge
	✓ Explain how ESD is generated
	✓ List four ways ESD can be prevented

Development: This is done by multiple curriculum developers throughout the corporation. Different departments may contribute to course curriculum, based on subject matter. (For example, the Personnel/HR department developed Harassment-Free Workplace; the Micron Fitness Center Physical Fitness Trainers developed Safe Work Practices; Information Systems developed Information Security.)

Implementation: Much the same as the development is handled, implementation is often handled by the subject matter experts who consulted with the curriculum developers.

Maintenance: The course content is maintained and modified by subject matter experts and instructors, and sometimes the final edit is completed by curriculum developers.

LESSONS LEARNED ALONG THE WAY

Developing an orientation program sooner rather than later is highly recommended. Once a company starts to grow and gets comfortable without a program, it can be difficult to implement a full-fledged program. We found many of our departments were reluctant to join the new orientation program when it was first developed.

RESULTS, FEEDBACK, AND MEASUREMENTS

Rapid company growth:

Micron grew from 2,000 employees in 1988 to 4,200 employees in 1993, which prompted the development of a corporate-level orientation program. Since 1993, the program has been measured and evaluated carefully and in detail. Program results at a high level include:

- Communication of Micron's culture, values, and business strategy

- Consistent content delivery through subject matter experts

- Lower turnover rates compared to state and industry averages

Please use the contact information provided to request any materials.

Company Size: Approximately 10,000 at Micron's main site—Boise, Idaho, USA (18,000 employees worldwide)

Number of New Employees per Month: 100–200

Frequency of Orientation: Weekly, on Mondays and Tuesdays, year-round.

Average Orientation Group Size: On average, we have about 25–50 people a week. This is an ideal size for our program. Variances in head count affect breakout classes in the training portion of the program.

Basic Orientation Logistics: Our program is held on-site, in various rooms dedicated for meetings and training. These rooms can be modified to seat varying audience sizes depending on the new employee volume for a particular week.

Troy Van Houten is a support analyst at Micron Technology Inc.

Contact Information   *8000 S. Federal Way*
P.O. Box 6
Mail Stop 308
Boise, ID 83707-0006
208-368-3767
tvanhouten@micron.com

Chapter 20

Wyndham International Beginnings

Orientation for Multiple Locations at Wyndham International, Incorporated

Wyndham International has developed a new employee orientation program called "Beginnings" for employees at each hotel and resort location. Beginnings is a three-phase process comprised of instructor-led workshops, one-on-one meetings, and self-study designed to orient employees to the company, their jobs, and their locations. Upon hire, employees spend time with their local representatives regarding the necessary paperwork and critical detail orientation (i.e., employee parking, employee entrance, clocking in). Employees also receive a copy of the employee handbook to review prior to orientation day.

Orientation day is an eight-hour instructor-led workshop. During orientation day, employees review the policies and procedures in the employee handbook, the benefits available to them, Wyndham's history and company culture, and its customer service philosophy.

The formal orientation process ends after 60 days of employment when employees come back to the human resources representative for follow-up interviews to assess their satisfaction with the workplace, their supervisors, and their training (see our checklist in Chapter 56). It is the responsibility of the local human resources representative to follow up on any issues raised during these one-on-one meetings.

THE BEGINNINGS TARGET AUDIENCE

Beginnings is designed for all employees at all levels of the organization. Every associate (from vice president to general manager to hourly employee) participates in the process. After employees complete the Beginnings program, the company also offers position-specific programs, entitled RightSTART, for their specific areas. For example, newly hired general managers attend a five-day RightSTART program in Dallas.

FREQUENCY AND AUDIENCE SIZE

Because our properties range in size from 37 employees to well over 1,000, *Beginnings* had to be designed to allow for flexibility on the part of the property. Optimally, employees attend orientation day prior to starting in their positions. In smaller properties, employees may complete the required portions of the process (new hire paperwork, benefits, etc.) and then wait several weeks until the next *Beginnings* class is offered. The program was designed in a modular format so local personnel at the property can teach as many of the modules per day as necessary.

MEASURING RESULTS

On our annual associate opinion survey, the average score for the orientation received upon hire was 58.11 percent, consistent with our company average of 59.06 percent. We will use this number as a baseline to track improvements year over year.

WYNDHAM'S TOTAL CURRICULUM

The number of classes attended by new employees varies greatly based on their positions. In some cases, training is required by local, state, or federal law (alcohol awareness, Hazmat, etc.). For some positions, Wyndham International has created a second, position-specific orientation. In such cases, the instructor-led workshops, entitled RightSTART, range in length from three to five days, and are typically held in Dallas.

All training is tracked centrally in our personnel software system. In this way, if employees transfer, their training histories transfer with them. The employee's training history is used in our succession planning process.

TESTING

In *Beginnings,* there are no formal tests that an employee must pass to continue employment. Frequent verbal discussions during the course of the day allow the instructor to determine the group's level of understanding. In addition, a follow-along quiz is distributed at the beginning of the day for employees to complete as they hear the correct answers.

The Wyndham International, Inc. *Beginnings* orientation curriculum is shown on the following page.

THE WYNDHAM INTERNATIONAL *BEGINNINGS* PROGRAM

Time	Topic or Activity	Facilitator	Comments
8:00–8:30	Welcome/Introduction	NEO Trainer	Select an icebreaker from *Beginnings* leader's guide.
8:30–9:00	Wyndham International— Who Are We?	NEO Trainer	Show video segments.
9:00–9:30	Our Division & Hotel	NEO Trainer	Show video segment 2.
9:30–10:30	Property Tour	NEO Trainer, Hotel Staff	
10:30–2:00	Employee Handbook	NEO Trainer	Review employee handbook in detail.
2:00–3:00	Employee Programs	NEO Trainer, Benefits Representative	
3:00–3:30	12 Right Moves for Safety	NEO Trainer, Risk Management	Show video segment.
3:30–4:00	Customer Service Representative	NEO Trainer, Wyndham Way	Show video segment.
4:00–4:30	Wrap-Up	NEO Trainer	

Steve Schuller is director of training for Dallas-based Wyndham International, one of the largest hotel management companies in the world. A recognized leader in the company's human resources department, Steve is responsible for the development and administration of training programs for Wyndham International's 300-plus hotels and 32,000 employees. Steve received his bachelor of arts degree from Cornell University's School of Hotel Administration in Ithaca, NY.

Current initiatives include the implementation of an advanced customer service training program as well as a leadership development program for all Wyndham-branded hotels. Steve is also involved in the development of global training programs for all Wyndham International employees, including a new employee orientation program, a supervisory development class, and a series of management development modules.

Contact Information   *1950 Stemmons Freeway, Suite 6001*
Dallas, TX 75207
214-863-1616
Sschuller@Wyndham.com

Chapter 21

New Crew Members "Take the Plunge!" at Red Lobster

Delivering a Consistent Orientation Message across Multiple Locations

Our need for new orientation was triggered by a need for consistent on-boarding to our company culture and a "first stop" before position-specific training begins for each employee. We explored several options for delivery (from video to read-only materials), and we decided to use a manager-facilitated multimedia orientation, using a variety of different materials such as videos, flip books, and graphics. We wanted personal involvement from managers without losing consistency or creating distance, and we didn't want new crew members oriented by someone they would not be dealing with daily in their own restaurants.

The result of our research into the best orientation delivery mode for hundreds of different locations is a consistent message delivered in a program we call Take the Plunge!, which is presented to every crew member by the highest-ranking manager on-site. The materials support the message while allowing each manager to customize his or her own presentation.

The method and content of the program were presented to and approved by our executive team, who then fully supported the program development and implementation. The program was piloted in several local restaurants (those near our Restaurant Support Center) to best determine the sequence of content material. The orientation program was launched at our annual General Manager Conference. General managers first attended sessions as participants viewing the Take the Plunge! orientation, then worked through questions and practice for facilitating the program.

Take the Plunge! covers the Red Lobster Brand, Our Compass (bringing our vision to life), and Making Wraves (*Wraves* is part of the customer service and crew member vocabulary at Red Lobster). The format allows managers to set out their expectations clearly while letting new crew members know what to expect as members of the crew. Take the Plunge! usually lasts two hours, and is provided within one week of joining the restaurant crew.

HUMAN OR MATERIAL RESOURCES USED

The program is contained in an A-frame four-color flip book with talking points for the manager/facilitator and graphics and visuals for the new crew attendees. There are two supporting videos. The first video is designed to help the general manager understand how to present Take the Plunge! A second video, presented to the new crew members, includes live-action footage and an explanation of crew life at Red Lobster. A new crew handbook is also part of the package and serves as a resource and reference to crew members for any questions regarding policies explained during Take the Plunge!

Take the Plunge! is reviewed annually by Red Lobster Crew Training and Development personnel. Any needed changes are made, and new materials are sent to each restaurant.

LESSONS LEARNED ALONG THE WAY

All in all, our Take the Plunge! orientation is hitting the mark by providing necessary information to our crew in an easy, friendly environment with a high-impact presentation. The fact that our general managers present the program is a strong indicator to our new crew of their value and the importance Red Lobster places on keeping our promises to crew members and guests.

Originally, the flip book used during the orientation program was more "scripted." We've changed it to more of a "talking points" format, based on feedback from managers.

RESULTS, FEEDBACK, AND MEASUREMENTS

Take the Plunge! was the most recognized program when we recently polled our restaurants. Managers were aware of the complete process and could clearly provide detail on the schedule they followed to ensure orientation presentations to their crew.

Executives and managers of Red Lobster are very supportive of our Take the Plunge! program. Here is what they have to say about the value it provides for the company:

John Ducey, Senior Vice President of Operations, Suncoast Division

"I cover the topic of orientation whenever I promote a new general manager. I explain that orientation must be done by the general manager—not delegated—for two very important reasons. The first is that the material helps the general manager communicate our company standards and provide the clear direction needed to start a new job. Second, spending two hours with new crew members gives the general manager a way to really connect with them.

"Research shows crew members want a boss who cares about them and is good to work for. If a connection exists between the general manager and the new crew member, when a question or negative situation comes up early in the job, the new crew member may decide to go to the general manager and talk about it rather than leave the job. The Take the Plunge! Program helps the GM show he or she is good to work for.

"Our business is hard. We experience larger turnover and lower retention of crew than we'd like. People don't take a new job simply to leave it quickly; something happens or doesn't happen to make them leave. General manager orientation delivers an early connection to new crew members, making it easier to question what's happening and thereby impacting retention."

Marge Phillips, Director of Operations

"Since the Take the Plunge! program was implemented, our crew members are much more informed. They understand how serious we (Red Lobster) are about Our Compass and our standards. So many parts of the orientation make them closer to their general managers and their jobs.

"I love it when managers add their own spirit and energy. This is a great orientation."

Karl Schiner, General Manager

"As they say, the speed of the leader determines the rate of the pack. The Take the Plunge! program gives the GM the opportunity to make the best first impression of Red Lobster possible, and to really set the pace and the standard to live by. If we didn't do this orientation, we'd lose people simply because they didn't understand the job. Take the Plunge! starts the Red Lobster experience off on the right foot."

Steve Weigel, Director of Operations

"One thing that sets really great organizations apart from the others is the time they invest in dealing with the people who take care of the organization's customers and guests. Our Take the Plunge! program really helps managers bond with their new crew members from the beginning. It's a powerful tool that makes new crew members feel at home and helps them become productive quickly. It also provides an opportunity to clear up any questions about the job, and sets out a clear vision for new crew members when they start."

THE TAKE THE PLUNGE! CURRICULUM

The Take the Plunge! program is designed to allow on-site managers to conduct the program based on the restaurant's schedule. Therefore, the program components include the recommended steps for managers to follow, and a flip book with talking points for the manager to use as a delivery outline.

The primary components of the Take the Plunge! Program include:

1. The new crew Take the Plunge! video,

2. The Red Lobster Brand,

3. Our Compass (The Red Lobster Vision), and

4. Get Ready to Make Wraves (Red Lobster's Crew Guidelines).

Employees then receive job-specific training from a certified trainer in the restaurant.

Other Information about Red Lobster: Red Lobster is a company of restaurants with over 650 locations. In the past four years, we have redesigned our new crew orientation and training programs (along with much of our management training) to better align and support each other and Our Compass (Red Lobster's vision).

Company Size: 60,000-plus employees in the USA and Canada.

Number of New Employees per Month: Approximately 6,000 new employees each month, averaging 10 new employees per restaurant monthly.

Frequency of Orientation: Individual restaurant managers determine the frequency of orientation. It is held as often as once per week.

Average Orientation Group Size: Red Lobster will hold orientation for one new crew member or as many as a dozen new crew members at once.

Basic Orientation Logistics: Our orientation program is held in our restaurants, usually in the dining area before it is opened to guests for the day. Red Lobster delivers orientation in over 600 Red Lobster restaurant locations.

Krista Rice is manager of crew training and development at Red Lobster. She holds a BS in Hospitality Management from Florida State University. She has several years of experience in food and beverage operations with a focus on training. Krista began teaching hospitality management in a private technical college before she returned to school for graduate studies. She joined the Red Lobster People Development group just before earning a master's degree in Human Resource Management with an emphasis on training.

Shannon Maurice is training specialist of crew training and development at Red Lobster and holds BS degrees in Business and Psychology from the University of California. Shannon also has several years of experience in food and beverage operations experience, working with multiple companies and locations. She was promoted from crew level to manager to corporate training facilitator with Planet Hollywood. Shannon joined the Red Lobster People Development group and immediately began work on the Take the Plunge! new crew orientation program described in this chapter.

Contact Information   *Krista Rice, Manager, Crew Training and Development*
Red Lobster People Development
7101 Lake Ellenor Drive
Orlando, FL 32809
407-245-4680
krice@redlobster.com

Chapter 22

Self-Directed Orientation Modules

No Computer or Trainer Required!

Many companies have multiple locations but not multiple computers and Internet access to orient their new employees in a consistent manner. This chapter describes a prepackaged but completely customizable, booklet-based program for new employee orientation, training, and management, called Getting in Gear. The heart of the Getting in Gear program is a series of almost 30 self-directed learning assignments organized into five modules. The modules are designed to be completed by the new employee, with one-on-one supervisor meetings scheduled between each module for additional learning and to review the employee's progress with the orientation program. *The program requires no computers, no human resource personnel, and no training personnel.*

The learning assignments are to be completed by the employee while on the job. They are designed to help the employee learn what is needed to become successful on the job as quickly as possible. The employee completes the learning assignments during the normal workday, and while learning and doing regular job duties.

Anchoring the completion of one module and the start of the next are six meetings between the new employee and his or her manager, supervisor, or team leader. The agenda for each meeting is provided, making each meeting a preprogrammed dialogue between the manager and the employee. The purpose of each meeting with the supervisor is to review and confirm what the employee has learned over the prior week, and to prepare the employee for the learning assignments in the next module.

RECOMMENDED USERS

While Getting in Gear can be used in any size company in any industry, it is especially perfect for:

- Retail stores and branch offices that are located remotely from the corporate office's orientation program

- Companies that have so few new employees each year that it doesn't make sense to have an instructor-led classroom program

- Employees who may not have easy access to a computer in the workplace, making an online orientation program unsuitable

- Companies without formal training personnel or with few human resource personnel; companies that rely on supervisors to train new employees

- Companies that want an additional, customized, on-the-job training component for employees and supervisors to use, to complement their generic classroom program

PROGRAM LENGTH AND DETAILS

Getting in Gear recommends that the modules be completed in the sequence provided; each module takes about a week to complete. As recommended, the complete learning cycle would then take about five weeks to complete. However, because the manager or supervisor decides what learning assignments to use and when to schedule the meetings, the total time required is at the supervisor's discretion.

The Getting in Gear program comes in the form of an *Employee Handbook* and a *Leader's Manual*. The *Employee Handbook* contains all the learning assignments and becomes the employee's self-directed learning workbook. The new employee is given this in the employee's first formal meeting with the supervisor, which often occurs on the employee's first day on the job. The *Leader's Manual* contains not only the learning assignments given to the employee, but also several other sets of materials, all packaged together for easy and convenient use. The materials include:

- The plan and overview for the complete Getting in Gear program

- Guidelines for enlisting coworker support in orienting the new employee

- Scheduling forms and completion checklists (which can serve as an official record of the employee's completion of orientation training)

- A learning plan for each module, including the complete set of learning assignments included and the learning objectives for that module

- A complete agenda for each meeting with the employee

- Instructions for how each learning assignment is to be completed, which may include training guidance for how the supervisor can prepare for certain assignments (for example, one learning assignment directs the supervisor to communicate the mission of his or her unit to the new employee; a short instructional piece in the *Leader's Manual* explains how to develop a mission statement for the unit if there is none).

The general schedule for implementing Getting in Gear occurs in two phases. In phase one, the supervisor completes various identified learning assignments. In addition to developing the mission statement, the supervisor should alert coworkers and others of the new employee's arrival, prepare an on-the-job structured learning plan, and complete a Leader–Follower Assessment.

Once these activities are completed, the supervisor can go through the Getting in Gear program repeatedly with any number of new employees without further preparation. In short, investing an hour or so of the supervisor's time in completing this material will pay off many times over.

Phase two starts when the new employee arrives at the workplace. See the program outline chart in this chapter for a more complete schedule.

One other note: Getting in Gear is a program that can be used to complement and supplement existing formal orientation programs that might be provided by Human Resources. In that case, the learning assignments covering topics that are dealt with in the formal orientation can simply be skipped.

Getting in Gear is a single-source program for new employee orientation, training, and management. There are nearly 30 separate learning assignments that cover virtually every conceivable item that a new employee should learn in order to be successful in his or her new job. Because the supervisor decides which assignments to use, the program can be used with employees at all levels and in all capacities. In effect, Getting in Gear allows each employee to receive a customized, individual learning plan that is the foundation for an effective working relationship between the new employee and his or her boss.

FREQUENCY AND AUDIENCE SIZE

Getting in Gear is designed to be offered on a just-in-time, as-needed basis. Whenever a new employee arrives, Getting in Gear can begin. Even though it can be used in group settings, the program is designed to be used with employees on a one-on-one basis.

TESTING

Getting in Gear includes several different forms of testing and assessment over the course of the program. However, the testing is nonevaluative and used for diagnostic purposes only. The assessments are not intended as tools to determine whether a new employee should be retained or terminated.

By reviewing these learning assessments, the supervisor has a chance to assess how well the employee has learned the materials in the previous module during the follow-up meeting. There are several training modules throughout the program that require the employee to make correct responses.

For example, in one learning assignment there is a generic set of training instructions on proper phone etiquette. In the follow-up activity, the supervisor can provide examples of various problem phone calls the employee may receive, to which the employee must respond with the correct principles. Finally, there are other diagnostic devices such as the Leader–Follower Assessment, which provides a basis for the supervisor to indicate what behaviors are expected of the new employee in difficult situations.

DIFFERENT ORIENTATIONS FOR DIFFERENT FOLKS

New employee orientation is probably the most universal training program in the workplace, and the training program with the most variation in delivery. A self-directed program like Getting in Gear meets the orientation needs of large companies looking for a more personalized, one-on-one orientation component to be used with the supervisor; and it provides a resource for the small office or retail store that lacks easy access to computer online programs or to large classroom orientations.

Dr. Alan Clardy, Ph.D. is an assistant professor of human resource development at Towson University and a principal of Advantage Human Resources. He has over 25 years of corporate and professional experience in human resources, having worked as a corporate training director, a vice president of human resources, and a private HR consultant. His doctorate is from the University of Maryland College Park. He is the author of *50 Case Studies for Management and Supervisory Training* (HRD Press) and *Studying Your Workforce* (Sage). He continues his consulting practice through Advantage Human Resources, where he specializes in the custom design and implementation of performance management and service quality systems, along with Getting in Gear, his new employee orientation, training, and management program.

Contact Information   *Towson University: Psychology/HRD Program*
8000 York Road
Towson, MD 21252
410-704-3215
aclardy@towson.edu
www.towson.edu/~aclardy

THE GETTING IN GEAR OUTLINE

Module	Learning Assignments	Schedule
Module One: **Working Here**	■ Knowing your office ■ Standards of conduct ■ Our mission ■ The work we do ■ Meeting your coworkers ■ Your job duties ■ Job update ■ Learning your job ■ Telephone skills	■ Meeting on first day ■ Follow-up meeting about a week later
Module Two: **Working Knowledgeably**	■ About our organization ■ How our organization works ■ Understanding our competition ■ Products and services ■ Customer service skills	■ Follow-up meeting near the end of second week on the job
Module Three: **Working Successfully**	■ Job specifications ■ Clarifying job expectations ■ Performance appraisals ■ Skills of a competent employee	■ Follow-up meeting near the end of third week on the job
Module Four: **Working Together**	■ Understanding your boss ■ Leaders and followers ■ Communication skills ■ Reporting and control	■ Follow-up meeting near the end of fourth week on the job
Module Five: **Working Smarter**	■ Managing time and priorities ■ Work planning ■ Improving the quality of your work ■ Streamlining the work you do ■ Asking for feedback ■ Competency improvement plan	■ Follow-up meeting near the end of fifth week on the job

LEARNING ASSIGNMENT 2-4

Sample Page

Products and Services

LEARNING ASSIGNMENT COMPLETED

It is important for you to know the products and services that we sell to our customers and clients. These products and services generate sales and revenue for our company, and they provide value to those people we serve. As an employee of our company, any function you choose to serve in will add value to these products and services, either directly or indirectly.

Your manager or leader will indicate what our primary products and services are. Write those products in the spaces below.

To Do	Product or Service	Source of Information

Use the enclosed worksheets to learn more about the products or services noted. Make more copies if necessary.

Worksheet

PRODUCT OR SERVICE: _____

Description of the Product or Service	_____ _____
Distinguishing Features	_____ _____ _____
Price and Purchasing Options	_____ _____
Guarantees or Warranties	_____
Complementary Products and/or Services	_____ _____
Typical Customer	

Sample Page

LEARNING PLAN

The Contents of Module Three:

In this module, you create the foundation for successful job performance by establishing the performance management conditions under which the new employee will work. This module covers:

WORKING SUCCESSFULLY

- The specific expectations for job performance.
- The performance appraisal process.
- How performance will be compensated.
- The skills needed for competent job performance.

Rationale

A "performance management system" requires three basic parts:

1. Identified expectations for job performance
2. Methods for evaluating job performance
3. Recognition and rewards based on performance

In addition, the employee should have help in learning the skills needed to perform effectively.

When to schedule the meeting

This meeting should be scheduled sometime during the employee's second to fourth week on the job.

Learning Objectives

As a result of completing this module, the new employee should be able to:

- Identify the specific expectations for job performance.
- State how his or her job performance will be evaluated.
- Describe how job performance will be compensated.
- List the competencies needed for successful performance of the job.

LEADER'S GUIDE TO MODULE THREE: WORKING SUCCESSFULLY

Sample Page

MEETING AGENDA

The following agenda is recommended for meeting with the employee about Module Three. The learning assignments from the Employee Handbook are shown beside each agenda item in parentheses.

YOUR NOTES

NOTE:

The first few weeks on the job are often stressful for new employees. The adjustment process can frequently create confusion, doubts, and even regrets.

Be sure to pay attention to how well the employee is adjusting at this time. It would be a good idea to spend a few moments asking how the employee is adjusting. Look for signs of frustration or dissatisfaction. Since the greatest chance of an employee quitting is often during this initial period, look for danger signals and be ready to help the employee.

1. Begin by reviewing the prior Learning Assignments; clear up any questions about:
   - Organization history (2-1)
   - Organization structure (2-2)
   - Operations (2-3)

2. Review the Job Specification Worksheet in Module 1 (1-6). To Clarify Job Expectations (3-2), review any standards and/or objectives with the employee; make sure the employee knows what the specific expectations are by either recording expectations on the form or giving the employee a prepared copy.

YOUR NOTES

3. For the Performance Appraisal Process (3-3), discuss how you will formally evaluate the employee's job performance. If your organization has a performance appraisal system, tell how that system operates. If not, you may want to establish your own procedures (3-3).

_____

4. Identify the Skills of a Competent Employee (3-4) that the employee needs to perform his or her job competently.

_____

5. Give the employee the assignments for Module Four. Set up the meeting date to review that module.

_____

INSTRUCTIONS FOR
LEARNING ASSIGNMENT 3-1:
CLARIFYING JOB EXPECTATIONS

Sample Page

INSTRUCTIONS:

The purpose of this assignment is to make sure your new employee knows as clearly as possible what you expect from his or her job performance, and how you will evaluate and respond to his or her performance.

For learning assignment 3-1:

1. Refer to the Job Specifications worksheet, Module 1-6. Both you and the employee should have a copy.

2. Review the lists of job duties (especially any critical duties) and customers to make sure this information is accurate. If not, be sure to update and correct the information.

Chapter 23

Designing an Annual Residential Orientation Program

THE USDA ANNUAL RESIDENTIAL ORIENTATION*—AN OVERVIEW

The National Agricultural Statistics Service (NASS) has been conducting an in-depth new employee orientation program for its professional employees for more than 25 years.

Because NASS hires only a few new professional employees each month, a decision was made to hold an annual intensive and comprehensive six-day residential program in Washington, D.C. for all statisticians and specialists who have been hired in the past year. This approach makes the best use of the organization's resources, while providing an opportunity to build relationships between critical professional employees.

The NASS new employee orientation is a six-day residential course conducted in Washington, D.C. It is designed to enable the participants to understand the agency's mission, goals, and objectives as well as the functional responsibilities of its headquarters units. All employees hired within the past year attend the course.

When not restricted by a federal government hiring freeze, the U.S. Department of Agriculture (USDA) NASS hires approximately two to three new employees each month, with the majority being in one of the three mission-critical positions of agricultural statistician, mathematical statistician, and computer specialist.

Generally, NASS conducts one NEO session each year. Each USDA NASS residential orientation program has approximately 25 to 30 participants. However, when hiring is slow, a session might be delayed until the following year to ensure a full complement of participants. Alternatively, when hiring is unusually heavy, back-to-back orientation sessions are conducted. In such a case, two sessions, starting one day apart, are conducted in one fiscal year.

The reasons behind the development of this orientation program are expressed in the Program Goals, which are listed here.

*Developed by the U. S. Department of Agriculture (USDA), National Agricultural Statistics Service (NASS).

The USDA NASS new employee orientation program is designed to enable the participants to:

1. Understand the agency's mission, goals, and objectives.

2. Know about their roles and responsibilities in carrying out the mission.

3. Acquire basic information related to: ethics, workplace diversity, benefits, training and career development, security, and legal and confidentiality requirements.

4. Understand the organizational structure and the relationships between and among the agency's headquarters divisions and its field operations.

5. Know how the organizational alignment enables them to carry out the operations necessary to accomplish the mission.

PROGRAM OBJECTIVES

There are three primary learning objectives of the program.

By the end of the program, participants will have had the opportunity to:

1. Obtain an overview of NASS mission and organization.

2. Understand the functions and concepts of headquarters units.

3. Meet and build relationships with NASS management and staff.

The NASS NEO is part of a larger program—the NASS Technical Development Program—that provides training and development activities for the three technical positions of agricultural statistician, mathematical statistician, and computer specialist. The NASS Technical Development Program provides the necessary knowledge, skill, and competence training needed for successful job performance. All courses and developmental experiences in the NASS Technical Development Program are provided to all agricultural statisticians, mathematical statisticians, and computer specialists.

Specifically, the NASS NEO program provides a formal, structured, state-of-the-art course designed for employees who have been on the job for 6 to 18 months, with the average student having one year of experience. Most of the content is technical in nature. Therefore, NEO participants must have had some survey experience, usually acquired by having worked in one of the 46 field offices, in order to understand the organizational units and headquarters functions.

NASS management is very supportive of the NEO program and its objectives. This is evident in the amount of staff resources and time allocated to the planning and implementation.

MANAGEMENT PARTICIPATION

Managers at the USDA NASS not only support this annual orientation program, they also fully participate in the program. All top managers meet with the NEO participants several times during the agenda.

First, managers will officially welcome the new employees at the reception. Next, managers personally present key topics on the first morning and participate in the management panel discussion on the last morning. NASS leaders are also present at key events throughout the NEO: Lockup Tour, Secretary's Briefing, Administrator's Reception, and lunch in the Secretary's Dining Room. (Note: "Lockup Tour" refers to the most secure aspects of how key NASS headquarters employees handle confidential agricultural data. These NASS employees are literally "locked up" for several hours prior to the report briefing to the Secretary of Agriculture, or his or her representative, and the release of the data analysis and report to the public.)

ORIENTATION LOGISTICS

Both the morning session on the first day and the closing session on the sixth day are conducted at the hotel in which the participants reside. The hotel location has traditionally been near a subway station in either Northern Virginia or Washington, D.C. The rest of the sessions are conducted in conference rooms and office areas at the two USDA NASS sites in the Washington metropolitan area.

Using NASS facilities is congruent with the workshop goals of familiarizing the NEO participants with NASS headquarters functions and networking with staff. Housing NEO participants in the Washington metropolitan area enables them to experience the city during six workdays and one weekend day, which is important to these young professionals because their career tracks will include a tour of duty in Washington, D.C. Many of the new staff have never been to the nation's capital, and the NEO program corrects any misconceptions and eases their concerns about working in D.C. later in their careers.

ANNUAL PROGRAM PLANNING AND PREPARATION

Each year, several months before the annual orientation program will be conducted, a new NEO planning committee is formed, led by a member of the training unit. This committee is comprised of representatives from each of the NASS headquarters divisions; the field office operation also provides input in NEO planning. This working committee, under the guidance of the training specialist, reviews and adjusts the workshop goals and learning objectives.

The committee receives and discusses the program evaluation results of the most recent NEO session and, where appropriate, incorporates the feedback into the program for continuous improvement. The committee updates and finalizes the NEO agenda, ensuring the inclusion of all new and critical topics. The committee agrees on trainers, speakers, presenters, and managers who will represent the headquarters organizational units.

Each individual trainer, speaker, or presenter decides the instructional methodology. The committee appoints a different chairperson for each of the six days, who ensures that the conference rooms, audiovisual equipment, participant handout materials, and presenters are ready. On his or her NEO training day, a chairperson acts as a moderator, introducing presenters, giving times for breaks and lunch, and directing participants where to go if several rooms are used.

The committee also arranges an informal mentoring program for the NEO participants. Mentors are employees located at the organization's headquarters who are more advanced in their statistical careers than the NEO participants. Each time an NEO is conducted, headquarter employees in all divisions are given the opportunity to volunteer.

Once selected and approved by upper management, the mentors are oriented to their roles and responsibilities, which include:

1. Attending all NEO mentor functions (there are at least two functions on the agenda for them).

2. Pairing with an NEO participant with similar interests and career aspirations.

3. Inviting the mentee to use the mentor's office as needed during the NEO for such basics as telephone and computer use, storing coats, and so on.

4. Giving the mentee a tour of the USDA two-building complex and the surrounding D.C. mall area, and highlighting special features such as the two cafeterias, several informal eating places, the Secretary's Dining Room, the Secretary's Office, the bank and underground shopping mall, the nearby museums, and the subway system.

5. Introducing the mentee to NASS headquarters staff, managers, and leaders.

6. Having an informal lunch with the mentee at least once during NEO.

7. Helping the mentee understand how to establish his or her own network.

8. Optionally, socializing with the mentee during the evenings and weekends.

Finally, the NEO committee is responsible for investigating the current Washington, D.C. social, dining, and sports options and producing a list of suggestions for NEO participants to avail themselves of during their six-day stay in the national capital. NASS has a social organization, the NASS Club, that usually takes the lead in this effort, producing a useful folder of current city information that is given to participants at the Welcome reception on the first evening. NASS committee members urge their coworkers to spend lunch, evening, or weekend time socializing with the NEO participants.

THE RESIDENTIAL ORIENTATION PROGRAM AGENDA

Exhibit 1 contains the agenda for the most recent NEO session. It should be noted that the agenda covers all NASS headquarters divisions, functions, and core processes. It is comprehensive and holistic in nature. Further, it is unique among federal statistical organizations. While each statistical agency orients its new employees according to its organizational needs, none provide such a comprehensive approach as NASS does.

EXHIBIT 1: THE NASS 6-DAY AGENDA

NASS EMPLOYEE ORIENTATION

Day 1 Chairperson: Training Coordinator

A.M. LOCATION:	Residence Inn-Thomas Circle	
8:00–8:30	Introduction	NASS Associate Administrator
8:30–8:45	Objectives / Agenda	Training Director
8:45–9:15	USDA/REE Overview	Under Secretary Research/ Education/Economics
9:15–9:45	NASS Overview	NASS Associate Administrator
9:45–10:00	Break	
10:00–10:30	Use of NASS Data	USDA Economics Research Service Economist
10:30–11:00	International Programs Office (IPO)	IPO Director
11:00–11:15	Preparation for Afternoon	Training Coordinator
11:15–12:00	Travel to South Building and Meet Mentors in Room 5152	
12:00–1:00	Lunch	
P.M. LOCATION:	Room 5152—South Building	
1:00–2:00	Administrative and Financial Management (AFM) Overview	AFM Specialists
2:00–2:30	Ethics	AFM Ethics Specialist
2:30–2:45	Break	
2:45–3:00	Civil Rights	NASS Civil Rights Director
3:00–4:15	Budget and Administrative Services Office	Budget Manager
	Training and Career Development Office	Training Director
4:15–4:30	Wrap-Up and Next Day Preview	Training Coordinator

Day 2 Chairpersons: Information Technology Managers

LOCATION:	Room 5152—South Building	
7:30–8:15	Lockup Tour/Security Briefing	Marketing/Information Services Managers

8:15–9:30	Secretary's Briefing	NASS Deputy Administrator
9:30–9:45	Break	
9:45–10:15	Marketing/Information Services Office Overview	MISO Director
10:15–10:45	Marketing—Group A	MISO Marketing Manager
	Customer Service—Group B	MISO Customer Service Rep.
10:45–11:15	Marketing—Group B	MISO Marketing Manager
	Customer Service—Group A	MISO Customer Service Rep.
11:15–1:00	Lunch	
1:00–1:30	Information Technology Division Overview	ITD Director
1:30–4:00	The group is divided into three groups of approximately 10 people each for branch tours and introductions to branch employees.	
4:00–4:15	Wrap-Up and Next Day Preview	ITD Manager

Day 3 Chairpersons: Statistics Division Managers

A.M. LOCATION: Room 1623—South Building

8:00–8:15	Statistics Division (SD) Overview	SD Director
8:15–9:30	Statistical Methods Branch (SMB) Activity	SMB Statistician
9:30–9:45	Crops Branch (CB) Overview	CB Chief
9:45–10:00	Break	
10:00–11:30	Crops Branch (CB) Interaction Activity	CB Statisticians
11:30–1:00	Group Lunch (Secretary's Dining Room)	

P.M. LOCATION: Room 5152—South Building

| 1:00–1:30 | Environmental, Economics, and Demographics & Branch Chiefs Livestock Branch Overviews (EED & LB) | LB Director |
| 1:30–2:45 | Environmental, Economics, and Demographics & EED Statistician Livestock Branch Group Participation Activity | LB Supervisor |

2:45–3:00	Break	
3:00–4:00	Conclude Activity	
4:00–4:15	Wrap-Up and Next Day Preview	SD Manager

Day 4 Chairperson: Research Division (RD) Statistician

LOCATION: Research Division

When directed, divide into two groups.

8:00–8:30	Fairfax Office Reception and Introductions	RD Director

	Group A	**Group B**
8:30–10:15	Research Sections Demonstrations	Area Frame Development Demonstrations
10:15–10:30	Break	

	Group A	**Group B**
10:30–11:45	Research Sections Demonstrations	Area Frame Sampling Demonstrations
11:45–1:00	Lunch	

	Group A	**Group B**
1:00–2:45	Area Frame Development Demonstrations	Research Sections Demonstrations
2:45–3:00	Break	

	Group A	**Group B**
3:00–4:15	Area Frame Sampling Demonstrations	Research Sections Demonstrations
4:15–4:20	Wrap-Up and Next Day Preview	RD Statistician
4:20	**—Special Activity—**	

Day 5 Chairperson: Census & Survey Division (CSD) Statistician

LOCATION:	Room 5152—South Building	
8:00–10:00	Mentoring Activities	ITD Manager
10:00–10:45	Census and Survey Division and Branch Overview	CSD Director CSD Branch Chiefs
10:45–11:30	Data Collection Branch/ Sampling Branch	CSD Branch Chiefs

	Sampling Activity	
11:30–12:30	Lunch	
12:30–1:45	Finish Sampling Activity	CSD Branch Chiefs
1:45–2:00	Break	
2:00–3:45	Census Planning Branch and Survey Administration Branch Bingo Activity	CSD Branch Chiefs
3:45–4:00	Wrap-Up and Next Day Preview	CSD Statistician

Day 6 Chairperson: Assistant to Associate Administrator

A.M. LOCATION: Room 1623—South Building

Hotel Checkout

8:00–8:15	Overview and Objectives	Assoc. Deputy Administrator
8:15–8:45	NASDA/NASS Program	NASDA Executives—President and COO National Association of State Departments of Agriculture
8:45–9:00	Human Resources	HR Manager
9:00–10:00	Field Operations	Deputy Administrator— Field Operations
10:00–10:15	Break	
10:15–11:15	Management Questions and Answers	Associate Administrator Deputy Administrators Division Directors Assoc. Deputy Administrators
11:15–11:45	Closing Remarks	NASS Administrator
11:45–noon	Completing and Collecting Evaluations	Training Coordinator

HUMAN OR MATERIAL RESOURCES USED

NASS NEO uses the usual materials needed for a classroom course: physical class space, participant folders or binders, handouts, and so on. NASS instructors usually have supporting audiovisual materials.

In addition, because the NEO participants travel from field offices and are housed in a hotel, NASS incurs hotel lodging fees and air transportation costs, as well as daily expenses for food, local travel, and incidentals. When the Welcome Reception is held in a hotel, there are the usual expenses for food and a reception room. Any sessions conducted in the hotel require a hotel classroom, which carries a modest usage fee.

In addition to NASS planning committee members, leaders, managers, presenters, mentors, NASS Club officers and some members, and headquarters staff who choose to socialize with NEO participants, NASS always includes at least one (but often more than one) leader from outside the NASS organization to present a larger USDA perspective. For example, in the NEO program illustrated by the agenda included in this chapter, Dr. I. Miley Gonzalez was a guest speaker. At the time of the NEO, Dr. Gonzalez was the Under Secretary of the Research, Education, and Economics (REE) Mission, and led an organizational entity comprised of NASS and three other related agencies.

In addition, the NEO agenda usually includes an individual from one of the NASS-related agencies or elsewhere who attests to the criticality and usefulness of NASS data products and reports. For example, in the NEO program illustrated in this chapter, Merritt Padgitt filled this role. At the time of the NEO, Merritt Padgitt was an employee in USDA's Economic Research Service, which is a related agency in REE. Dr. Padgitt frequently used NASS census and survey data for economic modeling.

LESSONS LEARNED ALONG THE WAY

USDA NASS has been conducting NEO and incorporating formal participant evaluation feedback, as well as informal feedback from many others involved in the NEO program, for more than ten years. Currently, participants and other interested parties rate the program components as highly successful and effective. The key points of advice are fundamental to all effective training:

1. Conduct a needs assessment to find out what is required by the organization and the prospective program participants.

2. Based on the needs assessment analysis, establish specific program goals and learner objectives.

3. Obtain organizational commitment and resources.

4. Sequence the NEO appropriately in existing developmental curriculum.

5. Plan to conduct NEO at a time that fits best for both the organization and the participants.

6. Involve as many of the organizational leaders and staff as possible in the planning and implementation.

7. Throughout the process, seek and incorporate broad participation and feedback.

8. Conduct a thorough end-of-course evaluation and incorporate the results as lessons learned for the next NEO session.

RESULTS AND EVALUATION OF THE PROGRAM

Exhibit 2 contains the participant evaluation form used for the most recent pair of NEO sessions, which ran simultaneously, starting one day apart. This thorough evaluation approach, and incorporating its feedback into the planning of the next NEO, is unique among Federal statistical agencies. While each statistical agency orients its new employees according to its organizational needs, none provide such a comprehensive evaluation approach as does NASS.

Some comments from recent NEO participants regarding the overall value of the program are listed below:

"Thank you for this wonderful opportunity. It had an impact on my life and career."

"The training has been great! I had the ability to meet many interesting people while gaining a greater knowledge of NASS as a whole."

"The sense of being part of something successful is important—good in intentions and follow-through."

Linda M. Raudenbush holds a BA in Mathematics and Secondary Education from St. Joseph College, an MS in Applied Behavioral Science from Johns Hopkins University, and an Ed.D. in Human Resource Development from George Washington University. Linda has more than 25 years of marketing, managing, training, and consulting experience in both private and public sectors.

Linda has been an adjunct professor at National-Louis University and Strayer University in the Washington, D.C. area, and is in her twelfth year of part-time teaching at the University of Maryland, Baltimore County. She authored a chapter of the 1996 Sage publication, *The Adjunct Faculty Handbook*; published an article in a 2000 issue of *Human Resource Development Quarterly*, a journal published by Jossey-Bass; and coauthored an article in *The 2001 Annual: Volume 2–Consulting*, published by Jossey-Bass/Pfeiffer.

Linda has been a regular session presenter at the annual University System of Maryland Women's Conference for the last six years, and has presented sessions at other human resource development and organizational development conferences. She also consults in the HRD/OD field, and is currently an HRD/OD specialist at the U.S. Department of Agriculture in the National Agricultural Statistics Service.

Contact Information   *USDA NASS DAFO TCDO—Room 4133*
1400 Independence Ave., S.W.
Washington, D.C. 20250
202-720-6016
lraudenbush@nass.usda.gov

NASS EMPLOYEE ORIENTATION EVALUATION

Directions: Circle your response on the scale. Comment where applicable.

1. *Length of Program*

    A. The program length, 5 1/2 days, was:

1	2	3	4	5
Too Short		About Right		Too Long

    Comment: _____

2. *Schedule of Program*

    A. The program schedule that extended from midweek to midweek in Washington, D.C. was:

1	2	3	4	5
Preferable		Didn't matter		Not preferable

    Comment: _____

3. *Content of Program as a Whole*

    A. The program content was:

1	2	3	4	5
Poor	Fair	Good	Very Good	Excellent

    Comment: _____

    B. Rank the top three Orientation Program activities that you valued the most. Place a 1 next to the activity you most valued, a 2 next to the second most valued activity, and a 3 next to the third most valued activity.

    __ 1 = Overview of NASS mission and organization.

    __ 2 = Communication of functions/concepts used in D.C.

    __ 3 = Asking questions of NASS management and staff.

    __ 4 = Meeting members of NASS management and staff.

    __ 5 = Networking during free time.

    __ 6 = Social aspects of the program.

    __ 7 = The mentor arrangement.

___ 8 = Enhanced morale or esprit de corps.

___ 9 = Other:

C. What comments do you have regarding the mentoring program?

D. What changes, additions, or deletions would you recommend for the program?

4. *Objectives*

Indicate the degree to which each of the following objectives was met for you.

A. To obtain an overview of NASS mission and organization.

1	2	3	4
Not met at all	Some of objective met	Most of objective met	Objective fully met

Comment: _____

B. To understand the functions and concepts of D.C. units.

1	2	3	4
Not met at all	Some of objective met	Most of objective met	Objective fully met

Comment: _____

C. To meet and build relationships with NASS management and staff.

1	2	3	4
Not met at all	Some of objective met	Most of objective met	Objective fully met

Comment: _____

5. *Program Materials*

A. The overhead transparencies were:

1	2	3	4	5
Poor	Fair	Good	Very Good	Excellent

Comment: _____

B. The other visuals, such as charts, were:

1	2	3	4	5
Poor	Fair	Good	Very Good	Excellent

Comment: _____

C. How useful were the handouts to your learning?

1	2	3	4	5
Not useful		Moderately useful		Very useful

Comment: _____

6. *Sessions*

Use the following scale to rate each session's value to you. Enter the number that best describes your reaction in the box to the right of the session title. Comments about each session can be entered in the far right column.

0	1	2	3	4	5
No Value or Don't Remember		Low Value		Moderate Value	High Value

Session Titles	Value	Comments
USDA/REE Overview		
NASS Overview		
Use of NASS Data		
International Programs Office		
AFM/Human Resources Overview		
Ethics Overview		
Civil Rights		

Session Titles	Value	Comments
Budget and Administrative Services Office		
Training and Career Development Office		
Lockup		
Marketing and Information Services Office Overview		
Marketing		
Customer Service		
Information Technology Division Overview		
Information Services Branch		
Technical Services Branch		
Systems Service Branch		
Research Sections Demonstrations		
Area Frame Development Demonstrations		
Area Frame Sampling Demonstrations		
Statistics Division Overview		
Statistical Methods Branch Activity		
Crops Branch Overview		

Session Titles	Value	Comments
Crops Branch Activity		
Environmental, Economics, and Demographics Overview		
Livestock Branch Overview		
Environmental, Economics, and Demographics & Livestock Branch Group Participation Activity		
Mentoring Activities		
Census and Survey Division Overview		
Census Planning Branch Overview		
Survey Administration Branch Overview		
Sampling Branch Overview		
Data Collection Branch Overview		
Data Collection Branch and Sampling Branch Sampling Activity		
Census Planning Branch and Survey Administration Branch Bingo Activity		
NASDA/NASS Program		

Session Titles	Value	Comments
Field Operations		
Management Q&A		

7. *Logistics:* Circle your response on the scale. Comment where applicable.

A. The hotel accommodations were:

1	2	3	4	5
Poor	Fair	Good	Very Good	Excellent

Comment: _____

B. The hotel meeting facilities were:

1	2	3	4	5
Poor	Fair	Good	Very Good	Excellent

Comment: _____

C. The D.C. office meeting facilities were:

1	2	3	4	5
Poor	Fair	Good	Very Good	Excellent

Comment: _____

D. The Fairfax, VA office meeting facilities were:

1	2	3	4	5
Poor	Fair	Good	Very Good	Excellent

Comment: _____

8. *Demographics* (Check the appropriate response.)

   A. Select your present position:

   __ a = ADP Statistician

   __ b = Agricultural Statistician

   __ c = Mathematical Statistician

   __ d = Computer Specialist

   __ e = Other:

   B. How many months have you been in your present position?

   __ a = 0 to less than 6 months

   __ b = 6 months to less than 12 months

   __ c = 12 months to less than 18 months

   __ d = 18 months to less than 24 months

   __ e = 24 months to less than 30 months

   __ f = other: _____ months

   C. How many years have you been with NASS?

   __ a = 0 to less than 1 year

   __ b = 1 year to less than 2 years

   __ c = 2 years to less than 3 years

   __ d = 3 years to less than 4 years

   __ e = 4 years to less than 5 years

   __ f = other: _____ years

9. *Overall Comments*

Thank you for taking the time to complete this evaluation. Your feedback will be considered when planning future programs.

QUESTIONS FOR NASS MANAGEMENT

On the last day of the Orientation Program, your group will participate in a Q & A session with NASS management. Please list any questions or concerns you have that you would like the Associate Administrator, Deputy Administrator for Field Operations, and Division Directors to discuss.

1.

2.

3.

4.

5.

Part 4

Orientation for New Managers

INTRODUCTION

Some companies choose to have their new supervisors and managers attend a management orientation program in addition to the company's new employee orientation program, to ensure they know applicable federal employment laws and the company policies and procedures for managers.

Part 4 provides the following tools:

- *The Management Orientation Shopping List*—This is a comprehensive checklist of potential topics for a management orientation program. Simply review the list and check the topics that pertain to your company. Then use the customized list to form the basic outline for your program. (Chapter 24)

- *Orienting the New Executive*—New company officers and executives have special needs to quickly integrate into and lead employees in the new company. This chapter discusses a partnership between Personnel Decisions International (PDI) and Parkland Hospital in Dallas, Texas. PDI conducts assessments with all of Parkland's internal and external executive candidates, and conducts customized, one-on-one coaching with each new executive at Parkland. (Chapter 27)

- *Sample Management Orientation Program Designs*—The following companies have provided their unique Management Orientation program designs for this section:

  - Exel Logistics (Chapter 25)

  - Kahunaville Management, Inc. (Chapter 26)

■ *Management Orientation Games and Table Discussions*—This section includes activities that can be used to enhance your management orientation program by making it more interactive and thought-provoking:

- Sexual Harassment Table Discussions (Chapter 32)

- Employment Law Hangman (Chapter 28)

- Company Ethics Baseball (Chapter 29)

- Effective Interviewing Tools (Chapter 30)

- Writing Effective Job Description KSAPs (Chapter 31)

Chapter 24
The Management Orientation Shopping List

Check the topics that are appropriate to include in your company's management orientation program or in your management procedure guides.

Note: See Chapter 13, The New Employee Orientation Shopping List, for other potential management orientation topics.

Company Culture/Integration Topics

❑ The Company's Mission Statement

❑ The Company's Vision Statement

❑ Company Strategy/Goals

❑ The Company's History

❑ Company Leaders/Executives

❑ Organizational Chart(s)

❑ Lunch with Company Leaders

❑ Parent Company Information

❑ Company Subsidiary Information

❑ Recognition and Reward Systems

❑ The Company's Leadership Competencies

❑ Company Values

❑ The Company's Products/Services

❑ The Company's Customers

❑ Company Logo(s), Marketing Plans

❑ The Company's Competitors

❑ NYSE Symbol/Information

❑ Company Locations/Size(s)

❑ Executive Presentations

❑ Company Growth, Past and Future

❑ Company Patents

Employment Law

❑ Civil Rights Act

❑ Americans with Disabilities Act

❑ Equal Pay Act

❑ Family Leave and Medical Act

❑ Sexual Harassment Definitions

❑ Handling a Sexual Harassment Report

❑ Preventing Harassment

❑ OSHA Requirements

❑ COBRA Requirements

❑ Age Discrimination Act

❑ Your Industry Regulations

❑ Worker's Adjustment and Retraining Notification Act (WARN)

❑ Definition of a Contractor

❑ Workers' Compensation/Safety

❑ Insider Trading Laws

❑ Affirmative Action

❑ Understanding Exempt versus Nonexempt

❑ FLSA Pay/Overtime Regulations

Management Policies/Procedures

❑ The Hiring and Orientation Process

❑ Generating/Renewing Contracts

❑ Performance Appraisals

❑ Purchasing Procedures

❑ Compensation/Salary Increase Policies

❑ Confidentiality Policies

❑ Vendor/Supplier Policies

❑ Tuition Reimbursement Policies

❑ Personnel Requisition Procedure

❑ Stock Option Policies/Exercise Procedure

❑ Management Bonus Plan

❑ Exiting Employee Procedures

❑ Travel Policies and Procedures

❑ Budget Reports and Procedures

❑ Conflict of Interest Policies

❑ Processing an Employee's Status Change

❑ Proprietary Information/Property

❑ Progressive Discipline Procedures

❑ Intellectual Property Policies

❑ Management Training Programs

❑ Profit and Loss Reporting Processes

Basic Management Skills

❑ Interviewing

❑ Delegating

❑ Developing Mission/Vision

❑ Effective Meetings

❑ Coaching, Feedback, and Appraisals

❑ Diversity/Communication Styles

❑ Setting Goals and Action Plans

❑ Writing a Job Description

❑ Basic Finance/Business Skills

❑ Motivating Employees

With 14 years of experience in training and development, Doris Sims was a contributor to Mel Silberman's 1999, 2000, 2001, and 2002 *Training and Performance Sourcebooks,* as well as *The Consultant's Toolkit.* Her ideas have also been published in *Creative Training Techniques* newsletters, *Training Magazine,* and *Training Directors Forum* newsletter. Doris served as a presenter at the Training Director's Forum Conference, Training '99, IQPC Employee Orientation Program Conferences, and the 1999 ASTD International Conference. Doris is a human resource development director at Alcatel. Doris earned an MS in Human Resource Development from Indiana State University in 2001.

Contact Information   *2301 Bennington Avenue*
Flower Mound, TX 75028
972-539-1649
dmsims@home.com

Chapter 25

New Managers Learn the Business

Using Customer Requests for Proposals as Learning Tools at Exel Logistics

Exel Logistics is one of the top five providers of logistics services—air, sea, rail and road freight, contract warehousing and distribution, and a host of value-added services—for blue-chip companies. A descendant of air freight, the culture was operationally oriented in a low-margin business, with a relatively low turnover at the management level.

Due to a shift in strategy and a succession of acquisitions and mergers, the company could no longer be managed using the same skills in the same manner. However, new management recruits needed to gain a solid footing quickly to be effective and to gain credibility with current-line managers. The management orientation process described in this chapter was developed to address this issue.

THE EXCEL MANAGEMENT ORIENTATION PROGRAM

The target audience for the orientation is entry-level and middle-level managers. If all aspects of the orientation were conducted continuously, the program would encompass 3.5 days.

The first half-day of the program sets the scene with the typical mission, strategy, and "how-you-fit-in" session.

The next full day introduces new managers to administration procedures and processes, primarily a talk-and-chalk session with subject matter experts from departments such as Accounting, Accounts Payable, and Administration. Participants review housekeeping topics such as expense guidelines and reporting, performance management processes, and forecasting and budgeting cycles.

The innovative two days remaining are based on a regular business event that involves a number of departments or functions, requires detailed company information to execute, and is critical to future service performance. This business event is the project of responding to a customer's Request for a Proposal, or RFP.

The Request for Proposal (RFP) is a document issued by a prospective customer that specifies the type and level of service the customer would like a potential supplier to provide. The RFP is later used as the basis of a contractual agreement with the customer, and its information is used as a guideline to implement new business into the company. Thus, a new manager's familiarity with the RFP and appropriate responses not only offers exposure to a number of functional areas and company information, but is also preparation for implementing services into the operation.

In this program, a series of five sessions is facilitated by a manager or instructor acting as a source of direction or information. Sessions vary in length from an hour to half a day, depending on the complexity of the RFP and the nature of the information needed to address the customer requirement. An actual customer RFP is used, with the name changed to ABC Company or something equally innocuous.

After each task, appropriate sections or pieces of the actual response from Exel MSAS to the customer are distributed and critiqued. Therefore, instructor preparation is minimal.

An example of one of the session tasks is shown here.

Task One—RFP Analysis

Your task will be to analyze a sample RFP and answer the following questions:

1. What are the business goals of the customer; what do they hope to achieve by outsourcing this service?

2. What factors do they believe are critical to implementing this service successfully; in other words, what will cause the supplier to succeed (or fail)?

3. How does the customer's request for service differ from our usual practices? Are there any discrepancies between their request and our terms and conditions of contract, legal liabilities, security provisions, etc.?

4. What other issues can you identify from the RFP?

The output of this session is a list of the issues to be addressed and the departments or areas of the company that will need to contribute information, and an outline of the response to the RFP.

The remaining sessions follow a similar format to concentrate on implementing the service, measuring our performance, and handling the most common disputes (invoicing, service failure). Similar customer documentation is used throughout the case studies as a foundation of the business requirements; subsequent exercises (referred to as case studies) either deepen or broaden these requirements.

For example, in one case study, customer review documentation was analyzed to determine the top three causes of service failure. As our top blue-chip customers conduct regular quarterly reviews with all suppliers to determine service performance and variance, the information was readily available. Participants were given a few paragraphs describing a classic service failure and they were asked to analyze service data to determine the root cause of the problem. As a group, they were to outline an approach not only to solve the service problem but also to recommend management controls to prevent the reoccurrence of the failure.

FREQUENCY AND AUDIENCE SIZE

The management trainee program has an intake of six new candidates every six months. The initial orientation is followed by three months in various aspects of operations: one month with the account manager of a key customer, and two months or more of assisting in the implementation of new pieces of business. The pace is hectic and the travel is frequent as we try to give trainees a broad spectrum of experiences at different sizes and types of facilities. At the end of this period, trainees should expect to assume their first supervisory management positions, depending on their maturity and previous business experience.

RESULTS AND EVALUATION OF THE PROGRAM

New recruits have been described as having a broad grasp of our business and are able to be productive in researching, responding to, and helping to implement new pieces of business. In particular, they have been instrumental in critiquing RFP responses and identifying insufficient levels of detail before implementation.

For example, trainees implementing a new assembly line for a manufacturer of cell phones recognized that given the setup, the phones would be produced in twice the quantities of their battery packs and final packaging. This would have resulted in only half the product being ready to be shipped to market at any time.

In a second instance, trainees mapped out the proposed international routing (Singapore/SFO/Amsterdam) for a maker of telecommunications gear, and realized that the transit times specified in the RFP were unrealistic given existing transportation modes.

Ryder Jones is director of operations development at Exel Logistics. She joined the recently merged Exel Logistics 11 years ago to implement a proprietary transaction system for this $5.8 billion international logistics provider. A shift in company strategy two years ago brought an opportunity to head a project to identify, recruit, and develop entry-level managers with skills and capabilities different from the traditional freight forwarding model. Experience in the operations, training and development, and finance areas helped Ryder design the project and the implemented programs with a more strategic perspective.

Contact Information Ryder Jones
Exel Logistics
4120 Point Eden Way, Suite 200
Hayward, CA 94545
510-731-3365
ryder.jones@msasglobal.com
www.exel.com

THE EXEL MANAGEMENT
ORIENTATION CURRICULUM

Time	Topic or Activity
Day 1 30 minutes	➤ Discuss the objectives of the program: • To align managers with the vision, mission, and strategic direction (Case Study 1: Exel in the Marketplace) • To define and support the operations management role • To develop the skills and sources of information needed to resolve operational and customer problems
2 hours	➤ Overview of the Exel Logistics vision, mission, and strategic direction ➤ Global Logistics: The new organization structure
1 hour	➤ Manager of the Future—Profile and Role ➤ The support role of the Management Trainee (MT) ➤ The format of the Management Orientation program - an RFP is given for homework
3 hours (May extend into Day 2)	➤ Discovering customer requirements, goals, and critical success factors (Case Study 2: RFP Analysis) ➤ Responding to Customer Requirements ➤ Creating and implementing a Service Plan (Case Study 3: Implementing the Service) ➤ Fine-tuning our service offering (Case Study 4: Measuring Performance) • Identifying areas of liability and risk • Defining management information requirements • Setting performance metrics • Interpreting SOPs (standard operating procedures)
Day 2 2 hours	➤ Handling Service Failures (Case Study 5: Handling Customer Complaints) • Analyzing performance metrics • Identifying the root cause of a customer service failure • Determining information needed to resolve a problem • Identifying correct sources of information and expertise
2 hours	➤ Optimizing freight movement and pricing structures (Case Study 6: Maximizing Freight Movement)
2 hours	➤ Administration Policies and Procedures

Time	Topic or Activity
Day 3 All Day	➤ Projects and Processes • Overview of Strategic Direction and Strategic Goals • Approach to Strategic Planning • Linking Business Processes to Overall Goals • The Role of Strategic and Key Business Projects • ISO 9000 Implementation • Tools and Techniques • Project Management Methodology • IT Support Systems • Measurement and Monitoring • Publishing and Communicating Results ➤ Business Processes
Day 4 3 hours	➤ Review of Performance Standards ➤ Performance Review Process ➤ Roles and Responsibilities ➤ Wrap-Up of Program

Chapter 26

A Focus on Culture for Managers

Kahunaville's Award-Winning Management Orientation Program

Kahunaville is currently a ten-unit, tropically infused restaurant chain, based in Wilmington, Delaware. It is one of the hottest up-and-coming restaurants in the country. In the past year, Kahunaville received two of the IAAPA 2000 Spirit of Excellence Awards, for Best Supervisory Training Program and for Service Excellence. In the same year, Kahunaville also received two of the First Annual Industry of Choice Awards, for Training & Education and Food Service Operations.

David Tuttleman, Mayor of Kahunaville, and his team of Imagineers have created an environment that complements the imaginative island décor. The architecture and imagination that are inherent in the creation of a Kahunaville restaurant are present in great detail, including Kahunaville's signature magical dancing waterfalls, animatronic turtles, an interactive sports bar, performing Cast Members, and a high-tech arcade. Kahunaville was also named "Hot Concepts!" Winner by *Nation's Restaurant News* in 1999.

Kahunaville is in the business of creating fun, not only for its guests, but also for each of its Cast Members and managers. How do you create and maintain a top-of-the-line corporate culture on a small business budget? Simple! You create a culture based on traditional values that support progressive ideals. You build on principles such as open and honest communication, integrity, honesty, pride, respect, teamwork, enthusiasm, passion, and a proactive approach to management. Kahunaville builds this planned culture by infusing its new management training program with the values and philosophies of the company.

KAHUNAVILLE'S INTRODUCTORY MANAGEMENT SEMINAR—IMS

The focus of the Introductory Management Seminar is Culture First! Culture First! is a value statement we live by at Kahunaville; it is not a specific class or program. Our entire concept and work ethic revolve around a good corporate culture. Our goal is to make sure every manager understands the expectations of Kahunaville's culture, first and foremost. When managers understand the culture "soft skills" as to why we do the things we do, we then provide them with the operational "hard skills" in the training program.

A component of our comprehensive eight-week management training program, Kahunaville's five-day Introductory Management Seminar (IMS) provides essential classroom training, as well as a welcome to the organization. While most management orientation programs focus solely on the systems and processes of the operations, IMS is a culture-based program that allows new managers to assimilate our beliefs in areas such as life balance, conflict resolution, coaching and counseling, motivation, and situational leadership, as well as learning to navigate the legal minefields of doing business in the ever-changing restaurant industry.

Lectures, group projects, labs, and guest speakers complement fun activities that lay the foundation for our expectations of Kahunaville's newest leaders. Several reading, writing, and goal-setting assignments help to carry the learning into the operations, while quarterly follow-up training visits (dubbed Whirlwind Tours) ensure that critical areas are being addressed and followed up on.

IMS began just several months after the first Kahunaville was built. At that time, Kahunaville had one restaurant, located directly across the street from the Home Office, so IMS was piloted at this location, with one class conducted each week for twelve weeks. As Kahunaville has evolved and grown, currently having units in six different states, so has the program's agenda.

THE KAHUNAVILLE MANAGEMENT
ORIENTATION CURRICULUM

Day 1:

- *Use of Authority and Communication—Classroom*

  External versus Internal Authority, External versus Internal Control, Barriers to Communication, Characteristics of Listeners

- *Perception Is Reality—Classroom*

  Johari Window, Self-Disclosure Questionnaire, You're Signaling Activity

  Note: The "You're Signaling" Activity is a great exercise that we found in *The ASTD Trainer's Sourcebook—Leadership*, by Anne F. Coyle Ph.D. (pages 81, 158–159). The concept of this activity is to create an awareness of the signals we send. We may not realize that by everything we do, we send signals—the way we dress, our arm gestures, tone of voice, actions, and so on. Part of our success in communication is sending the "right" signals. In reality, the people we deal with on a daily basis act and react based on the signals we send. The activity focuses on intent versus impact.

- *Loss Control, Insurance—Guest Speaker*

- *Security, Safety, Accident Documentation, Workers' Compensation*

- *Cast Resources, Training—Lab*

  New Cast Member Training, Cast Member Certification, Expectations of Trainers, Expectations of Management Involvement in Cast Training

Day 2:

- *Sexual Harassment—Classroom*

  Prevention—Our Responsibility, Be Proactive, Definition, Improper Conduct, When a Complaint Is Filed, Complaint Assessment, Conducting an Investigation, Interviewing the Complainant, Interviewing the Harasser, Interviewing the Witnesses, Documentation Needed, Credibility, Apply Company Policy, Follow-Up Sessions, Resolution Options, Important Tips

- *Millennium Management Issues—Classroom*

  Internet Usage, INS, I-9, FMLA, EEOC, HIPPA, COBRA, PCN, W-2, W-4, FLSA, BFOQ, ADA, Title 7

- *Conflict Management—Classroom*

  Conflict Attitude Questionnaire, Management of Conflict Exercise, Types of Conflict, Styles of Conflict Resolution, How to Confront

- *Marketing—Lab*

  The Importance of Word-of-Mouth Marketing, How to Execute Promotions, How to Get Your Cast Excited about Promotions

Day 3:

- *Benefits—Guest Speaker*

  How to Take Advantage of Your Own Benefits, How to Help Cast Members Take Advantage of Their Benefits, How and When to Complete Paperwork

- *Interviewing Skills—Classroom*

  Preparation for the Interview, Establishing Rapport, Getting Information, Giving Information, Closing the Interview, Evaluation of Candidate, Legalities of Interviewing, Interviewing Skills, Nondiscriminatory Interviewing

- *Motivation—Classroom*

  Factors That Motivate, What Motivates Me, Maslow's Hierarchy of Needs, Herzberg's Hygiene Factors and Motivators, Giving Credit, The Self-Fulfilling Prophecy

- *Accounting—Lab*

  Weekly and Daily Procedures, Cash Handling, Sales Audits, Reports

- *Payroll—Lab*

  How to Distribute Paychecks, Assist with Lost Checks, Attend to Payroll Questions, Review Payroll Detail, and Correct Discrepancies, How to Forecast a Schedule

Day 4:

- *Win–Win Counseling (A Problem-Solving Process)—Classroom*

  Win–Win Performance Agreements

- *Discipline and Termination—Classroom*

  The Effects of Termination, The Process of Termination, Reasonable Cause Checklist

- *Situational Leadership—Classroom*

  Reading List—Bob Nelson, Kenneth Blanchard, Sheldon Bowles, Dale Carnegie, Thomas Peters, Robert Waterman, Ron Zemke, Max DePree, Warren Bennis, Stephen Covey, Zig Ziglar, Steven Brown

- *Life Balance—Classroom*

  Our Commitment and Your Commitment, Where Are You Today?, Action Plan to Get Where You Want to Be

- *Food Trak, System Program—Lab*

  Weekly and Daily Procedures, Sales Import, Updating Statistics, Compacting the Database, Running Reports

Day 5:

- *ServSafe Training—Guest Speaker/Classroom/Lab*

  A National Restaurant Association Educational Foundation ServSafe Instructor provides a national certification course in safe food handling. This eight-hour course provides accurate, up-to-date information on all aspects of handling food, from receiving and storing to preparing and serving. This science-based information will guide managers on how to run a safe establishment.

- *Graduation Ceremony!*

HUMAN AND MATERIAL RESOURCES NEEDED

Kahunaville is able to keep the costs of the training program low by using internal subject matter experts and internally developed materials. The training manager is also a certified ServSafe instructor, so an external training vendor is not needed.

Materials and costs include:

- The IMS Binder at $15 per manager

- Guest speaker costs: Internal $0; Labs: Internal $0, ServSafe Certification: $25 per manager.

- Travel/Lodging/Pens/Pencils/Notebooks/Gifts/Candy/Material for Icebreakers: These costs vary.

IMS costs approximately $2,000 per person, and each newly hired Kahunaville manager is required to attend. Feedback from managers attending has been outstanding (we require a feedback form to be sent to the president of Kahunaville upon completion of the course), and we have found our managers to be significantly better prepared to handle the barrage of human resource issues that face them on a daily basis.

In the year 2000, 20 managers graduated from this program. With the growth anticipated for 2001, we approximate that more than 45 managers will attend over the next 12 months.

LESSONS LEARNED ALONG THE WAY

Looking back over the past six years, there have been several lessons learned along the way. Our first big lesson was finding out that not setting clear expectations on the very first day can leave too much room for interpretation. Setting very clear expectations on the commitment level needed and the participation expected lays the foundation for maximizing the learning potential of participants.

The biggest lesson we learned was that the facilitator needs to "clear the air" with all attendees at the very beginning of the course. Since the IMS is taught quarterly, most managers attending have already been with Kahunaville for at least a month or two. Therefore, when they come into the program, they usually already have questions.

This month or two of training prior to IMS has probably raised some questions as to why Kahunaville has specific core beliefs and values set in place. "Why can't I fire someone if they come into work late?" "Why do I have to make sure my Cast is having fun? After all, they are here to work, aren't they?"

If the managers attending have issues or concerns on their minds at the beginning of the course, it is hard for them to capitalize on what is to be accomplished. There is a very strong chance they will take their past experiences and close their eyes to conflicting pieces of learning, making those pieces about their issue or concern. For this reason, all concepts taught need to be followed through at the unit level when the managers return "home" from IMS. The senior managers and Home Office must support 100 percent of the culture and philosophies introduced and discussed in IMS.

RESULTS, FEEDBACK, AND MEASUREMENTS

Each member of the IMS class fills out a Feedback Survey, rating the class on:

- Delivery of Instruction

- Training Facility

- Printed Materials

- Participation

- Activities

- Level of Learning

- Applicability to the Job

With this feedback information, the IMS has been molded into what it is today. Feedback isn't limited to this survey; all managers and Home Office support personnel give constant feedback about how our managers need help. All feedback is taken seriously, with the intent always to break the mold and make it better.

Comments received from managers who have attended the program include the following:

"I feel that I am a much better leader and manager. This will help me positively affect my Cast in every way!"

"I'm inspired both personally and professionally!"

"I can honestly say that the last several days have been some of the most exciting and fun days I've had in a long time. The people I met and the time we shared created such a memorable experience. Thank you for giving me the opportunity to share in the Kahunaville experience!"

"I really appreciate the time put into us! Have been in the restaurant business for 12 years and this is the first time anyone showed me how to manage a crisis situation. The Win–Win Performance Agreements will help immediately with a peer of mine!"

"I am going to save my IMS binder and use it for the rest of my life!"

"This (IMS) was so valuable to my training as a young manager. My values of how I want to manage have been reinforced. Yes! I now have more confidence in myself to do a fantastic job. Knowing more about my support systems, I can't wait to grow with the company."

"IMS really opened up a light inside of me, and now I realize how important *my* life really is!"

Number of New Managers per Month at Kahunaville: 4 managers

Frequency of the IMS Orientation: Quarterly

Average IMS Orientation Group Size: 12 Managers

Basic Orientation Logistics: Orientation takes place in the Home Office using class-room training and designated areas of the office where labs take place.

Company Size: 10 units...and growing! Future locations are destined for Treasure Island Casino, Las Vegas in July 2001; Tampa, Florida in September 2001; and Orlando, Florida in March 2002.

Shawna McNamee is a graduate of the University of Delaware; she has worked in the restaurant business for 12 years and has been an integral member of the Kahunaville management team. Shawna has been with Kahunaville for six years and serves as a training manager. She plans, coordinates, and directs training and cast/management development programs, prepares budgets, formulates training policies, selects appropriate training methods, organizes and develops training manuals, trains instructors and supervisory personnel, and plans and organizes training for all new restaurant openings.

Shawna began working at The Big Kahuna Nite Club & Deck as a server and has opened all ten Kahunaville locations. She is a certified National Restaurant Association Foundation ServSafe Instructor and a member of the American Society for Training and Development, the Society for Human Resource Management, and the Council of Hotel and Restaurant Trainers.

Shawna has received numerous awards, including the first annual Industry of Choice Award 2000 for Training and Education and the International Association of Amusement Parks and Attractions 2000 Spirit of Excellence Award for Supervisory Training.

Contact Information   *500 South Madison St.*
Wilmington, DE 19801
302-571-6200, x16
smcnamee@Kahunaville.com

Chapter 27

Orienting the New Executive

Integrating an Executive into a New Culture Using Transitional Coaching

When new executives begin a new position, they need orientation and integration assistance to be successful in their new roles. Recognizing the impact that the executive group can and does have on the success in the organization, Parkland Health and Hospital Systems, a health care facility in Dallas with over 6,500 employees, partnered with Personnel Decisions International to:

1. Assess all executive candidates (both internal and external) to determine if they have the basic competencies needed to be successful in the new position. Licensed psychologists conduct the one-day assessments at PDI. In addition, individuals complete a number of psychological instruments prior to the day of the assessment.

2. Provide each new executive with transition coaching, which is based on the development needs identified through the assessment.

The coaching process, based on the assessment results, is designed to address development needs and to ensure a smooth transition to the culture of Parkland Hospital. The transitional coaching process described in this chapter takes place as new executives are hired (vice presidents and above). An average of six new executives are hired each year at Parkland.

THE TRANSITIONAL COACHING PROCESS

The process begins with a one-on-one feedback session with the new executive. The PDI consultant gives detailed feedback to the new executive concerning his or her strengths and weaknesses identified through the assessment process. At the end of the session, a development plan is discussed and the coachee is given resource material, a model, and instructions on how to create a development plan for him or herself.

Both the new executive and his or her manager receive a copy of the assessment report. Then, a development planning meeting (DPM) is scheduled with the new executive, his or her boss, and the PDI coach. In this meeting, the executive presents his or her development plan to the boss. The development plan is then discussed, modified if necessary, and agreed to.

After this session, the executive and the PDI coach schedule a number of two-hour coaching sessions (usually at the PDI offices in Irving, Texas) to assist the person in focusing on the plan and making a smooth transition to the Parkland culture. The number of sessions can vary, but an average of five sessions occur for each new executive.

The vice president of human resources, who coordinates this process at Parkland, is the contact point for Personnel Decisions. He is the first to receive a copy of the assessment report, and he distributes it to the appropriate people. The vice president of human resources is occasionally involved in the DPM and is always kept informed of the executive's progress toward completing his or her plan.

The chief operating officer of Parkland is an avid supporter of this process and has committed to requiring that each executive hired will go through transitional coaching. He sees this as critical to the success and growth of the organization. He believes that each person must fit into and support the culture and grow in his or her skills if the organization is to continue to be successful.

In addition, each of the existing executives is going through the same process of being assessed and receiving coaching for development. This ensures that all executives are developing themselves (enhancing strengths and addressing developmental needs), so that the entire executive group can function in a highly effective manner to pursue and achieve the goals of Parkland Health and Hospital System.

THE EXECUTIVE COMPETENCY MODEL

The competencies that are measured and developed through coaching, according to individual plans, include:

- Seasoned Judgment

- Shaping Strategy

- Visionary Thinking

- Financial Acumen

- Global Perspective

- Aligning the Organization

- Driving Execution

- Inspiring and Empowering

- Influencing and Negotiating

- Attracting and Developing Talent

- Driving Continuous Improvement

- Fostering Teamwork

- Building Organizational Relationships

- Fostering Open Dialogue

- Drive for Stakeholder Success

- Adaptability

- Career and Self-Direction

- Cross-Functional Capability

These are leadership competencies that PDI has identified as critical for successful leaders to possess, based on more than 30 years of research. Through pre-assessment discussions with the supervisor of the targeted position, the assessment and coaching are focused on specific leadership requirements of the position. The PDI consultants involved in the assessment (usually about six) are thoroughly briefed by the lead consultant, who has a long-standing relationship and thorough understanding of Parkland's culture and the specific demands of the new position.

The coaching process is initiated once a person has been assessed, is recommended for hire, and has accepted the position. The process is individually focused. Transitional coaching is designed to ensure that the individual, who is critical to the success of the organization, is brought up to speed quickly. The process ensures that talents are identified and maximized and development areas are addressed quickly. The process is not only focused on the near term, but is also future-focused. The chief operating officer sees the process of assessment and coaching as critical to succession management.

RESULTS, FEEDBACK, AND MEASUREMENT

This program has been in effect since 1999, and the COO and CEO are pleased with the results. They both feel that this process has improved the transition of new executives to the team and improved the caliber of hires.

McGregor Day, chief operating officer of Parkland, said: "We are committed to accelerating the performance of our new executives and to the development of our entire executive staff. We are doing this so that top management can develop our organization to meet the challenges of the future. We want our executives not only to develop their areas of need, but to continue to grow and take advantage of their strengths."

Kirk Calhoun, M.D., the new medical director for Parkland Hospital, states: "I found the assessment and the transitional coaching very valuable. It made me focus and take the time to consider the strengths and weaknesses I bring to the organization. This process gave me the opportunity to rapidly find my niche in the organization. My boss (Ron Andersen, M.D., Chief Executive Officer) cautioned me in our development planning meeting not just to focus on my weaknesses, but to build on and take advantage of my strengths. I found that to be excellent advice."

HUMAN OR MATERIAL RESOURCES USED

Parkland Hospital has partnered with Personnel Decisions International (PDI), a management and human resources strategy consulting firm. The vice president and chief operating officer of Parkland, in consultation with a senior consultant at Personnel Decisions, identified the competencies considered to be critical for executives at Parkland to master. PDI conducts (at its own offices) a one-on-one, half-day assessment of individuals identified by Parkland as qualified for the executive position that is open.

Once the person has been hired, a consultant from PDI is matched to the executive and he or she provides coaching focused on key areas. The executive's immediate supervisor provides ongoing support and coaching to the executive, and is kept informed by the PDI coach of progress, issues, and any changes in the plan.

The cost of this type of executive assessment and coaching varies depending upon the position, the level of the position, the type of assessment, and the coaching services needed.

BASIC ORIENTATION LOGISTICS

The initial coaching takes places at Parkland with the individual's boss, the person being coached, and the consultant.

John Welsh is a consultant for Personnel Decisions International (PDI) in Dallas, Texas, where he provides consulting and training services in the areas of: organizational development and effectiveness, executive and leadership development, management development, Total Quality Management and Continuous Quality Improvement, team building, strategic planning, assessment, and individual coaching. John also has 20 years of experience as a middle manager, corporate director, vice president, chief operating officer, and board member of various organizations.

John earned a BA in Mass Communications and an MA in Educational Research and Psychology from the University of Missouri. His Ph.D. is in Human Resource Development, from the University of Nebraska. He also holds a certification in Total Quality Management from George Washington University and a certification in Health Services Administration from the University of Alabama.

John has served as a guest lecturer or adjunct faculty member to Vanderbilt University, the University of Nebraska, and the University of Missouri at Kansas City. He has published numerous articles in both regional and national publications, including a monthly column, "Workplace Issues" in *McKnight's Long-Term Care News,* and he is the author of *The Quality Improvement Team Facilitator/Team Leader Handbook.*

Contact Information   *Personnel Decisions International*
Suite 1700, LB142, 600 E. Las Colinas Blvd
Irving, TX 75039
972-401-8109
jwelsh@pdi-corp.com

Chapter 28
Employment Law Hangman

Teaching Employment Law and Sexual Harassment Law in an Interactive Way

Employment law is an important part of any new supervisor or management orientation training program. But it can be less than exciting, and participants don't retain the information, if the instructor relies on the lecture training method.

Employment Law Hangman is a fun and interactive way to introduce all of the major employment laws. It will greatly reduce any lecture time needed to fill in details after the game, and it generates discussion and high interest.

Use this game when you begin the topic of employment law. The participants won't know all the answers, but that increases the competitive nature of the game, and increases their interest in learning the answers.

Appropriate Group Size for the Activity: This activity works best for a group of 10 to 25 people.

Approximate Length of Time: 30 to 60 minutes (depending on the amount of discussion during the game)

You'll Need:

- At least one flip chart and markers

- Employment law questions (You can write your own, or use the questions included in this chapter.)

- A bell or buzzer that is hit with the hand to generate sound (e.g., the type of bell used at a hotel check-in desk to alert an employee of your arrival)

- Prizes for the winners

Preparation: Brush up on your knowledge of employment law to make sure you are up to date. Review the latest information and actual cases on the Equal Employment Opportunity Commission Web site at www.eeoc.gov.

CONDUCTING THE GAME

1. Divide the class into two teams.

2. Draw an empty hangman frame for each team. If you have two flip charts, draw one on each; otherwise, draw both frames next to each other on one chart. The frames should look like this:

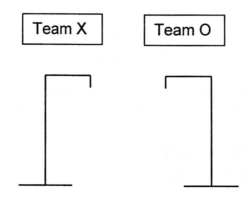

3. Then draw a completed hangman (stick figure) on the flip chart to show the figure that teams want to avoid obtaining. The team that loses is the team that has a complete figure first. It normally works best to have a stick figure with a head, body, two arms, two legs, two eyes, a mouth, and two ears—so it takes 11 points (or parts) to lose the game.

4. Explain the rules of the game to the class:

   ■ One player from each team will come up to the front of the class for each question. They will each choose a friend from the audience **before** the question is read. If they choose to, they may call on the friend for help with the answer to the question. (Note: Make sure the students choose different friends each time so everyone gets a chance to answer the question or to be a friend to help answer a question.) The rest of the team cannot help to answer the question.

   ■ Tell the class that you will read the question until you hear the bell ring; tell them you will stop reading the question when the bell rings.

   ■ The player who rings the bell first can choose to answer the question, call on the friend for help, or pass the question to the other team.

   ■ If a team answers incorrectly, the instructor draws a body part on the team's frame. The object of the game is to have a complete person drawn on the *other* team's frame first.

5. After giving the instructions to the class, call up the first two players (normally everyone in the class gets a chance to play, unless you have more than 40 people in the class) to the front table with equal access and opportunity to ring the bell. Read the question, and follow the bulleted steps in item 4.

6. It is very important to have a brief (1- to 3-minute) discussion regarding the answer after each question. Discuss actual lawsuits that pertain to the law, and emphasize what the manager needs to know and do to follow the law. This al-

lows you to capture a learning point during a time when participants' attention is strongly focused on the information. Discussion points are included in the handout that accompanies this chapter.

7. Once a completed person is drawn, award prizes and ask the participants to stand up and shake the hands of the players on the opposite team with a "Good game" comment!

DEBRIEFING THE GAME

After the game is over, you can go over the laws and their definitions fairly quickly, filling in gaps that weren't discussed during the game and providing a second opportunity to retain the information and ask questions.

With 14 years of experience in training and development, Doris Sims was a contributor to Mel Silberman's 1999, 2000, 2001, and 2002 *Training and Performance Sourcebooks,* as well as *The Consultant's Toolkit.* Her ideas have also been published in *Creative Training Techniques* newsletters, *Training Magazine,* and *Training Directors Forum* newsletter. Doris served as a presenter at the Training Director's Forum Conference, Training '99, IQPC Employee Orientation Program Conferences, and the 1999 ASTD International Conference. Doris is a human resource development director at Alcatel. Doris earned an MS in Human Resource Development from Indiana State University in 2001.

Contact Information   *2301 Bennington Avenue*
Flower Mound, TX 75028
972-539-1649
dmsims@home.com

EMPLOYMENT LAW GAME QUESTIONS

Note: This text is designed to be used for training purposes only, and is not intended to be used as legal advice. Federal regulations are updated regularly, and interpretations of these regulations change based on court cases. This could change the information presented here at any time. Instructors and human resource professionals are advised to continuously obtain information and training to stay current on employment law and federal regulations affecting the workplace.

1. Should an interviewer ask applicants if they are authorized to work in the United States?

   - ■ Yes!

   - ☞ Discussion Point: The interviewer should always determine if the applicant is authorized to work in the United States, because it is against the law to hire an illegal immigrant.

     However, the interviewer should *not* ask if the applicant is a United States citizen (unless the employee will be working on government contracts or government activities that require U.S. citizenship). Asking about an applicant's citizenship implies possible discrimination based on national origin, which is prohibited by the Civil Rights Act. But a person does not have to be a U.S. citizen to be authorized to work in the United States.

2. If a jury awards the plaintiff in an employment law discrimination case payment for wages lost after the employee was wrongfully terminated, would that be an example of compensatory relief or punitive damages?

   - ■ This is an example of compensatory relief.

   - ☞ Discussion Point: The Civil Rights Act of 1991 added a provision to allow punitive damages, which are designed to punish a defendant who acted intentionally and/or with malice. The punitive damage option is not available against state or local governments. Normally, when you hear about a very large jury award provided for a plaintiff, you are hearing about punitive damages.

3. Is it legally advisable to have weight and height requirements for jobs that require good physical condition, such as police officers, emergency personnel, etc.?

   - ☜ No!

   - ☞ Discussion Point: It is better to require physical tests that pertain to *the essential job functions*. Weight and height requirements can imply discrimination under the Americans with Disabilities Act, and although physical appearance is not covered under the Civil Rights Act, many lawsuits have been filed (and these cost the employer money, time, and embarrassment) on the basis of weight discrimination.

     Physical tests that can be proven to pertain to the essential job functions virtually eliminate this problem, and they will help you hire better candidates. It is very possible for a person who might be perceived as overweight to be in better physical condition than a person who is considered to be of normal weight. What you are really looking for is the best candidate who can perform on the job, so that is what you should to test for.

---

4. If an employee reports a sexual harassment complaint to you, but asks you not to do anything about it, should you still report it to your human resource representative?

   - ■ Yes!

   - ☞ Discussion Point: You are obligated to report the complaint, and/or go with the employee to report the alleged incident to the human resources representative for the company. Explain to the employee that the report will be confidential, on a need-to-know basis. Only those who are required to be involved in the complaint investigation and resulting actions will know about the complaint.

   Important: If a company is aware of a potential or actual sexual harassment situation and does nothing, punitive damages may be awarded if a lawsuit ensues.

5. A male supervisor sends his male workers out of town for seminars but does not send his female workers, citing their need to care for their children. What law does this violate?

   - ■ The Civil Rights Act.

   - ☞ Discussion Point: The Civil Rights Act of 1964 prohibits discrimination on the basis of race, sex, national origin, color, and religion. This can pertain to employment, promotions, training opportunities, and benefits.

   In this situation, the employer is out of compliance with the Civil Rights Act because he is denying the female workers a training opportunity (which can lead to advancement in position and pay). Also, the supervisor is setting himself up for a sexual harassment—hostile work environment complaint due to his stereotypical statements.

6. A supervisor asks an applicant if she owns a car to get to her job as a bank teller. Why was this question inappropriate?

   - ■ It does not pertain to the essential job functions.

   - ☞ Discussion Point: It is only appropriate to ask an applicant if he or she owns a car if the position requires employees to have a car to fulfill their responsibilities. Examples might be pizza delivery personnel or courier service personnel. However, as a bank teller, an employee will not need a car to fulfill his or her job functions.

     When interviewing candidates, make sure you stick to questions that pertain to the responsibilities of the job. In the bank teller's situation, it may be appropriate to ask candidates if they have transportation to work (avoiding the issue of *owning* a car, which is not required for employment for most jobs), *but only if the interviewer asks each candidate the same question.*

7. An employer of 50 people fails to send continuation of benefits information to a worker who was laid off. What law does this violate?

   - ■ COBRA.

   - ☞ Discussion Point: The Consolidated Omnibus Reconciliation Act requires employers with 20 or more employees to provide information regarding continuation of insurance to former employees and retirees and their dependents. This is one of the many reasons it is important for managers to notify their human resources personnel immediately when an employee terminates employment with the company.

Note: If an employee is terminated for gross misconduct, COBRA benefits may not be required; however, a human resource professional should review the situation and make this determination.

8. The I-9 form must be obtained from an employee within how many days of employment?

   ■ Three.

   ☞ Discussion Point: The I-9 form and the appropriate identification documents (appropriate documents are listed on the I-9 form) must be obtained from the employee within three days of employment. For this reason, many employers require these forms to be completed in their new employee orientation programs.

   If the employee does not fulfill this obligation within three days of employment, the employer must terminate the employee to avoid being in noncompliance with the Immigration Reform and Control Act of 1986 (IRCA). Special circumstances may exist that would require an employee to provide proof of situations such as an extended work authorization in lieu of these normal requirements.

9. An employer pays below the current minimum wage amount. Which law does this violate?

   ■ The Fair Labor Standards Act.

   ☞ Discussion Point: The Fair Labor Standards Act includes the Equal Pay Act, minimum wage compliance, child labor laws, and regulations pertaining to overtime and the classification of employees into either exempt or nonexempt status.

10. An employee who has been with the company for three years goes on medical leave. The employee demands paid time off during her leave under the Family Medical and Leave Act of 1993. Is she correct?

    ☞ No!

    ☞ Discussion Point: The Family Medical and Leave Act Act provides for protected job leave to care for a newly born or adopted child, a family member with a serious illness, for placement of a child for adoption or foster care, or for the employee's own serious illness.

    The law states specific eligibility requirements for the employee to be covered under the act. This law provides for up to 12 weeks of unpaid time within a 12-month period of time. It does not provide for any paid leave time, which is what the question included. Employees may have benefits from their employer that will provide a full or partial paid leave period, such as disability benefits, vacation time, or sick time, but the Family Medical and Leave Act does not require paid leave benefits—only job protection.

11. A 20-year-old woman is turned down for a job as a model for a senior citizen vitamin supplement. The company cited a need for an older model for the job. Is the company in violation of the Age Discrimination Act?

    ☞ No!

    ☞ Discussion Point: First, the Age Discrimination Act of 1967 (ADEA) prohibits employment discrimination against individuals over the age of 40. This woman is not over the age of 40; therefore, the company has not violated this law. In addition, the company would have a very valid argument that it is an essential job function to have a model for a senior citizen vitamin supplement who has the appearance of a senior citizen, and virtually all jury members would likely see the validity of this job requirement.

12. A job applicant is asked, "You have an unusual accent. Where are you from?" Is this a legally advisable interview question? Why or why not?

   ☞ No, this is not a legal question. It suggests potential discrimination based on national origin.

   ☞ Discussion Point: It is a common mistake for interviewers to ask this question, usually out of curiosity or simply to make conversation. But it can imply that the interviewer is seeking information to determine the candidate's national origin, and discrimination based on national origin is prohibited by the Civil Rights Act.

   Even if the interviewer is asking to determine the *part* of a country or nation a person is from (e.g., a New York accent versus a Texas accent), this is not a legally advisable question to ask during an interview. Of course, it also has nothing to do with the essential job functions.

13. A company of 500 employees has to lay off 250 full-time employees at one work site immediately. They provide one week of severance pay for each year each employee has worked. Is this legal?

   ☞ No!

   ☞ Discussion Point: In this situation, the employer would need to provide either 60 days advance notice of employment termination, or 60 days severance pay. This is covered under the Worker Adjustment and Retraining Notification Act (WARN) of 1989. This law pertains to employers with 100 or more full-time employees (employees who work 20 or more hours per week) who have worked for the company for at least six months, when layoffs of specified numbers or percentages as defined within this law occur.

14. True or False: The Equal Pay Act of 1963 requires that the same compensation be paid for men and women who are working in the same position with the same job title.

   ☞ False!

   ☞ Discussion Point: This law provides for differences in compensation between employees of any gender when the difference is based on valid criteria such as differences in productivity or performance levels, differences in experience or background, and differences in educational levels. The law is intended to prohibit differences in compensation between men and women that are not based on any valid and accepted criteria.

15. An employee complains that other workers are using racial slurs and jokes in the workplace. What law is being violated?

   ■ The Civil Rights Act.

   ☞ Discussion Point: Using racial jokes or slurs in the workplace is a form of harassment on the basis of race, which is covered under the Civil Rights Act. The law prohibits a hostile work environment on the basis of race, sex, national origin, color, or religion.

16. A security guard is fired because he has a religious practice of wearing a cap at all times. What law is violated?

   ■ The Civil Rights Act.

☞ Discussion Point: This question is based on an actual Equal Employment Opportunity Commission (EEOC) lawsuit in 1999. The jury found in favor of the plaintiff and determined that the employer violated the Civil Rights Act on the basis of religion.

Managers need to take care not to design or try to enforce a dress code that does not respect clothing or attire requirements on the basis of religion, national origin, color, sex, or race. Employers are required to respect religious practices of employees, providing they do not create an undue hardship on the employer or violate the rights of other employees.

17. Due to financial difficulties, an employer requires all employees over 60 to retire. Is this legal? Why or why not?

☞ This is not legal. This falls under the Age Discrimination in Employment Act of 1967.

☞ Discussion Point: This question was also based on an actual EEOC lawsuit in 1999. The Age Discrimination Act protects employees over the age of 40. In this case, the employees were terminated based solely on the basis of age, not on performance or any other criteria.

18. An employer decides not to hire a candidate who cannot leave a wheelchair for the flight attendant position the candidate applied for. Did this violate the Americans with Disabilities Act (ADA)?

☞ No!

☞ Discussion Point: The ADA requires employers to make reasonable accommodations for persons with disabilities that will allow the employee to complete the essential job functions. In this case, two of the essential job functions of a flight attendant are to be able to direct and to assist passengers in the event of an emergency on the plane; a person who could not rise from a wheelchair would not be able to accomplish this effectively. Also, airplane aisles currently would not allow a flight attendant in a wheelchair to serve beverages and food to passengers, and no accommodation could be made without undue hardship on the employer.

However, most often an employer *is* able to make an accommodation for an employee with a disability without undue hardship. Examples include installing equipment or ramps needed for wheelchair access or providing Braille computer keypads.

19. A company defines all of its assembly line employees as exempt, so they can take compensatory time instead of being paid overtime, per their own request. Is this legal? Why or why not?

☞ No. This is a Fair Labor Standards Act violation.

☞ Discussion Point: The Fair Labor Standards Act (FSLA) contains specific definitions of exempt employees (who would not receive overtime pay) and nonexempt employees. Nonexempt employees must be provided overtime pay according to the laws of their state.

It would be virtually impossible for assembly line workers (who are not supervisors or managers) to qualify for exempt status as defined in the FSLA. Therefore, even if the employees prefer and request "comp time" rather than overtime pay for extra hours worked, the law requires that they be paid the overtime amount.

20. Name any two federal laws that prohibit employment discrimination.

- Possible answers include:
    - The Civil Rights Act of 1964 and the amended CRA of 1991
    - The Equal Pay Act
    - The Age Discrimination Act
    - The Americans with Disabilities Act
    - Section 501 of the Rehabilitation Act of 1973

☞ Discussion Point: The Equal Employment Opportunity Commission (EEOC) oversees all of these laws. Supervisors and managers may think that knowledge of these laws is important only for human resource professionals. It's true that the supervisor and manager should partner with and rely on the HR professional to handle the situations that require expertise. But supervisors and managers need to have a basic understanding of what is covered in the laws to avoid making compliance errors during the normal course of business, and to work more effectively with the HR professional.

Chapter 29

Company Ethics Baseball

Score a Home Run While Teaching Ethics and Sexual Harassment Policies

It's true that lectures on ethics and sexual harassment policies are not the most dynamic and interesting talks, but it is critical that managers learn and lead others to follow these policies, rather than just covering the material as a matter of standard procedure.

So why lecture when the managers will have better retention and attention if the material is presented in an active and competitive format? This indoor classroom baseball game provides the perfect format to make sure your company ethics receive the focus they deserve.

Appropriate Group Size for the Activity: This game can be played with a group size ranging from 10 to approximately 50 employees.

Approximate Game Length of Time: The amount of time needed for the game is greatly affected by the number of questions and the number of innings played, which are the choice of the orientation facilitator. An average time range is 30 to 60 minutes.

You'll Need:

- Small index cards with one ethics question on each card (Sample questions you can modify to suit your company are included in this chapter.)

- Post-It Notes, 1 per employee, 3" x 3" size (You'll need two colors.)

- A flip chart and flip chart markers

- A plastic baseball bat

- Optional but recommended to add to the experience: Bases and a home plate to place on the floor, peanuts for everyone (or hot dogs!), and if the budget allows, baseball caps with the company logo for everyone

- It is recommended that the instructor dress as a player, an umpire, or a catcher, complete with a whistle to quiet the class as needed when it is time to "pitch" the question to the next "batter."

- A fishbowl, hat, or box to hold the question cards

- Prizes

Preparation: Before the class, write or print one company ethics question (and the answer) on each index card, and place the cards in the fishbowl, hat, or box. Identify the difficulty level of each question as a "single," a "double," a "triple," or a "home run," and mark the level on each question card. The instructor should be familiar with these questions and answers, to be able to expand on them and to answer related questions that the employees may bring up.

Prior to the actual game play, the instructor sets up the baseball props, passes out bags of peanuts, and so on. The instructor also dresses in the chosen costume, with a baseball cap, umpire mask, whistle, or whatever else has been planned.

The instructor then draws a large baseball diamond on the flip chart, showing first base, second base, third base, and home plate.

CONDUCTING THE GAME

1. Divide the class into two teams. Have each team come up with a name.

2. Distribute Post-It notes to each player, using different colors for the two teams. Ask the players to write their names on a Post-It note. They can also add the team's name to the note.

3. Present the rules of the game to the class. Define when the game will be over—either when all the questions are gone, or when a specified number of innings have been completed. The number of innings is up to the instructor, based on the time available.

   Explain that each team is provided with three lifelines. 1) They can ask for help from one person in the audience; 2) they can ask for a vote from the team before answering; or 3) they can ask the instructor to reduce the answer choices by 50 percent.

   The lifelines need to be used carefully, though; once they are gone, the team will have to answer all questions directly. The three lifelines should be drawn as symbols for each team on the flip chart, for the purpose of keeping track of when the team uses them.

4. Flip a coin or use any other method to determine which team will go first. This team's first player comes up to the front of the room to the home plate, and takes the plastic bat.

5. Draw a question card and "pitch" it to the player. (You may also wish to have a PowerPoint or transparency slide of each question ready, especially if the ques-

tions are lengthy, such as the sample questions in this chapter.) Identify whether the question is a single hit, a double, a triple, or a home run. Then read the question to the batter.

6. The batter can choose to answer the question directly; if the answer is correct, the player places his or her Post-It note on the base level that corresponds with the question. If there is already a Post-It note on that base from a previous player, all of the notes then advance around the diamond.

    If the player answers incorrectly, the instructor can answer the question and discuss the answer, or the question can go back into the box for another player.

OR

    Alternatively, the batter can choose to use one of the team's lifelines if he or she is not sure of the answer. If the player uses a team lifeline, cross out that lifeline symbol on the flip chart.

7. The team keeps control of the game and continues to swing at question pitches until they have three outs or five runs, whichever comes first. Then, the next team comes up to bat and this cycle is repeated for them.

8. The game continues until the questions are gone, or until the number of innings specified at the beginning are completed. The instructor may choose to distribute prizes to the winning team, or to both teams for "good sportsmanship."

DEBRIEFING THE GAME

Clear up any confusion regarding the correct answers to the questions, and expand on any ethics topics as needed. Ensure that all questions concerning the ethics policies are answered.

Trudy Whitmore is a senior trainer with Comcast Cablevision in Southfield, Michigan. Her ideas have been published in the *Creative Training Techniques* newsletter.

Contact Information   *248-204-4738*
Trudy_whitmore@cable.comcast.com
www.comcast.com

SAMPLE ETHICS
AND SEXUAL HARASSMENT QUESTIONS

1. Which federal law defines and prohibits sexual harassment?

   A.   The Equal Rights Act

   B.   The Sexual Protection Act

   C.   The Civil Rights Act

   D.   The Work Environment Protection Act

   Answer: C—The Civil Rights Act

2. Which of the following is *not* an example of intellectual property owned by a company?

   A.   Patents

   B.   Trademarks

   C.   Copyrighted Documents

   D.   Company Facilities

   Answer: D—Company Facilities

3. Quid pro quo sexual harassment refers to:

   A.   A corporation that consistently fails to promote females into leadership positions.

   B.   A supervisor who requests sexual favors in exchange for employment or promotional opportunities.

   C.   A work environment that allows slander of other employees based on their gender.

   D.   Both A and C

   E.   All of the above

   Answer: B—The supervisor who requests sexual favors in exchange for an employment or promotion. A quid pro quo sexual harassment situation exists when sex is requested, required, or implied to keep a job, or to obtain a job, to obtain a promotion.

4. Which of the following are correct ethical behaviors to follow if you possess inside information that could potentially affect the company's stock price?

   A.   Refrain from trading any company stock you own yourself until the information is made public.

   B.   Refrain from advising anyone else to trade in the company stock until the information is made public.

C. Refrain from discussing the information with anyone else (including your spouse, family, and friends.) until it is made public.

D. Both A and B

E. All of the above

Answer: E—All of the above

5. Sexual harassment can take place between:

A. Men and women

B. Women and women

C. Men and men

D. All of the above

Answer: D—All of the above

6. Which of the following is an example of a potential conflict of interest?

A. A bank employee also sells quilts at craft shows on the weekends.

B. A sales employee owns company stock and she feels this motivates her to work harder to sell the company's products to customers.

C. An employee works in a mortgage company as a loan officer and also has his own small mortgage brokerage company on the side.

D. An employee works for a large retail grocery chain but buys her own groceries at the corner grocery store on a regular basis.

Answer: C—A potential conflict of interest exists if an employee engages in a business that competes directly with that of his or her employer.

7. Which of the following evidence is required to prove a hostile work environment sexual harassment case being reviewed in a court of law?

A. The plaintiff's attorney must show evidence that the defendant(s) deliberately intended to offend and harass the plaintiff.

B. The plaintiff's attorney must show evidence that the defendant's words, behaviors, or possessions offended the plaintiff.

C. The plaintiff's attorney must show evidence that the plaintiff lost his or her job or was denied another type of employment opportunity.

D. All of the above

E. None of the above

Answer: B—It does not matter whether the harasser intends to harass; all that matters is that the other person or persons are offended by the behavior, words, or graphic item. The court is concerned with the impact of the behavior, not with the intent of the behavior. Also, a person's job or position doesn't have to be threatened for a hostile work environment to exist.

8. When working with suppliers and vendors, which of the following could potentially be considered unethical behavior?

    A. The employee receives a rebate on a home computer system if she engages that supplier for the purpose of supplying the company's computer needs.

    B. The employee receives a free cruise vacation if he signs a contract with a relocation services vendor.

    C. The employee engages his brother-in-law as a company consultant without comparing pricing or services of comparable consultants.

    D. Both A and B

    E. All of the above

Answer: E—All of the above. Employees should refrain from accepting substantial gifts from vendors. They should also refrain from retaining relatives as vendors or suppliers, or at least disclose the relationship to senior management or to the company's legal department.

9. Which of the following statements is true?

    A. If an employee submits to a sexual situation, then harassment definitely has not taken place.

    B. If an employer is not aware of a sexual harassment situation, then the employer is not liable for it.

    C. If the sexual harassment situation takes place at a location away from the work facility, the employer is not liable for it.

    D. None of the above

Answer: D—None of the above. A) An employee may feel pressured and then submit to a sexual situation to keep his or her job, but sexual harassment has still taken place. B) The court holds an employer liable for a sexual harassment situation even if the employer was not aware of the situation. C) As one example, if the sexual harassment behavior occurs during a business trip between two employees, the employer still retains liability.

10. Which of the following behaviors is ethical?

    A. Making copies of a vendor's copyrighted material as long as it will be used only for internal training purposes.

    B. Making copies of a software package for coworkers if they need the software to do their job.

    C. Offering customers a discount if they order a package of products rather than purchasing products singularly.

    D. Discussing aspects of your own compensation package with another employee.

Answer: C—It is an ethical and normal business practice to offer a discount for products that are packaged together or purchased in bulk. A) It is never ethical or legal to make copies of copyrighted materials for use within the organization; this is equal to stealing the vendor's intellectual property. B) The company must purchase either a software package for each employee or a license agreement that specifies (and charges a fee for) a number of users for the software. D) It is never appropriate to discuss any aspect of your compensation package with another employee.

11. Which of the following behaviors is ethical?

    A. Taking your company laptop home to work on your e-mail messages.

    B. Using the company's e-mail system to sell your Avon products.

    C. Accessing Internet Web sites with content that might be offensive to others or sexual in nature.

    D. Discussing the company's pending acquisition with a coworker during a business flight on an airplane.

    Answer: A—It is appropriate to use your company laptop to work on company business at a variety of locations, within the workplace and outside of the workplace. B) Employees should not use the workplace to sell products that are not associated with the employer. C) Accessing inappropriate Web sites in the workplace is cause for disciplinary action. D) A conversation concerning a company's pending acquisition can be overheard on an airplane, which could affect the stock price or the acquisition itself.

12. Which of the following is an unethical question that could portray potential discrimination during an interview with a job candidate?

    A. Do you have your own car to drive to and from our work facility?

    B. Will you ever need to take time off from work to care for your children?

    C. Would you describe yourself as having a physical handicap?

    D. Both B and C

    E. All of the above

    Answer: E—All of the above. A) It is not appropriate to determine whether the employee owns a car to get to work; however, it may be appropriate to discuss the work hours and whether the employee would be able to work during those hours. B) It is inappropriate to refer to child care needs during an interview. C) This statement may be perceived as a violation of the Americans with Disabilities Act (ADA). It is appropriate to discuss the essential job functions and ask all candidates for the position if they would be willing and able to perform these job functions.

13. Which of the following behaviors would be considered gross misconduct?

    A. Carrying a firearm onto the company property.

    B. Threatening to assault another employee.

C. Illegal drug usage.

D. All of the above

Answer: D—All of the above

14. Which of the following is *not* a legal and ethical interview question?

A. The position you are applying for is a second shift position. Would you be able to work the hours of 3 p.m. to 10 p.m.?

B. Where are you from originally?

C. Are you legally authorized to work in the United States?

D. What other companies are you interviewing with?

Answer: B—Asking this question can be perceived as fishing for information about the candidate's national origin. The Civil Rights Act makes it unlawful to discriminate based on national origin.

15. Which of the following is unethical or potentially illegal use of the company's computer systems?

A. Intentionally forwarding an e-mail message with an attachment containing a computer virus.

B. Forwarding chain e-mail letters to other employees using the company's e-mail system.

C. Intentionally deleting company documents or programs on individual computers, on servers, or on networks.

D. All of the above

Answer: D—All of the above are definitely unethical or are violations of federal, state, or local law.

16. If an employee reports a sexual harassment situation but asks you not to do anything about it, what should you do?

A. Tell the employee that you will not report the situation but that he or she should come back to you immediately if the problem is not resolved.

B. Tell the employee that the situation will not be reported, but instead a sexual harassment policy will be reissued companywide and sexual harassment training will take place.

C. Explain that you are obligated to report the situation so an investigation can take place, but that the investigation and information about the situation will be confidential, on a need-to-know basis.

D. Conduct the investigation yourself to prevent rumors from starting in the company, and to alleviate the concerns of the employee.

Answer: C—As a manager, you are obligated to report the situation to your human resource representative to allow an investigation of the claim.

17. Which of the following is unethical behavior with a vendor or supplier?

   A. Asking the vendor or supplier for tickets to an upcoming concert because you know they are the audiovisual crew for the event.

   B. Accepting money from a vendor or supplier.

   C. Asking a vendor to come into the company to demonstrate their product, even though you aren't sure if you want to purchase the product.

   D. Both A and B

   E. All of the above

   Answer: D—Both A and B are inappropriate behaviors. An employee should never solicit a vendor gift, and accepting money from a vendor is never ethical. Answer C is a perfectly appropriate request, because a demonstration can help the company decide whether they want to purchase a vendor's product.

18. Which of the following factors should be considered before accepting a gift from a vendor to ensure acceptance of the gift would be ethical?

   A. Does the cost of the gift exceed my company's limit for unsolicited gifts from vendors?

   B. Could my acceptance of this gift cause me to feel obligated to purchase products or services from this vendor?

   C. Would I enjoy using this gift?

   D. Both A and B

   E. All of the above

   Answer: D—Both A and B are ethical issues to be considered before accepting a gift from a vendor.

19. Which of the following people might be considered to have inside information that should not be used to influence stock purchase decisions?

   A. A sales employee who is involved in obtaining a new, significant client with the business potential to double the company's revenue in the next two years.

   B. A cocktail server who overhears a conversation between two business executives about a multi-billion-dollar company merger that has not been made public yet.

   C. The CEO's spouse who is aware that the company's financial results, which are about to be released, are not as high as the company projected to shareholders.

   D. All of the above

Answer: D—All of the above. Anyone who gains access to significant information about the organization that has not yet been announced to the public is a potential insider. Insiders do not have to be employees of the company. If the information you learn (that has not been made public yet) causes you to want to either buy or sell stock in the company, then the potential for violating insider trading laws exists.

20. Which of the following behaviors has (have) the potential to create a hostile work environment?

    A. One manager in the company requests sexual favors of an employee in exchange for a promotion.

    B. Racial slurs are heard frequently in the company.

    C. Many of the employees in the company have screen savers depicting sexual situations or scantily clothed models.

    D. Both A and B

    E. Both B and C

Answer: E—Both B and C. A) This is an example of quid pro quo sexual harassment, but it is not an example of a hostile work environment. A hostile work environment is characterized by "frequent and pervasive" harassment. **B)** A hostile work environment does not pertain only to sexual harassment; it can also pertain to racial harassment, age harassment, or national origin harassment. **C)** Harassment can occur in the form of visual items that are degrading or sexual in nature.

Chapter 30

Effective Interviewing Tools

Assessment Tools and Activities for Improving Interviewing Skills

Conducting effective interviews and selecting top-notch candidates are two of the most important skills a manager can have. After all, if the manager hires excellent employees, the need for coaching is reduced (never eliminated—everyone needs coaching), and the need for progressive discipline is definitely reduced. Excellent employees are more productive, demonstrate more positive attitudes, and work more effectively with their team members and their manager. Once a hiring decision is made, it is generally a long-term commitment, so it is critical for a manager to use time and interview questions wisely and to select employees carefully.

The tools and activities in this chapter can be used in a management orientation program for managers to assess their interview behaviors and their interview question techniques, to determine their current interviewing competencies, and to identify areas of improvement.

Appropriate Group Size for the Activity: The information and assessments can be used as self-study tools for an individual manager, or they can be used as activities in an instructor-led management orientation class. If the activities are used as classroom tools, they can be used for groups of any size.

Approximate Length of Time: Managers can use the tools on their own as individuals, or a facilitator can use the tools in a classroom environment as group activities—small groups can discuss the assessment items and choose responses together. If the activities are done in a classroom setting with small-group discussions, allow approximately 60 minutes for the discussion, activities, and debriefing. The instructions in this chapter assume the activities are completed in a classroom setting.

You'll Need:

- Copies of the handouts found in this chapter, one set of handouts per participant

- Pens or pencils for the participants
- Two flip charts and markers

PREPARATION

To prepare for the activity, make copies of the handouts prior to the class. Also, become familiar with the information in the handouts and research additional background information on various types of interviewing questions, so you will feel comfortable presenting the information and answering questions.

CONDUCTING THE ACTIVITY

1. Begin the topic of effective interviewing by writing "The Best Interviewer I Have Encountered" at the top of one flip chart and "The Worst Interviewer I Have Encountered" at the top of the other flip chart.

2. Ask the participants to share their most memorable interview experiences, and record their responses on the correct flip chart. Emphasize points that are raised by the participants and how they pertain to the class today.

3. Ask the participants to take a few minutes to complete the Effective Interviewing Self-Test handout. After the participants check the actions they are currently using during their interviews, ask them to record the top three items on the list they feel are their most effective interviewing techniques, and three items on the list they would like to improve about their interviewing techniques.

4. Emphasize that the items they identified that they would like to improve about their interviewing methods now become their action plans to implement back on the job.

5. If desired, conduct a group discussion and record the responses of the participants regarding their effective interviewing techniques and the items they wish to improve. This will allow a period of time for the managers to learn from each other based on real experiences.

6. Next, discuss the importance of developing a list of standard questions to be used for each job function, using the Developing a List of Standard Questions handout.

7. Then, present the various types of interview question by reviewing the Interview Question Styles handout. Emphasize the importance of using a variety of interview question types in order to create a comprehensive set of standard interview questions for each job function.

8. Ask the participants to work in small groups of 3 to 6 (depending on the total class size) to discuss and identify each type of interview question listed on the Interview Question Styles Challenge handout.

9. After the groups complete the Challenge handout, bring them back together as a class to discuss their responses and to correct any misconceptions.

10. As a last exercise, ask the participants to choose a job function in their group that they might interview for in the future. Ask them to create a list of standard questions for that job function with at least one of each interview question type, using the handout. If time allows, after the participants complete this exercise, have the participants work with partners to review each other's lists and provide feedback.

DEBRIEF THE ACTIVITY

Debriefing discussions have been included after each activity listed in the section on conducting the activity. However, to wrap up the entire topic of effective interviewing, you may choose to have the participants share the action items they will be applying back on the job based on what they learned today. Or, refer back to the "Best" and "Worst" interview experiences that were recorded on the flip charts at the beginning of the session, to emphasize the issues brought up by the participants that were addressed in the session today.

With 14 years of experience in training and development, Doris Sims was a contributor to Mel Silberman's 1999, 2000, 2001, and 2002 *Training and Performance Sourcebooks,* as well as *The Consultant's Toolkit.* Her ideas have also been published in *Creative Training Techniques* newsletters, *Training Magazine,* and *Training Directors Forum* newsletter. Doris served as a presenter at the Training Director's Forum Conference, Training '99, IQPC Employee Orientation Program Conferences, and the 1999 ASTD International Conference. Doris is a human resource development director at Alcatel. Doris earned an MS in Human Resource Development from Indiana State University in 2001.

Contact Information   *2301 Bennington Avenue*
Flower Mound, TX 75028
972-539-1649
dmsims@home.com

EFFECTIVE INTERVIEWING SELF-TEST

Place a check mark in front of the items you are currently doing as part of your normal interview process.

❑ If applicable, I ask candidates to bring samples of work they completed at other companies to the interview.

❑ I start my interviews on time, and I check with the candidates to see what their time limitations are before beginning the interview.

❑ I review the candidate's application and resume completely prior to the actual interview.

❑ I have developed a list of questions that I use for each candidate applying for the same job.

❑ At the beginning of the interview, I take steps to help the candidate feel comfortable and at ease.

❑ During the interview, I focus on what the candidate has done elsewhere (this is the best indicator of what he or she will do for you).

❑ During the interview, I ask a variety of different types of interview questions to obtain a thorough picture of the candidate's qualifications and other success indicators.

❑ During (or at the end of) the interview, I provide information about the job, the company, and our benefits. I work to "sell" strong candidates on the position and on the company.

❑ I let the candidate know what the next step is in the interview process at the end of the interview.

❑ I feel confident that my interview questions all comply with all Equal Employment Opportunity Commission laws; I am especially careful of my questions in more informal settings, such as during lunch with the candidate or driving the candidate to the airport.

❑ I check multiple references on final candidates before making a decision.

❑ I ensure the candidate signs all Consent to Release Information forms prior to checking references, and prior to conducting a background check on the candidate.

❑ I ensure that final candidates for a position meet at least one or two other company employees during the interview process, and I check with those employees regarding their opinions before making a hiring decision.

❑ I check with the department or building receptionist (whoever initially greets individuals and asks them to complete an application form) to determine what the candidate's behavior was toward him or her, before making a hiring decision.

My top three strengths as an interviewer are:

1. _____

2. _____

3. _____

The top three areas of improvement I discovered during this exercise (items not checked on the list) are:

1. _____

2. _____

3. _____

My action plans to implement improvements back on the job are:

Action Plan Description	Target Date	Comments

DEVELOPING A LIST
OF STANDARD QUESTIONS

If you take the time to develop a set of questions for each type of position you may interview for, you will realize the following advantages:

- You will be prepared for interviews ahead of time.

- Your preparation will impress the candidate, as opposed to your appearing unprepared, late, or scatterbrained. (Remember, a job interview is a two-way sales process.)

- Your interviews will be more consistent, resulting in a more accurate comparison of job candidates.

- If a candidate who is not selected for a job sues for employment discrimination, you will be able to show in a court of law that you use a consistent list of questions for each job applicant.

- After the interview, you will have a consistent list of notes that you can place on file so you can review all responses at a later time when you are ready to make a decision.

INTERVIEW QUESTION STYLES

This table shows different types of questions you will want to use in your interview meetings.

Type	Purpose	Examples
Open-Ended Questions	Open-ended questions greatly reduce prejudgment on the part of the interviewer. Also, the interviewer obtains more information, because the candidate can't answer with a simple "yes" or "no."	Under what types of conditions do you learn best? How would you describe your relationship with your last supervisor? As a manager, how would your direct reports describe you?
Integrity-Based Questions	To determine the candidate's judgment and integrity when handling an out-of-the-ordinary situation.	A customer begins yelling obscenities at you. How would you handle this? A coworker calls in sick. She told you the day before she would be taking the day off today to go to the beach. What would you do?
Case Interview Questions	To set up a scenario that the candidate will likely face if he or she is hired for the position, to see how the candidate would handle the situation.	You have just been assigned to handle new customer accounts. You have been told that one of the customers on your list would really benefit from a new service the company offers. However, you have also been told that this customer complained about the previous account manager as being "too pushy" and as always trying to "nickel and dime" them to buy more services. What would you say and do to convince the customer that the new service would save them money, while building a positive relationship with them?
Knowledge and Skill-Based Questions	To obtain specific information about the candidate's knowledge and skills that will be needed in the new position.	Your resume indicates you have used Word software in the past. What types of documents did you create using Word? What type of microfiche equipment did you use on your last job?
Behavioral Interviewing	To find out more about a candidate's past job performance, because past job performance is the best indicator of future job performance.	Describe things or situations that seem to cause you the greatest amount of stress on the job. How do you respond when these situations arise? Describe a time when you worked with a team of coworkers to complete a project or a task.

INTERVIEW QUESTION STYLES CHALLENGE

Use the following codes to identify each interview question type (you may use more than one code per question):

O = Open-Ended Question

I = Integrity-Based Question

C = Case Interview Question

K/S = Knowledge- and Skill-Based Question

B = Behavioral Interview Question

(These questions can be also used to build your own interview question lists when you return to your job.)

1. _____ In your current or last position, what did you enjoy most about your job?

2. _____ How did you help increase revenue at your current or previous position?

3. _____ What do you know about our company?

4. _____ Why are you interested in this position?

5. _____ Imagine that you have just started as a new supervisor of a group of employees who were also all just hired within the last six weeks. How would you begin working with these employees?

6. _____ What important trends do you see in our industry?

7. _____ A coworker confides in you that she is being sexually harassed. How do you handle this situation?

8. _____ Describe a time in your career when you had to respond quickly to changes in your job priorities. How did you handle the situation, and what impact did the change have on you?

9. _____ Describe your most challenging experience in convincing management to accept a new idea. How did you do it, and what was the outcome?

10. _____ You overhear a conversation between two of your coworkers. One of the employees is asking the other employee to clock his time card out for him at a later time, because he has to leave work early. What are your thoughts and actions regarding this conversation?

11. _____ Describe three accomplishments you are the most proud of.

12. _____ Describe the tasks you were fully responsible for in your last position.

13. _____ What will you be looking for in this job that you didn't find in your last job?

14. _____ If you could have changed things at your last company, what would you have changed?

15. _____ Describe the one most important and the one least important course you took in high school or college. Explain why you chose these two courses in your answer.

16. _____ Describe a situation when you had to help people with differing viewpoints reach a constructive solution. What did you do, and what were the results?

17. _____ You have just been assigned to teach new employees coming into your department to learn to use the computer system they will need to use daily on the job. How will you approach this assignment? How will you know if your teaching is successful?

18. _____ What are your long-range goals?

19. _____ On your resume, you note that you have extensive customer service experience. What are the most important things a customer service representative can do during a phone conversation with a customer to meet the customer's service and satisfaction needs?

20. _____ Your resume indicates you have five years of experience as a data entry operator. What do you estimate your typing speed to be?

21. _____ Describe a time when you needed to work extensively with employees in other departments to solve a problem for a customer. How did you approach your coworkers to meet the customer's needs, and what were the results?

22. _____ What prompted you to apply for this position?

23. _____ The person who will fill this position will need to have an extensive and thorough understanding of our company's services. What steps will you take to learn about our company's services?

24. _____ Are you better with figures or with words? Explain your answer.

ANSWER KEY:
INTERVIEW QUESTION
STYLES CHALLENGE

Note to the facilitator: All the questions are open-ended questions, so that response is always correct. For many of the questions, participants should also be able to identify the type of open-ended question, using the choices listed.

O = Open-Ended Question

I = Integrity-Based Question

C = Case Interview Question

K/S = Knowledge- and Skill-Based Question

B = Behavioral Interview Question

1. In your current or last position, what did you enjoy most about your job?—O

2. How did you help increase revenue at your current or previous position?—B, K/S

3. What do you know about our company?—K

4. Why are you interested in this position?—O

5. Imagine that you have just started as a new supervisor of a group of employees who were also all just hired within the last six weeks. How would you begin working with these employees?—C

6. What important trends do you see in our industry?—K or O

7. A coworker confides in you that she is being sexually harassed. How do you handle this situation?—I, K

8. Describe a time in your career when you had to respond quickly to changes in your job priorities. How did you handle the situation, and what impact did the change have on you?—B

9. Describe your most challenging experience in convincing management to accept a new idea. How did you do it, and what was the outcome?—B

10. You overhear a conversation between two of your coworkers. One of the employees is asking the other employee to clock his time card out for him at a later time, because he has to leave work early. What are your thoughts and actions regarding this conversation?—I

11. Describe three accomplishments you are the most proud of.—O

12. Describe the tasks you were fully responsible for in your last position.—O, K

---

13. What will you be looking for in this job that you didn't find in your last job?—O

14. If you could have changed things at your last company, what would you have changed?—O

15. Describe the one most important and the one least important course you took in high school or college. Explain why you chose these two courses in your answer.—O, K

16. Describe a situation when you had to help people with differing viewpoints reach a constructive solution. What did you do, and what were the results?—B

17. You have just been assigned to teach new employees coming into your department to learn to use the computer system they will need to use daily on the job. How will you approach this assignment? How will you know if your teaching is successful?—C

18. What are your long-range goals?—O

19. On your resume, you note that you have extensive customer service experience. What are the most important things a customer service representative can do during a phone conversation with a customer to meet the customer's service and satisfaction needs?—K/S

20. Your resume indicates you have five years of experience as a data entry operator. What do you estimate your typing speed to be?—K/S

21. Describe a time when you needed to work extensively with employees in other departments to solve a problem for a customer. How did you approach your coworkers to meet the customer's needs, and what were the results?—B

22. What prompted you to apply for this position?—O

23. The person who will fill this position will need to have an extensive and thorough understanding of our company's services. What steps will you take to learn about our company's services?—C

24. Are you better with figures or with words? Explain your answer.—O

Chapter 31

Writing Job Descriptions

Writing Effective KSAPs (Knowledge, Skills, Abilities, and Personal Characteristics)

How many people go into a car dealership and say, "I'd like to buy a car—any old car will do"? Would you ever say to a real estate agent, "I need to buy a house. It doesn't matter where it is located, what size it is, how much it costs, or what amenities it has"?

Of course, no one would think of making these major decisions without first thinking about what they are looking for, what their requirements are, and what features would be nice to have. But managers do hire new employees every day without putting forethought into the competency requirements of the position, and the competency "nice-to-haves" for the position. Anyone who has ever made a hiring decision and later regretted it (or anyone who has *taken* a job and later regretted it) can appreciate that taking the time to think about employee qualifications before hiring can save much more time, headaches, and money later on.

The activity in this chapter will help managers practice determining the knowledge, skills, abilities, and personal characteristics (KSAPs) that pertain to a job. These KSAPs should be listed on job descriptions, personnel requisitions, and career competency charts.

Appropriate Group Size for the Activity: The ideal group size for this activity is between 8 and 50 participants.

Approximate Length of Time: 25 to 30 minutes

You'll Need:

- Copies of the handouts found in this chapter, one set of handouts per participant

- Pens or pencils for the participants
- Two flip charts and markers

PREPARATION

To prepare for the activity, make copies of the handouts prior to the class. Also, become familiar with the information in the handouts and research additional background information on competencies and KSAPs, so you will feel comfortable presenting the information and answering questions.

CONDUCTING THE ACTIVITY

1. Open the topic of determining job position requirements by asking the participants to share a time in their lives when they made a major decision or purchased a major item, but later the decision or product did not match their needs and they were disappointed with it. Come prepared with your own story, to break the ice and start off the discussion.

2. Next, lead the participants into the need for managers to spend time before hiring employees to determine the knowledge, skills, abilities, and personal characteristics (KSAPs) they require in a candidate for a job position. The KSAPs would be written in the job description for the position, and they may also be included on personnel requisitions that human resource personnel use to screen candidates. Distribute the Knowledge, Skills, Abilities, and Personal Characteristics handout to provide a visual and reference aid for the managers.

3. Break the class up into groups of 3 to 6 (depending on the total size of the group). The participants will need to rearrange their seating so each group can hold a discussion.

4. Pass out copies of the Name That KSAP! handout.

5. Instruct the groups to select a job, choosing from the list at the top of the handout. Move around the room to encourage each table to select a different job, which makes the discussion and debriefing more effective.

6. Tell the groups that they are responsible for hiring a person in the position they have selected. As a group, they should discuss the KSAPs that would be needed for this position. Each group should list multiple items in each of the four categories. Allow 10 to 15 minutes for this portion of the activity. You may wish to provide blank flip chart paper and markers at each table for the groups to record their answers for a presentation to the rest of the class. Have a spokesperson for each group tape the completed flip chart paper on the wall.

DEBRIEF THE ACTIVITY

1. Ask a spokesperson from each group to review the items the group came up with. Make comments and observations as needed during the presentations to reinforce learning points.

2. Now select one of the job descriptions to use for the next step in the debriefing process. Ask the class which of the KSAPs are *job requirements,* and which are *"nice-to-have."* It is important for managers to be able to differentiate between absolute candidate qualifications and preferred qualifications.

With 14 years of experience in training and development, Doris Sims was a contributor to Mel Silberman's 1999, 2000, 2001, and 2002 *Training and Performance Sourcebooks,* as well as *The Consultant's Toolkit.* Her ideas have also been published in *Creative Training Techniques* newsletters, *Training Magazine,* and *Training Directors Forum* newsletter. Doris served as a presenter at the Training Director's Forum Conference, Training '99, IQPC Employee Orientation Program Conferences, and the 1999 ASTD International Conference. Doris is a human resource development director at Alcatel. Doris earned an MS in Human Resource Development from Indiana State University in 2001.

Contact Information   *2301 Bennington Ave.*
Flower Mound, TX 75028
972-539-1649
doris.sims@usa.alcatel.com

KNOWLEDGE, SKILLS, ABILITIES, AND PERSONAL CHARACTERISTICS (KSAPS)

To determine the requirements of a job position, it is helpful to divide the needs into four categories, as defined below. Note that an employee may be at an entry level or at an advanced level within each of the same categories.

Knowledge—A body of information related to a specific subject or industry. For example, salespeople need to know the specifications of the product or service they are selling. A customer service representative in a call center needs to know the company's policies and philosophies on handling customer complaints.

Skill—An observable capability to perform; a learned motor act. For example, the new salesperson may need computer skills in order to communicate through e-mail or in order to be able to enter customer orders.

Abilities—The present power to perform a physical or mental activity. For example, we may need our salesperson to possess the ability to make charismatic presentations to groups of varying sizes, or we may need him or her to be able to close a sale effectively. Abilities are often natural talents, but they can also be developed or enhanced through training and practice.

Personal Characteristic—A special, specific personal characteristic *that applies directly to the essential functions of the job.* For example, it may be a requirement for our salesperson to be able to lift 30 pounds, because the equipment taken on sales demonstrations weighs 30 pounds. The salesperson will also need to have a professional appearance and be perceived as credible to potential customers. The manager may want a detail-oriented person for a copyeditor position. It is critical, though, that personal characteristics are tied directly to the required, essential job functions.

Hire for abilities and personal characteristics—hire talents, not skills that can be trained easily! Knowledge and skills can generally (although not always) be trained. But it is more difficult to train and coach someone to have the abilities or talents you need for a position, and it is even more difficult to train personal characteristics. For example, it is difficult to teach the detail-oriented person to become big-picture oriented, and vice versa.

NAME THAT KSAP!

1. First, circle the job your group chooses to focus on for this activity:

    Pizza Delivery Person   **President of the United States**

    Professional Wrestler   **Shamu the Whale Trainer**

    First Grade Teacher   **Movie Actor**

    TV Infomercial Director   **Video Game Designer**

2. Next, work as a team to identify the knowledge, skills, abilities, and personal characteristics (both required and preferred) a job candidate applying for this position should have. Record your answers below, and on the flip chart paper provided by your instructor.

    KNOWLEDGE:

    SKILLS:

    ABILITIES:

    PERSONAL CHARACTERISTICS:

Chapter 32

Sexual Harassment Table Discussions

Talking about Sexual Harassment Issues Increases Understanding

Many companies post their sexual harassment reporting procedure, give presentations on sexual harassment, and show videos on sexual harassment. These are all valid activities in the prevention of sexual harassment, but for true understanding, employees need to discuss the gray areas of potential sexual harassment behaviors and situations that pose a question in people's minds—is it or isn't it sexual harassment?

The purpose of this activity is to pose these questionable situations to stimulate discussion about when the line is crossed from acceptable behavior to sexual harassment.

Appropriate Group Size for the Activity: The ideal group size for this activity is between 8 and 50 participants.

Approximate Length of Time: 20 to 30 minutes

You'll Need:

- Copies of the handout found in this chapter, one per participant
- Pens or pencils for the participants
- Two flip charts and markers

PREPARATION

To prepare for the activity, make copies of the handout prior to the class. Also, become familiar with the information in the handout and discuss responses and potential issues that could arise during the activity with the organization's human resource personnel and/or corporate attorney, to obtain a complete understanding of sexual harassment law (covered within the Civil Rights Act) and the organization's policies.

CONDUCTING THE ACTIVITY

1. Use this activity as part of a larger presentation on sexual harassment. This activity works well after the factual information concerning sexual harassment has already been presented.

2. Break the class up into groups of 3 to 6 (depending on the total size of the group). The participants should rearrange their seating as needed so each group can hold a discussion.

3. Pass out copies of the Sexual Harassment Table Discussions handout.

4. Instruct the groups to discuss each question and determine if the action listed is sexual harassment or is not sexual harassment. Participants should write down the discussion points and positions in the spaces provided.

5. After the groups have completed their responses to each question, bring the class back together as a total group.

DEBRIEFING THE ACTIVITY

Bring up one question at a time, and ask the groups if they answered yes or no. The following points can be made during this discussion (*Check with your human resource personnel or corporate attorney for additional discussion points and appropriate responses to customize the session to your company's policies and procedures.*):

■ The best answer to each of these questions is yes—each situation *could* be a sexual harassment behavior leading to a hostile work environment (some more immediately than others), and a hostile work environment is one form of harassment. Much depends on how something is said, the body language and facial expressions used, and how often the behavior occurs in the workplace. Frequency, severity, and pervasiveness are all factors the courts review when determining if a hostile work environment exists.

■ When discussing each situation, describe a scenario when it would normally not be considered sexual harassment (e.g., a coworker simply compliments someone on a new outfit), and when the "line is crossed" and sexual harassment might exist (e.g., "Hey, baby, that new skirt really shows off your great legs"). Some of the situations are inappropriate in any scenario (e.g., making a racial joke in the workplace).

■ Sexual harassment can take many forms—physical, verbal, graphics or photos, roaming or "elevator" eyes.

- It doesn't matter whether the sexual harasser *intended* to offend or harm the harassed person. If someone is offended, a potential harassment situation exists.

- Harassment is covered under the Civil Rights Act and includes all types of harassment, including racial harassment and gender harassment.

- The reason some of these issues are gray areas is that a potential sexual harassment situation may depend on *how* a person says something, rather than *what* was said. Also, it is not possible to list every potential sexual harassment situation in the law, so the law is subject to interpretation by juries and courts.

- Harassment can take place between a male and a female, a female and a male, a female and a female, and a male or a male.

With 14 years of experience in training and development, Doris Sims was a contributor to Mel Silberman's 1999, 2000, 2001, and 2002 *Training and Performance Sourcebooks*, as well as *The Consultant's Toolkit*. Her ideas have also been published in *Creative Training Techniques* newsletters, *Training Magazine*, and *Training Directors Forum* newsletter. Doris served as a presenter at the Training Director's Forum Conference, Training '9, IQPC Employee Orientation Program Conferences, and the 1999 ASTD International Conference. Doris is a human resource development director at Alcatel. Doris earned an MS in Human Resource Development from Indiana State University in 2001.

Contact Information   *2301 Bennington Ave.*
Flower Mound, TX 75028
972-539-1649
doris.sims@usa.alcatel.com

SEXUAL HARASSMENT
TABLE DISCUSSIONS

Consider and discuss these questions with your table group. Take notes regarding the main points or issues brought out in the discussion under each item. Then the group needs to agree on an answer choice. Circle YES if the situation is potential sexual harassment behavior and NO if the situation is not potential sexual harassment behavior.

The Situation	Discussion Notes	Circle YES or NO	
1. An employee makes a racial joke in the workplace.		YES	NO
2. One employee compliments another employee on a new outfit or hairstyle.		YES	NO
3. An employee has a photo of her boyfriend in a string bikini on her desk.		YES	NO
4. A manager in the workplace states that women should stay at home with their kids.		YES	NO
5. Two coworkers from different departments have been dating for three months.		YES	NO
6. A manager is dating an employee who reports directly to her.		YES	NO
7. An employee discusses his gay activist views in the workplace.		YES	NO
8. One employee hugs another employee to congratulate her on a recent engagement.		YES	NO
9. A consultant working with an employee in the company asks the employee for a date.		YES	NO
10. A regular customer of a retail store frequently makes sexual comments to the female cashiers.		YES	NO
11. A male manager refers to the female employees as "girls" or "honey."		YES	NO
12. A female employee makes sexual advances toward another female employee.		YES	NO

Part 5

Orientation Games and Activities

INTRODUCTION

New employee orientation is filled with information, multiple benefit decisions, forms to complete, new people to meet—and all of this normally takes place on the employees' first day of work in a new company, when they are already feeling a bit overwhelmed. Adding games and activities to your orientation will:

- Make employees feel more relaxed.

- Help new employees to meet each other.

- Add energy to your program.

- Increase learning retention.

- Keep the new employees focused and paying attention.

Part 5 contains 18 games and activities to help employees learn the culture, to help employees meet each other, to provide energy throughout the program, to review information, to help new employees feel valued, and to make your orientation program both fun and informative.

Chapter 33

Mission or Vision Telephone Game

A Fun Way for New Employees to Learn the Company's Vision or Mission

All trainers would agree it is important for new employees to learn the company's mission statement, vision, and values, but it may be difficult to motivate employees to memorize the company's mission statement and take it to heart. The Mission or Vision Telephone Game challenges employees to memorize the mission statement in an interactive way. It also increases the team-building effect that is so important to new employees who want to feel included in their new company's culture.

Best of all, the Mission or Vision Telephone Game requires only flip chart paper and markers; and because it is based on a game almost everyone has played in their childhood, the directions are simple and the game moves quickly.

The Mission or Vision Telephone Game works especially well in new employee orientation programs. It provides an excellent opportunity to include an activity in a training session that is often packed with lecture information about company benefits and policies, which can become overwhelming to a new employee.

Appropriate Group Size for the Activity: This activity works best with a minimum of 10 people and a maximum of approximately 100 people.

Approximate Length of Time: The time period depends on the number of people playing. With 10 people playing, the game will take about 15 minutes. With 100 people playing, the game will take 20 to 30 minutes.

YOU'LL NEED

- One blank piece of flip chart paper for each team

- One marker for each team

- One printed copy of your company's mission statement for each team

PREPARATION

No preparation is required prior to conducting the game, other than gathering the materials listed.

Important: If your company's mission statement is more than one sentence, just use the first sentence, or use the vision statement if it is shorter. You can even use the company's values instead of the mission or vision statements. If the statement you use is long, it's too difficult for the participants to remember much of anything and the game doesn't work well.

CONDUCTING THE GAME

1. Divide the class into two teams and have them line up on opposite sides of the classroom.

2. Ask the class if they remember the telephone game they played as children, when each person whispers a secret to the next person to see how different and silly the secret turned out as the last person repeated it out loud.

3. Give the first person in each team's line a printed copy of the company's mission statement. Instruct them to read the mission statement to the person in line behind them. (Encourage them to speak softly enough so the other team can't hear, rather than whispering in the other person's ear.) Emphasize that this is not a race; points will be awarded based on accuracy only. After the first person in line reads the mission statement to the second person in line, he or she sits down with the paper in hand.

4. The second person in line then repeats the mission statement (without benefit of the printed copy!) to the third person in line, who turns around and repeats it to the fourth person in line, and so on until the last person in line hears the mission statement. Each person in the line can repeat the mission statement only once to the person behind him or her. Have participants sit down once they've repeated the mission statement.

5. When the last person in line hears the mission statement, he or she moves to the flip chart and writes what was heard on the paper. It is best to position the flip charts so teams can see only their own chart. This game is fairly quiet at first, but the volume increases as the employees responsible for writing the mission statement are cheered on heartily by their teammates!

6. Ask the last two people to stay with their flip charts. Then, read the mission statement one word at a time, and instruct the people at the flip charts to record one point for each correct word. The team that has the most accurate mission statement, measured by the number of correct words, is the winner.

DEBRIEFING THE ACTIVITY

Now, display and review the company's correct vision or mission statement, while everyone's attention is clearly focused on it.

If desired, this game can be played at the beginning of the new employee orientation session as a "benchmark run." Then encourage the teams to learn the mission statement more thoroughly during the training session, with the game being played again at the end of the orientation program to see how well they have learned the mission statement.

A debriefing activity after the benchmark run can include a discussion regarding the importance of the mission to the culture, and what activities, programs, and action plans the company has in place to support the mission.

With 14 years of experience in training and development, Doris Sims was a contributor to Mel Silberman's 1999, 2000, 2001, and 2002 *Training and Performance Sourcebooks*, as well as *The Consultant's Toolkit*. Her ideas have also been published in *Creative Training Techniques* newsletters, *Training Magazine*, and *Training Directors Forum* newsletter. Doris served as a presenter at the Training Director's Forum Conference, Training '99, IQPC Employee Orientation Program Conferences, and the 1999 ASTD International Conference. Doris is a human resource development director at Alcatel. Doris earned an MS in Human Resource Development from Indiana State University in 2001.

Contact Information   *2301 Bennington Ave.*
Flower Mound, TX 75028
972-539-1649
dmsims@home.com

Chapter 34

Autographs Icebreaker

An Icebreaker Designed to Help New Employees Become Acquainted

The room looked desolate with its scores of chairs splayed against its outer walls. Into this barrenness entered 40 computer engineers with heads slightly bowed. One by one, they silently slid into their seats, and sat and stared. These were Leadership Potential Candidates specially selected from every division at a large corporation's two-week program. The candidates did not seem to know each other and looked vulnerable and fidgety in their chairs.

The trainer positioned herself in the center of the large room and smiled. After her brief welcoming statement, she handed out copies of one assignment sheet containing the well-known "autographs" icebreaker to each participant. The game requires players to find someone who fits each of the characteristics listed on the sheet. The object is to fill the sheet with autographs. The real objective, of course, is to get the participants to interact with each other and create a friendlier environment.

Even after the trainer started the exercise, many participants remained seated, reading the assignment sheet with curiosity and suspicion. Then, one or two of the braver ones turned to their neighbors, asking if they identified with any of the characteristics. A trickle of conversation emerged. Then, a few participants got up from their seats, boldly going to other parts of the room. Finally, all the participants left their chairs to mingle in the ongoing exercise.

In just a few minutes, the room became a raucous social gathering, with the animated chatter of 40 participants waving assignment sheets and moving through the group in search of the elusive autograph. Chatter and laughter were now the rule as pens flashed across the room. This mild pandemonium continued for 15 minutes, ending only when the trainer invited the participants to return to their chairs. It took a few joyful minutes to quiet the room as the participants reluctantly left their newfound friends and acquaintances.

While it is important to relax the environment for learning to take place in any training program, it is especially important in new employee orientation, when participants are already a little nervous about starting a new job and meeting new people. Use this highly interactive icebreaker to create enthusiasm and to "warm" the room with friendly introductions.

Appropriate Group Size for the Activity: This exercise works well with groups of 8 to 100 participants.

Approximate Length of Time: 20 to 45 minutes, depending on the class size.

YOU'LL NEED

- Game sheets and pencils or pens for each participant
- One timer (optional)
- Prizes (optional)

PREPARATION

1. Develop a set of descriptive statements that are pertinent to the audience. These descriptions can come from information on preregistration forms, from required prerequisites, or from target audience data.

2. List a set of statements on a handout.

3. Make one copy of the handout for each participant.

CONDUCTING THE GAME

Game Objective: To complete the list by obtaining the signatures of class members who fit the characteristics listed.

1. Tell participants that they will be involved in an exercise to learn something about other people in the course.

2. Distribute one worksheet and a pen or pencil to each person.

3. Explain the task: "Find another participant who fits each of the statements, and get the person's autograph on the line next to the statement that describes him or her. All signatures must be legible. No participant may sign his or her name on any one handout more than once. When your sheet is completed, have it validated by the facilitator." (The facilitator may give a prize to the first three to five participants with completed worksheets.)

4. Allow participants 15 minutes to complete the exercise.

DEBRIEFING THE GAME

By going over the statements, this is an excellent time to "harvest" both skills and perspectives that surface during play of the game.

1. This will allow all participants to meet each other and reinforces the concept that we all bring something to the learning environment. As the statements

are disclosed and participants are identified, players gain a greater understanding and appreciation of their fellow participants.

2. Extended debriefing time helps new participants learn about and identify with their fellow participants, allowing for better interaction during the ongoing class and increased networking possibilities.

3. Extended debriefing for in-place teams provides an excellent way to reveal new perspectives of team members.

   ■ On one occasion, a quiet, gentle female revealed that she had been one of the students who walked through a school segregation line. Other team members gained a new, and perhaps valuable, insight into one of their team members—a perspective that was never revealed or discussed before.

   ■ On another occasion, we listed the statement "Rides a Harley-Davidson." The debriefing not only identified the rider—a petite, 52-year-old grandmother—but uncovered underlying assumptions of participants, who admitted to looking for large male bikers.

VARIATIONS

1. Charge a penny for each worksheet. Declare that the first participant to fill in his or her worksheet receives the pot.

2. Use comparative statements that require participants to take note of similarities, such as "Born in the same month" or "Drives the same make automobile."

3. Use a Bingo format, such as a 5-by-5 matrix. Have participants autograph the square, and award prizes for Bingos.

4. Develop one or two statements in a foreign language. This requires players to 1) translate the statement, and 2) find someone who fits the characteristic.

Steve Sugar, president of The Game Group, is a writer and teacher of learning games. Steve is the author of *Games That Teach* (Jossey-Bass/Pfeiffer), and coauthor of *Primary Games* (Jossey-Bass) and *Games That Teach Teams* (Jossey-Bass/Pfeiffer). He has written game systems that are used worldwide, including QUIZO, X-O Cise, Management 2000, and LearnIt! (HRD Press). *Personnel Journal, Training & Development Journal,* and *Training Magazine* have all interviewed Steve about learning games.

Steve contributed chapters on game design to *The ASTD Handbook of Training Design and Delivery* and *The ASTD Handbook of Instructional Technology,* has written several ASTD Info-Line publications, serves on the Editorial Advisory Board of the *Thiagi Game Letter,* and is a frequent contributor to the Jossey-Bass/Pfeiffer *Annuals.* Steve is a faculty member at the University of Maryland Baltimore County (UMBC) and a frequent presenter at international ASTD, TRAINING, and ISPI conferences.

Contact Information   *The Game Group*
10320 Kettledrum Court
Ellicott City, MD 21042
410-418-4930
info@thegamegroup.com

AUTOGRAPH GAME

Autographs

I. Complete this list by obtaining the signature of a participant who matches each statement.

II. You are limited to one signature from any one participant. The signature must be legible.

III. When completed, return the list to the facilitator for validation.

Identify someone in the class who:

1. Has a gold filling. _____

2. Was born outside of the United States. _____

3. Has created his or her own Web site. _____

4. Plays bridge. _____

5. Has shaken hands with a celebrity. _____

6. Ballroom dances. _____

7. Can tie a bow tie. _____

8. Can use sign language. _____

9. Drives a Corvette. _____

10. Owns a pedigreed dog. _____

11. Has had root canal work. _____

12. Sings in a chorus. _____

13. Can ice skate or rollerblade. _____

14. Has purchased groceries on the Internet. _____

15. Has one or more grandchildren. _____

AUTOGRAPH BINGO

1	2	3	4	5
6	7	8	9	10
11	12	13	14	15
16	17	18	19	20
21	22	23	24	25

AUTOGRAPH BINGO QUESTIONS

Ask your new coworkers to sign the Bingo box that corresponds to the number of any item listed that is a true description of them. You must have two rows of signatures to win the game.

1. Has three or more brothers and sisters

2. Owns a Jeep or 4-wheel drive vehicle

3. Plays a musical instrument

4. Has season tickets to the symphony or opera (or sporting event)

5. Is a weekend sailor

6. Paints in oils or watercolors

7. Has a child in college ($$$)

8. Cooks French cuisine

9. Has ordered groceries on the Internet

10. Has Dave Brubeck or Miles Davis albums

11. Has a bird feeder

12. Wears contact lenses

13. Has a birthday in December

14. Plays racquetball

15. Has been married two years or less

16. Owns 78-rpm records or 8-track tapes

17. Sings in a choir or chorus

18. Skis (water or snow) or has gone snowboarding

19. Has had root canal work

20. Has visited Europe in the past year

21. Tap dances

22. Rides a motorcycle

23. Has his or her own Web site

24. Has earned a belt in karate

25. Has one or more grandchildren

Chapter 35

Spots and Signatures

Combine New Employee Introductions with an All-Day Energizer

The Signature Scramble icebreaker is unique because the activity takes place at periodic intervals throughout the training course, so students continue to get to know each other during the entire class. This activity provides a method for class participants to introduce each other, while also providing an energizer during the class as needed.

The activity includes all aspects of the concept we call BEN: **B**reak preoccupation (students can begin to focus on the current training, and mentally leave the demands of the office); **E**ncourage participation and interaction; and allow for **N**etworking opportunities. The game is simple for participants to play, but also fosters creative thought on the part of the participants. This activity is excellent for orientation programs, which tend to have dead air time as people are completing forms or reviewing benefit information. Use these time periods to energize the group with this activity.

Appropriate Group Size for the Activity: This activity works best with a group of 15 to 50 people.

Approximate Length of Time: Allow 3 to 5 minutes to present the game instructions. The actual game time will take place in periods of 5 to 7 minutes at times the instructor chooses throughout the entire class.

YOU'LL NEED

- One large index card per participant
- Sheets of colored sticker "dots"
- Some type of sound maker—a bicycle horn, bell, buzzer, or clapper
- Prizes

PREPARATION

No preparation is needed other than gathering the materials and becoming familiar with the game instructions.

CONDUCTING THE ACTIVITY

1. Tell the class that the object of the activity is to collect five signatures from their fellow participants, with the following stipulations:

   * You may not obtain a signature from someone at your table.

   * You may be called upon to introduce the person "behind the signature," so it is important to obtain information about that person.

   * Only one person can obtain a signature during an exchange. In other words, two people cannot "trade" signatures.

2. Tell the participants that the first way to win a prize during this game is to be among the first three participants to obtain five signatures. Once five signatures are obtained, the participant runs to the front table and blows a noise maker to be recognized. (This prevents confusion concerning who the first three winners were.)

3. The first three winners each receive a dot sticker from the facilitator to place on their name tents. From this point on, the object of the game is to obtain dots to stick on their name tents. Tell the participants that they will be able to buy prizes at the end of the training session based on the number of dots earned; the more dots a person earns, the better the prize received!

4. Write the dot earning system on a flip chart that can be referenced by participants throughout the course. Dots can be earned by any of the following actions:

   * Being one of the first three people to obtain five signatures (as described in step 2).

   * Asking and answering questions. (Dots can be awarded by peers or by the instructor.)

   * Sharing profound thoughts or ideas that could be used back at the employees' work units (awarded by peers).

   * Volunteering (especially if the participant does not know what he or she is volunteering for; this reinforces the concept that leaders often need to take risks to move forward).

   * If an entire table returns from a break on time, everyone at the table is awarded a dot.

   * Use a secret dot award. Before the lunch break, ask the group if anyone has awarded a peer with a dot for a profound thought, idea, question, or answer. Anyone who awarded someone else now obtains *two* dots for themselves! (*Note:* Do not place this dot-earning method on the flip chart.)

This reinforces the concept that leaders help each other and cheer each other on. It will also increase participants' focus on the contributions and questions their peers present in the class, and the number of dot awards given by peers will increase.

5. At periodic intervals during the training session, when the group needs a zap of energy, ask for volunteers to introduce someone whose signature appears on their card. Of course, volunteers are rewarded with a dot, so participants are eager to provide their introductions. Allow only one introduction per person at each interval. Continue this activity at intervals throughout the course until everyone in the class has been introduced.

6. At the end of the course, students "cash in" their dots for prizes, which are arranged and labeled in categories by the number of dots needed to "buy" them. If desired, the instructor can display the prizes and the number of dots needed to buy them at the beginning of the course, to increase the motivational level.

Al McClaney is an Employee Services Relationship Manager and vice president of First Tennessee Bank, one of *Working Mother Magazine*'s top 100 companies to work for in the United States. Al has worked in various supervisory, management, and training positions for the Texas Department of Transportation, the U.S. Army, and First Tennessee Bank.

Contact Information   *First Horizon Home Loans*
4000 Horizon Way
Irving, TX 75063
Amcclaney@fhhlc.com
214-441-7158

Chapter 36

Match That Number!

A New Way to Help Employees Interact and Start Conversations

This is an icebreaker that gets new employees on their feet and talking with others in the room. It requires participants to be creative and to talk with others to find things they have in common.

Appropriate Group Size for the Activity: This icebreaker requires a minimum of approximately 12 people and a maximum of approximately 100 people.

Approximate Length of Time: 15 minutes

YOU'LL NEED

- A copy for each participant of the Match That Number! handout

- Pencils or pens

- Prizes

PREPARATION

No preparation is needed other than gathering the materials listed.

CONDUCTING THE GAME

1. Distribute copies of the Match That Number! handout.

2. Explain that participants will have 10 minutes to talk with others in the room to find examples in which you both have the same number of items. For example, if you find someone else who has three children, you both write "children" next to the number 3, and write the name of the coworker you matched with. If you both have 12 coins in your pocket, write "coins" next to the num-

ber 12, and write the name of the coworker you matched with. Creativity is the key to success in this game!

3. Encourage the class to be creative and to make as many matches as possible—the top winner(s) will receive a prize!

4. Tell the group to start finding matches. Encourage them to get up out of their seats and talk with others.

5. Call time after 10 minutes and have everyone sit down. Ask the participants to raise their hands if they have three matches; most likely, everyone will raise their hands. Ask them to keep their hands up if they have 4 matches, then to keep their hands up if they have 5 matches, and so on, until the number of people with their hands up matches the number of prizes you have. Award the prizes!

With 14 years of experience in training and development, Doris Sims was a contributor to Mel Silberman's 1999, 2000, 2001, and 2002 *Training and Performance Sourcebooks*, as well as *The Consultant's Toolkit*. Her ideas have also been published in *Creative Training Techniques* newsletters, *Training Magazine*, and *Training Directors Forum* newsletter. Doris served as a presenter at the Training Director's Forum Conference, Training '99, IQPC Employee Orientation Program Conferences, and the 1999 ASTD International Conference. Doris is a human resource development director at Alcatel. Doris earned an MS in Human Resource Development from Indiana State University in 2001.

Contact Information   *2301 Bennington Ave.*
Flower Mound, TX 75028
972-539-1649
doris.sims@usa.alcatel.com

MATCH THAT NUMBER!

Talk with your new coworkers to find examples in which you both have the same number of items. For example, if you and someone else both have three children, you both write "children" next to the number 3, and write the name of the coworker you matched with. If you both have 12 coins in your pocket, write "coins" next to the number 12, and write the name of the coworker you matched with.

Number	Item	Coworker's Name
1		
2		
3		
4		
5		
6		
7		
8		
9		
10		
11		
12		
13		
14		
15		

Chapter 37

A Sweet Way to Meet!

A Unique (and Tasty!) Orientation Icebreaker

At DeRoyal, this icebreaker is conducted during the first few minutes of the orientation program, to help employees relax and have a little fun. It also provides an opportunity for everyone to get to know the other employees in the room.

At the end of the activity, each new employee will have a new "racehorse" name, which is used throughout DeRoyal's three-day orientation program (which has an "Off to the Races" theme), and everyone will have a small candy bar to eat. Sometimes the racehorse nickname sticks with employees throughout their careers at DeRoyal! (However, the candy doesn't usually last through the game!)

DeRoyal structured this game in the hope of creating lasting friendships that begin in the orientation program.

Appropriate Group Size for the Activity: This activity is ideal for a small orientation group of 20 employees or fewer. However, the activity can be done with a larger group if employees work in groups of 3 to 5 during the game.

Approximate Length of Time: The group size will affect the amount of time needed; factor approximately 5 to 7 minutes per employee or group.

YOU'LL NEED

- An Off to the Races! handout for each employee

- An assortment of the following candy bars: Mr. Goodbar, Hershey's Dark, Krackle Bar, and Hershey's regular chocolate bars. These are produced and sold by Hershey's in a single bag of assorted mini-bars. You will need at least one candy bar for each new employee. Employees always appreciate additional bars to enjoy after the game!

PREPARATION

No preparation is required other than obtaining the materials listed and becoming familiar with the steps to conduct the game.

CONDUCTING THE GAME

1. Give each employee a copy of the Off to the Races! handout.

2. Instruct the new employees to mingle and ask each other the questions on the sheet. If you have a large group, it may be better for people to work in groups of 3 to 5, rather than trying to mingle among too many people in a limited period of time.

3. After about 10 minutes, ask the employees to return to their seats, and give them each one miniature candy bar, making sure all types of candy bars are fairly evenly distributed.

4. Now each participant tells a story based on the type of candy bar received:

   * Employees with a Mr. Goodbar will tell the group about the nuttiest thing they've ever done.

   * Employees with a Hershey's Dark bar will tell the group about the "darkest" thing they've ever done.

   * Employees with a Krackle bar will tell the group about the funniest thing they've ever done.

   * Employees with a regular Hershey's bar will tell the group about the sweetest thing they've ever done.

   Note: If you have a larger group (more than 20 participants), have the employees go back to their groups of 3 to 5 to tell their stories, rather than having everyone in the class present to the entire class.

5. After the stories, either the entire class (for a group of 20 employees or fewer) or the small groups of 3 to 5 will confer to come up with their racehorse nicknames for the rest of the orientation period. (See examples on the next page.)

   Important: The trainer or facilitator must also share stories and answer the questions along with the new employees. When you begin with your story first, the group is able to see you as a person just like them.

DEBRIEFING THE GAME

At DeRoyal, the new employees' racehorse nicknames are used with a game board in which the new employee becomes a racehorse during the program. The movement of the horses on the game board is used to keep score for the various activities in the remainder of the program.

Employees can put their nicknames on their name tents or badges. In a large group, this would be especially helpful to keep track of all the nicknames.

And of course, the employees can now enjoy their candy bars (if they haven't already done so)!

THE STORIES WE HAVE HEARD AT DEROYAL

It is amazing what people will tell you when they feel comfortable with you. I've heard everything. One very funny story came from an employee who was a real sports nut. He attended a Philadelphia Phillies baseball game; he was extremely excited to get the tickets. He was so excited he became very comfortable in his surroundings and he started to pick his nose. He noticed people around him were staring not just at him, but also at a cameraman who had spotted him in the crowd—he was caught on camera at the game in front of thousands of people, picking his nose! If this wasn't embarrassing enough, he made the highlight films on the local news channel. What a moment of fame. All of his friends called to tease him—of course, everyone had seen him in his moment of glory. The entire class was in hysterics laughing from this story and decided to give him the race-horse name of *One Nose from Fame*.

Another story: One of our new hires told us the story of the sweetest thing he had done. His grandmother was alone and feeling lonesome, so he bought her a puppy to keep her company. His racehorse name became *Puppy Love*.

The story that I shared at the ASTD conference took place when I was a dancer at a local theme park, DollyWood. I was performing one evening, clogging to a song with a very fast tempo, and my shoe came off and hit a man seated in the front row. I had to keep going, because the song wasn't finished. I had to dance with one shoe on and one shoe off, with this poor man staring at me. After the program was over, I found the man in the audience and apologized. He thought the whole thing was funny, thank goodness. My racehorse name became *Kick a Rock* because when I kicked my shoe off, I hit a man whose head was hard as a rock!

Rebecca Harmon is director of corporate human resources at DeRoyal. Rebecca received her bachelor's degree in Psychology with an emphasis in Industrial Organizational Psychology from the University of Tennessee. Rebecca joined DeRoyal in 1997, where she is responsible for all hiring practices, for ensuring compliance with all federal contract guidelines, and for facilitating employee relations. Rebecca served as a presenter at the 2000 International ASTD Conference.

Contact Information   200 DeBusk Lane
Powell, TN 37849
865-362-2341
rharmon@deroyal.com

OFF TO THE RACES!

Ask your new coworkers for their answers to the questions below.

1.   What is your name?

2.   Where are you from?

3.   What is your favorite color?

4.   What is your favorite food?

5.   What hobbies do you enjoy?

6.   What was your most embarrassing moment?

Chapter 38

Have Your Passport Ready!

Creating an Interactive Tour of the Company

This is an interactive data-gathering activity that provides exposure to the organization's physical facilities and information on departments that will have an impact on the employees' roles and responsibilities. The information should be incorporated into every new employee orientation process on the first day of employment.

Appropriate Group Size for the Activity: Minimum of 2 participants, maximum of 15 participants; 10 participants is the ideal size.

Approximate Length of Time: 30 to 60 minutes

YOU'LL NEED

- Passport booklets (create your own using the template and directions provided in this chapter)
- Facility maps
- Department Information Sheets (optional)
- Stickers or stamps (optional)

PREPARATION

1. Using the passport template provided, duplicate one copy for each participant. Cut along the outer edges of the passport form, then cut one (or more if needed) blank sheets of paper to match the size and shape of the passport template. Fold both sheets in half, inserting the blank paper inside the printed passport form. Lay both sheets flat, and staple at the fold line. A "booklet" is formed when the stapled sheets are folded in half.

2. Prepare a map of the facility, showing the location of departments and listing the representative for each one. If time is limited or if the facility is large, designate the specific departments that the employees are to visit. Duplicate one copy of the map for each participant.

3. Notify the appropriate department representatives of the date and time frame in which employees will be visiting. Explain that each set of employees will ask the representative for a brief description of the department's function. After providing this brief description of the department, the representative is to enter his or her initials and the department name into each passport booklet. Or, each department could be identified by a sticker or stamp that can be used instead of initials, to increase the realism of traveling around the company and having the passport stamped.

4. *Optional:* Make copies of the Department Information Sheet and forward one copy to each designated department for completion, indicating a return date prior to the orientation session. Make copies of the completed information sheets for each participant as a follow-up resource.

CONDUCTING THE GAME

1. Explain to participants that one of the important features of an orientation program is gaining knowledge about the organizational facility and the people who work there. To this end, they will be completing a travel tour that will take them to various departments throughout the company.

2. Distribute one passport booklet and a facility map to each employee. Instruct each person to place his or her name on the front cover of the passport.

3. Direct the employees to form pairs (or trios, as necessary). State that each set of employees will locate and visit the departments indicated on the map. They are to ask the appropriate representative for a brief description of the department's function. After the question is answered, the representative will enter his or her initials (or stamp or sticker) and the name of the department into each person's passport booklet.

4. Announce the designated time limit (20 to 45 minutes) that the participants will have to complete the tour and return. Dismiss the participants.

5. At the end of the designated time, reassemble the returning participants.

6. If the size of the group and time allow, facilitate a group discussion as the participants share aspects of the information they gained from the various departments.

7. *Optional:* Distribute copies of the completed Department Information Sheets to each participant as a follow-up resource.

DEBRIEFING THE GAME

Lead a general discussion by asking the following questions:

■ What was your overall reaction to this activity?

- Which department did you find most interesting, and why?

- How will this information benefit you in doing your job?

Explain that an important part of new employee orientation is obtaining company-level information. This activity provided information about the physical facilities as well as the key functions of departments that will have an impact on the new employees' roles and responsibilities. More importantly, each employee was actively involved in gaining this knowledge. This approach sends the message that the organization expects employees to be proactive and take initiative in completing job tasks.

In addition, orientation programs provide socialization and support to new employees. Each person has been partnered with at least one other individual who will continue to be his or her "orientation buddy." These partners can be a resources for each other as employees settle in.

Lorraine L. Ukens is the owner of Team-ing with Success, specializing in team building and experiential learning. Team-ing with Success also provides performance improvement consulting, as well as training activity books and games. Lorraine received her MS degree in Human Resource Development from Towson University (Maryland), where she is currently an adjunct faculty member. She is the author of several training activity books (*Getting Together, Working Together, All Together Now!, Energize Your Audience!, Pump Them Up, Skillbuilders: 50 Customer Service Activities*), consensus activities (Adventure in the Amazon, Stranded in the Himalayas, Arctic Expedition), and a game (Common Currency: The Cooperative-Competition Game). Lorraine is the editor of and a contributor to *What Smart Trainers: The Secrets of Success from the World's Foremost Experts.*

Contact Information   *4302 Starview Court*
Glen Arm, MD 21057-9745
410-592-6050
ukens@team-ing.com
www.team-ing.com

DEPARTMENT INFORMATION SHEET

Department Name:

Department Head:

Department Function:

Products/Services:

Resource Contacts:

Hours of Operation (if applicable):

PASSPORT TEMPLATE

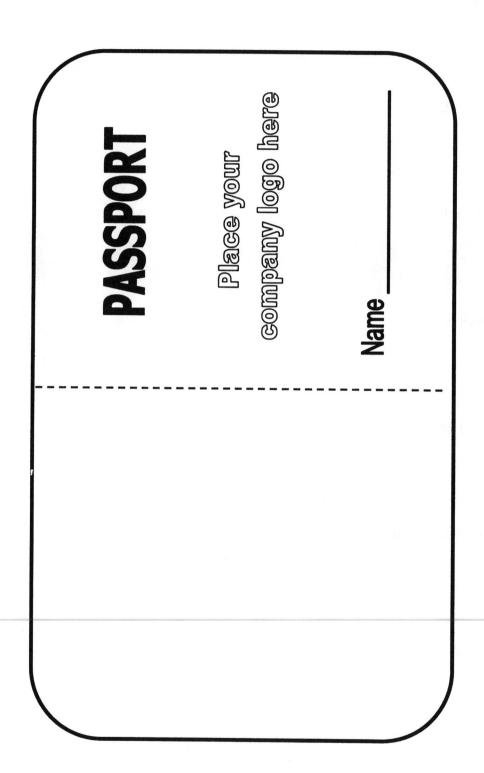

Chapter 39

New Job Butterflies

An Opening Activity to Emphasize the Importance of Orientation

Use this activity to open your orientation program in a very unique way that will get participants' attention immediately. Your new employees will know this is not the "same old" type of orientation they've been to at every other company. This activity emphasizes the purpose and importance of orientation, especially for those who've been through orientations at other companies and may feel they don't need to attend another orientation program.

This activity also serves as an initial icebreaker between the students and the facilitator, and helps participants recognize that everyone feels a little apprehensive as they start a new job.

Appropriate Group Size for the Activity: This activity works well with 5 people or 500 people, or any number in between.

Approximate Length of Time: 10 minutes

YOU'LL NEED

- Sheets of 8 1/2- by 11-inch colored paper for the instructor and for each employee

PREPARATION

Practice following the directions prior to class until you can smoothly, and without fail, make a butterfly that matches the illustration provided.

CONDUCTING THE GAME

1. Rather than walking into the room and welcoming employees to the company and so forth in the normal way of orientation programs, try this: Walk into the

room without saying anything at first, but simply pass out a sheet of colored paper to each new employee.

2. Ask the employees to follow your directions exactly, and let them know that you are not allowed to answer any questions or to give any further details on each direction. Then give the directions listed below, pausing between each sentence to follow the direction yourself to make your own butterfly, and allow the students a few seconds to follow each instruction.

"Fold your paper in half.

Tear off the upper right-hand corner.

Fold your paper in half again.

Tear off the upper left-hand corner.

Fold your paper in half again.

Tear off the lower right-hand corner.

Now open your paper and you will have a butterfly just like mine!"

(Of course, some of the participants will have a butterfly like yours, but others will have different shapes—some will even have a hole in the center.)

DEBRIEFING THE GAME

1. Have the participants all hold up their butterflies so all can see that there are several different versions of the butterfly.

2. Ask: "Why do some of you have different butterflies? I gave the same directions to everyone!" Listen to the responses, and make the point that every direction is subject to interpretation, and people listen from their own perspectives.

3. Say: "Have you ever felt like this when starting with a new company, when you were trying to figure out the company's 'butterflies'—things like the company's culture, company policies and procedures? Every company is different, and everyone who starts employment with a new company is trying to fit into a new place. Everyone wants their 'butterfly' to come out right. Our NEO program is designed to help provide a road map to our company's vision, values, policies, procedures, and benefits, to reduce those butterflies everyone feels when they begin a new job."

4. Now, introduce yourself, welcome the employees to the company, and go into the agenda of topics for the orientation program.

Mel Silberman is president of Active Training and a professor of adult and organizational development at Temple University, where he specializes in instructional design and team building. He is the editor of the annual McGraw-Hill *Training and Performance Sourcebooks* and *Team and Organizational Development Sourcebooks*, as well as the *Consultant's Toolkit*. He is also the author or editor of 17 other books, including *PeopleSmart, Active Training,* and *101 Ways to Make Meetings Active.*

Contact Information   *Active Training*
303 Sayre Drive
Princeton, NJ 08540
609-987-8157
mel@activetraining.com
www.activetraining.com

ILLUSTRATION:
THE COMPLETED BUTTERFLY

Before conducting this activity with a class, practice following the directions to produce a butterfly that looks like the shape below.

Note: The trick to making the butterfly is to tear off (initially) the upper right-hand corner and then rotate the paper so that each subsequent tear occurs in the same corner as the previous tear. Also, your first fold will be from top to bottom, not from side to side, as some participants will do. The completed butterfly has this shape:

Chapter 40

Visioning—The Power of One

A Format for Employees to Think Deeply about Their New Future

 Whenever people start new paths in their lives or make a fresh start, it is an excellent idea to take time to think about the goals they would like to achieve, the experiences they hope to gain, and the contribution they can bring to the overall plan.

This activity provides the time for employees to think deeply about:

- What they would like to contribute to an organization

- What they would like to gain from the time they spend in the organization

- What experiences they would like to have with their coworkers and in their jobs

- What value they can bring to the organization

Appropriate Group Size for this Activity: This activity can be conducted with groups of any size.

Approximate Length of Time: This activity can run from approximately 45 minutes to 60 or more minutes.

YOU'LL NEED

- A copy of the Personal Visioning handout for each participant

- Pens or pencils for all participants

- Flip chart and markers

PREPARATION

Before conducting this activity, make copies of the handout for each participant.

CONDUCTING THE ACTIVITY

1. Explain the importance of setting goals and spending a few minutes thinking about expectations whenever we make a fresh start or take a new path in our lives. Explain that participants will be taking a few minutes now to think about their future in the new company.

2. Distribute copies of the handout to each participant.

3. Give participants approximately 20 minutes to think quietly and deeply about their responses to the questions on the handout. Participants should record their thoughts directly on the handout.

4. Then ask the participants to share their thoughts with a partner—someone sitting next to them, behind them, or in front of them. Partnerships can be groups of three for a class with an odd number of participants. Provide at least 20 minutes for this portion of the activity. Notify the class when 10 minutes have passed so both partners will have time to talk about their responses.

DEBRIEFING THE ACTIVITY

Bring the class back together as a group. Ask the following questions and record responses on the flip chart:

■ What did you learn about your own expectations regarding the company and your potential contributions?

■ What did you learn about the other people in your group?

■ How did this exercise affect you?

■ What is the most important message you want to pass on to your new manager to help you work most productively and to increase your satisfaction in your new job?

■ Are there any other burning questions or thoughts to add to our discussion?

Encourage participants to keep their documents, to refer to at a later date, and also encourage them to share their responses with their managers. Then thank the participants for their willingness to share their thoughts on these topics, and move on to the next orientation topic or activity.

Sheila Armitage has worked internationally in the training and organizational development fields for over 13 years. She has been involved in all aspects of developing people, and specializes in cutting-edge management development. Sheila works with clients such as Sulzer CarboMedics, Sulzer Orthopedics, Zimmer Orthopedics, Janssen Pharmaceuticals, HMR, PPD, Columbia Healthcare, Iomega, AT&T, Southwestern Bell, IBM, Texas Rehabilitation Commission, Teacher's Retirement System of Texas, MHMR, Houston-Tillotson College, One World Music, and Confederation Life Insurance Company.

Contact Information   *512-263-8525*
Sheila@managementconnection.com
www.managementconnection.com

PERSONAL VISIONING

Take a few minutes to reflect quietly and deeply about your responses to the following questions. Record your thoughts for each question in the space below.

1. What contributions do you think you can make to this company?

2. How do you view your role in the company at this time? What is your understanding of why you were hired by the company?

3. What are some key milestones you have experienced in other positions or in your life that you can look back on and feel proud of?

4. When your association with the company comes to a close sometime in the future (the far future ☺), what can you envision will be the key milestones and accomplishments you will have achieved? What will you leave to the company as a result of your innovation and effort?

5. What three primary factors attracted you to this company?

6. What skills do you want to develop through your association with us? How do you envision using and obtaining these skills?

7. Under what conditions do you thrive and learn best?

8. What conditions are counterproductive for you, based on past experiences?

9. What advice do you have for your new supervisor or manager to help unleash your fullest potential?

10. Based on your past experience and your knowledge of yourself, what factors are important to keep you motivated and happy in your job?

11. How would you describe your ideal working relationship with a) your manager, and b) your team members?

12. What differences in working styles or communication styles can you envision at this point in working with your new supervisor or manager? What might you and your manager do to address these issues?

13. When you are stressed or overwhelmed, how does that show up in observable behaviors? What can others do to help reduce your feelings of stress?

14. List some books or films that have had an impact on your thinking or your life, and explain why they had this effect on you.

Chapter 41

Pom-Pom Power!

A Continuous Energizer for New Employee Orientation Programs

One purpose of this activity is to start the orientation program with a look that is more interesting than the average orientation. People don't expect to be handed a small plastic pom-pom as they go into a new employee orientation program.

The second purpose of this activity is to energize the new employee group (in only a few seconds) as needed throughout the entire program. It is tied to an ongoing point system throughout the program, to add a level of competition and to reward positive participation, coming back from breaks on time, winning other games in the program, and so on.

Appropriate Group Size for the Activity: This energizer method works best with at least 10 people, and can be used for up to 500 people.

Approximate Length of Time: This is not a "start and stop" activity; it is a way to add a sense of fun and energy throughout an orientation program that is one or two days in length. If your orientation program is longer than that, I recommend that this method be used for only a part of the program; otherwise, like a good joke that is told too many times, it will lose its punch.

YOU'LL NEED

Pom-poms in at least two colors, one pom-pom for each new employee. These can be ordered from Oriental Trading Company (*www.orientaltrading.com* or 1-800-875-8480). At this writing, they sell for $10.80 per dozen, and they are sturdy enough to be used over and over if your budget requires you to do so.

For a group of 10 to 30 new employees, buy two colors of pom-poms, for two teams. If you have more than 30 employees, consider using four or more teams, by choosing four or more colors of pom-poms.

You will also need a flip chart and markers to keep track of the points each team will earn throughout the program, and prizes for the winning team.

PREPARATION

No preparation is needed.

CONDUCTING THE ACTIVITY

1. Place pom-poms on the tables in the classroom so participants will each have one when they sit down (using an equal number of pom-poms in each color), or hand pom-poms to participants as they walk in the door.

2. As you begin the class, explain that the class has been divided into teams according to the colors of the pom-poms.

3. Explain that points will be given to teams throughout the program for enthusiasm, asking a good question (you will be the judge of a "good" question), coming back from breaks on time, and for games that will be played during the program. For each day of the program, the team with the most points will win prizes. The point system is cumulative and ongoing at all times.

4. Test to see if people were paying attention by asking, "Which team is most excited to be here this morning?" Then award a point to the team that waves their pom-poms and cheers. Even if only one or two people on the team wave their pom-poms a bit, reward this by providing a point to that team. As the stakes get higher throughout the day, even the more reserved people will join in to cheer and wave their pom-poms to get points.

5. As the orientation program is conducted, reward teams for:

   * Asking good questions.

   * Winning any other games included in the program.

   * Coming back from breaks on time; if the entire team is back on time, the team wins 5 points.

6. Orientation programs by their nature are packed with information. If you see that your group needs a quick pick-up, ask which team is learning the most or is the most intrigued by the information. If you have rewarded them for enthusiasm along the way, they will now compete for the loudest cheer to demonstrate their enthusiasm and gain a point. Reward the most enthusiastic team with at least one point, and then go on with participants who have been energized in only a few seconds and are ready to listen to more information.

   Note: Please don't assume that your company's employees won't accept this activity in an orientation class, if your culture is more reserved. This method has been used very successfully in a banking corporation for multiple years.

DEBRIEFING THE ACTIVITY

Reward the team with the most points with prizes at the end of the session. If you like, and if your budget allows, go ahead and reward the whole class with prizes for being enthusiastic participants!

With 14 years of experience in training and development, Doris Sims was a contributor to Mel Silberman's 1999, 2000, 2001, and 2002 *Training and Performance Sourcebooks,* as well as *The Consultant's Toolkit.* Her ideas have also been published in *Creative Training Techniques* newsletters, *Training Magazine,* and *Training Directors Forum* newsletter. Doris served as a presenter at the Training Director's Forum Conference, Training '99, IQPC Employee Orientation Program Conferences, and the 1999 ASTD International Conference. Doris is a human resource development director at Alcatel. Doris earned an MS in Human Resource Development from Indiana State University in 2001.

Contact Information   *2301 Bennington Ave.*
Flower Mound, TX 75028
972-539-1649
dmsims@home.com

Chapter 42

If They Snooze, You Lose

A Dozen Ways to Add Energy and Action to Your Orientation Presentations

New employee orientation is often packed with information and presentations covering various topics. By its very nature, it can be overwhelming and tedious for employees if the orientation facilitator doesn't actively identify and incorporate a variety of methods to keep the attention and energy levels of the new employees high.

If attention and energy levels drop, information retention and satisfaction with the orientation experience also drop. And, if employees don't retain information covered in the orientation program, phone calls and work hours increase for personnel in the company who deal with new employee issues, such as benefits personnel. So an orientation program filled with dull presentations is a lose–lose situation for everyone.

Adding energy and interaction to your orientation presentations doesn't take a lot of time. This chapter presents a dozen ways to quickly and simply increase the level of energy in your orientation presentations, and in the orientation environment overall.

IDEA #1: DON'T JUST SAY IT—DISPLAY IT!

When introducing new terms, policies, and concepts, use a unique visual aid to make your point. For example, during an orientation discussion on the company's quality programs and philosophies, displaying a compass or outdoor thermometer with a bent needle could emphasize the terms "reliability" and "validity"—the instrument readings will be reliable but not valid.

When discussing the company's executive organizational chart, distribute papers with the names of the executives in large print to the new employees. As you discuss the executives and their roles in the organization, ask the employee with that executive's name to tape it in the appropriate position on the wall or the flip chart.

IDEA #2: LET YOUR CLOTHES DO THE TALKING

Covering OSHA safety topics? Give your presentation wearing safety glasses, a back brace, gloves, and a dust mask and carrying safety signs. Include whatever safety gear is used within your company, to emphasize points and to increase attention to the presentation.

Presenting the company's employee referral program? Create a sandwich board made from two poster boards to wear as you enter the room, with text on the boards identifying the amount of money an employee receives if he or she refers a friend who is hired by the company.

IDEA #3: LET THEM FILL IN THE BLANKS

Most companies provide a manual or guidebook in an instructor-led orientation program, and spend significant amounts of time keeping the information in the book up to date. But savvy orientation instructors can increase the employees' retention and attention, while also saving hours of course material maintenance time, by placing fill-in-blanks in various places throughout the text for the employees to complete themselves as they listen to the presentation.

Fill-in-blanks can be used for benefit information that changes frequently or for company executive names. This technique requires the employees to pay close attention to avoid missing information, and retention is increased when they write the information themselves.

For example, if an insurance premium amount changes occasionally, the orientation guide text can read, "The insurance premium amount withheld from each paycheck is $_____." The employees can then enter the current amount when they attend the orientation program.

Note: If this technique is used, it is very important for the instructor to have the fill-in-the-blank information in writing for the participants to copy. The text should be on an overhead slide or in a PowerPoint presentation or on a flip chart. This prevents the instructor from having to repeat the information multiple times as employees copy it into their books.

IDEA #4: GET ON YOUR SOAPBOX

A fun way to demonstrate a strong passion for a particular topic in orientation, such as the company's vision or values, is to literally show the audience that you are "on your soapbox" during this part of your presentation.

Purchase a large cardboard box of laundry detergent, empty the soap contents into another container, and then either flatten the box so you can stand on it without crushing it, or if you have a little extra preparation time, cut out the panels of the soapbox and glue them onto a block of wood or other hard material that will hold your weight. As you begin your presentation, hold up the "soapbox" and explain that you will be "on your soapbox" for the next few minutes, and then stand on it as you speak. Doing the unexpected will energize the class and increase their attention.

IDEA #5: ARRANGE FOR AN INTERRUPTION

Before your orientation presentation, ask someone (not one of the new employees) to sit in the room, and to stand up at the appointed time to interrupt the presentation with an issue, a comment, or a question. Or, have someone in your work group (who enjoys hamming it up) burst into the room and interrupt your presentation to make a point.

For example, employees usually select their benefits during the orientation period. Most insurance carriers do not allow these selections to be changed except during open enrollment periods.

To ensure that new employees understand when they can and can't make changes to their benefits, ask someone to burst into the room suddenly during your presentation. Have the person say, "I just *have* to make a change to my benefit selections right now!" Ask the person to really act it up, pleading and begging to make the change. When the actor is told that the changes can't be made, he or she can slink off out of the room and your presentation can go forward—but no one will forget the point that was made. This technique is virtually guaranteed to wake up anyone in the room who is even thinking about snoozing.

IDEA #6: DRAW FROM YOUR OWN HOBBIES AND INTERESTS

Adding a personal touch to your presentation can help you connect to the class participants. Draw on ideas from your own outside interests. If you enjoy golf, bring in your golf club bag and "tee off" each point as it is made by taking a swing at an imaginary ball and calling the shot as the subject of each bullet point. If you enjoy cooking, you could enter the company values as "ingredients" in a mixing bowl, stirring carefully to create a culture that is a treat for both employees and customers.

IDEA #7: CREATE A TIMED MATCHING GAME

Do you need to present information about your company's products and services? Instead of telling them about the products and services, create a timed matching game.

Create a handout that lists the company's products and services on one side of the paper, and a definition or use of these products or services on the other side. Hand them out upside down (to avoid false starts) either to individuals or to teams. Instruct the employees (before they turn the paper over) that once you give the signal, they will turn the paper over, and the first team (or individual) to correctly match all of the products and services will win a prize. After the game, review the handouts to ensure that all the employees know the correct matches. They will be more likely to remember the products and services, and the room will be energized.

IDEA #8: ARRANGE THE ROOM FOR INTERACTION AND FUN

How much of a difference does it make when people enter a room and any of the following are in place?

- Small toys are on the tables.

- Hard candies are in bowls on the tables.

- Energetic music is played as new employees arrive.

- Confetti is scattered on the tables.

- An inviting breakfast and coffee area is waiting for the employees.

- The new employees are greeted as they enter the room.

- Current employees are invited to attend the first few minutes of the orientation, to grab a bagel and to introduce themselves to new employees.

Using even one or two of these ideas adds significant energy to the room and says to the new employees, "We are glad you are here. We've prepared for your arrival, and we celebrate you as valued new employees of our company!"

Classroom table and chair arrangements can have an amazing effect on attention and energy levels. When participants are sitting in a traditional classroom style, with all tables and chairs directly facing the front of the room, and participants can't see each other, the energy level is lower. When participants are seated at round or rectangular tables and they can see each other and work in small groups, the energy level is increased.

In addition, new employees often enter a room and try to sit in an isolated seat if the room size allows it; so it is up to the facilitator to arrange the tables and chairs in a fashion that encourages employees to greet each other, sit next to each other, and have group discussions.

The lighting in a room is critical. If the room is dim for too long while you show PowerPoint presentation slides or videos, energy also begins to dim. Ideally, the lighting is arranged so that the only dim area is directly around the projection screen or the television monitor. If this is not possible, the instructor should avoid extensive use of slides or videos.

IDEA #9: CREATE A "DO IT YOURSELF" TIMELINE

Rather than just presenting the company's history or timeline, involve the employees in the process. If your orientation is more than one day in length, new employees can be solicited to research company events and the dates when they occurred.

You can arrange this in an open fashion: "Research the company's history and identify a company event that was most impressive to you and the date it occurred." As the employees arrive the next day, they can tape their contributions to a timeline on the classroom wall, and explain what impressed them about the particular events. Timeline events can be researched on the company's Internet or intranet site, or by talking with other employees, or by researching company newsletters provided by the instructor.

Or, assign a date to employees, and ask them to research a significant company event that occurred in that year. If the orientation is one day in length, provide teams with a group of papers with one company event on each, and have the teams try to arrange the events in the correct order in which they occurred.

IDEA #10: BUILD YOUR ORIENTATION AROUND A THEME OR SLOGAN

Some companies build their entire orientations around one theme. The theme is carried in the graphics on the course materials, in the name of the program, in the activities, and so forth. The theme may tie directly into the company's industry, or it may tie into the company's values or culture, or it may be a metaphor for something that is at the beginning point to make a connection to the new employee's beginning point with the company.

Having a theme for your orientation program "packages" the presentations together in a fun way, and can assist in the employees' assimilation into the culture if the theme is tied to the industry or the company's values.

IDEA #11: GROUP DISCUSSIONS FOSTER SELF-DISCOVERY

An alternative to lecture format is the group discussion. Why lecture about the differences between private and public companies when the employees can discuss this with each other? Why lecture on what is and is not sexual harassment when employees can discuss potential scenarios and determine together what is and is not a sexual harassment situation? When conducting group discussion activities, it is important to follow three steps:

1. Provide a structure or specific questions or scenarios for the groups to discuss.

2. Provide adequate time for the groups to discuss.

3. Facilitate a debriefing time for the class to come back together as a whole group to identify and record what they learned from the group discussions, to clear up any issues or outstanding questions, and to emphasize key points.

IDEA #12: OBTAIN HONEST PRESENTATION SKILLS FEEDBACK

A critical factor in the success of the orientation program is the facilitator's presentation skills, including appropriate voice volume, voice inflection, eye contact, and gestures. Your presentation should make every new employee feel included. Ideally, each new employee should feel that you are talking to him or her personally. This is basic presentation information, but it is so important to all the other presentation ideas in this chapter that it must be emphasized.

Ask a trusted friend or colleague to attend the orientation for the sole purpose of providing totally open and honest feedback—both positive and constructive—after the class. Or, have the program videotaped so you can review your skills later. Join a Toastmasters group or attend a course on delivering effective presentations to hone your skills. Even if you are an experienced presenter, it is a good idea to refresh your skills at least annually using one or more of these suggestions.

A FEW LAST WORDS OF ADVICE

There are a few potential presentation errors to avoid. First, be careful not to overdo a good thing. The method you use to energize your presentation should tie directly to your content to emphasize information, not to detract from it. It is up to the facilitator to use time effectively and to keep the program on track.

Second, it is critical to avoid using group stereotypes or exploitation in an attempt to increase attention to your presentation. References to gender, ethnicity, race, religion, or age should never be used during a presentation. Find ways to use presentation aids to build good character, enhance learning, and provide enjoyment for everyone in the process.

Dr. Eldon Rebhorn received a BS degree and an MS degree from Northern Illinois University, and he obtained his Ed.D. from the University of Illinois. Over a long career in quality education and interaction with students, he has taught courses in Industrial Arts, Technology Education, Vocational Education, and Human Resource Development. Dr. Rebhorn is Professor Emeritus of Industrial Technology Education at Indiana State University.

Contact Information   *335 South Fruitridge*
Terre Haute, IN 47803
merebhorn@aol.com

Chapter 43

And the Category Is . . . Ford History!

Ford Motor Company Introduces Its History in a Game Format

Since Ford is about 100 years old, new employees need to understand how that legacy contributes to what the company is today, and to our industry and our competitors. But why lecture about company history when new employees can discover it in teams? With this approach, both information retention and enjoyment of the learning experience increase.

Appropriate Group Size for the Activity: This activity works well with groups of any size.

Approximate Length of Time: The length of the game depends on the number of history questions provided and the complexity of the quiz. Ford Motor Company's quiz activity is 45 minutes in length.

YOU'LL NEED

- A quiz sheet for each participant (see the sample Ford quiz sheet)
- A pen or pencil for each participant

PREPARATION

The quiz questions need to be prepared in advance. The Ford Motor Company quiz is lengthy. It includes about ten pages of questions, including fill in the blank, multiple choice, true/false, and matching. It includes product sketches, vehicle pictures, and brand logos.

The quiz can include historical questions, such as when a certain product was introduced to the public, or how many items a competitor sold during a particular year. Other questions can focus on subsidiary information and other statistical data about sales, products, and consumers. It can be as simple or complex as the designer finds appropriate.

CONDUCTING THE ACTIVITY

Participants should be seated at round tables or in teams. The new employee orientation program leader gives the participants the following instructions:

a) Please take the quiz out of your participant package.

b) For the next 45 minutes [adjust the time frame according to your quiz's length and complexity], work as a team at your table to answer the questions in the quiz. Record your answers on the quiz.

c) You will be in competition with the other tables to see who can answer the most questions correctly. After you are done, we will go through the answers with you. You can begin now!

DEBRIEFING THE ACTIVITY

Debrief the quiz by reviewing the answers and providing additional information to add to the learning. It is suggested that the answers be displayed on PowerPoint or on overhead slides, and *not* be located elsewhere in the participant's manual.

Have participants call out answers, and congratulate the participant contributing a correct answer. This is a light and fun method to celebrate the company's legacy, to point out fierce competition in a particular product line, and to acquaint new employees with current issues and trends in the industry.

SAMPLE QUESTIONS FROM THE FORD MOTOR QUIZ:

1. Match the automotive company name with the year it was established.

Ford Motor Company	1903
Toyota	1935
Honda	1948
General Motors	1908
Fiat	1899
Daimler Benz	1886
	1940
	1920

2. In 1999, the automotive industry sold _____ (number) vehicles.
   a. 54,400,000 units
   b. 78,000,000 units
   c. 12,100.000 units
   d. 8,300,000 units

3. Ford has _____ (number) of plants in _____ countries on _____ continents.

   Select your answers from these numbers: 460, 1000, 380, 112, 6, 5, 3, 25, 80, 72

4. What are the top five Ford Motor Company markets?

_____

_____

_____

_____

_____

5. What were the top five selling vehicles (all makes) in the U.S. last year?

_____

_____

_____

_____

_____

6. Match the number of units sold last year to the brand.

Lincoln (US)	400,834
Mercury (US)	75,312
Volvo	625 (1998)
Mazda (equity interest sales figures)	438,000
Aston Martin	176,493
Jaguar	1,005,000

Christine R. Day is a human resource business solutions partner at Ford Motor Company's Fairlane Training and Development Center in Dearborn, Michigan. As a manager, she supports global learning and performance deployment initiatives, performance management, transformation and growth, benchmarking, and new employee assimilation strategy.

Christine has traveled extensively, taught classes, and managed programs internationally. She served as a project leader for the team that was awarded the American Society for Training and Development Automotive Industries Program of the Year. She also teaches part-time in the MBA program at Eastern Michigan University. Author of *Discovering Connections,* Christine holds a Ph.D. in organizational communications.

Contact Information   *19000 Hubbard Drive*
Dearborn, MI 48121
313-390-5052
Fax 313-390-4666
cday4@ford.com

Chapter 44

Stories in a Jar

A Continuous Energizer for New Employee Orientation Programs

Rather than concentrating all of the employee introductions up front and all at once (and in the ordinary way), this game spreads the introduction of orientation class participants throughout the day, or throughout the entire orientation program. Each introduction includes a unique story about the individual.

This method allows the employees and the instructor to more easily remember the names of each participant, because they are not being bombarded with names all at once, and because it's easier to remember someone's name when you can tie it to a story. It also provides multiple fun and quick breaks throughout the information-filled orientation program.

Appropriate Group Size for the Activity: This energizer will work for group sizes from 3 to 100. However, if the group size is more than approximately 30 people, not everyone's story will be read, but everyone will have a *chance* for their story to be read, and therefore a chance to win a prize.

Approximate Length of Time: This is not a start-and-stop activity; it is a way to add a sense of fun and energy throughout an orientation program.

YOU'LL NEED

- A glass jar that is large enough for your hand to enter (or a bowl or large glass)

- Story Strips (see the handout)

- Prizes for the best story, the funniest story, the most unusual story, etc.

- A flip chart and markers to make note of each person's name and a "title" for the story each person told

PREPARATION

Make copies of the Story Strips handout and cut each question into a separate strip of paper. Place the strips on the centers of your classroom tables so there are plenty to choose from at each table.

CONDUCTING THE ACTIVITY

1. Ask participants to find at least one Story Strip that provides an idea for a true story about themselves—stories they are willing to share with the class.

2. Give the participants a chance to jot down the basic ideas of their stories on the Story Strips. They don't need to write the entire story out.

3. Gather the Story Strips and place them in the jar.

4. Start the day with a few Story Strips. Pull a strip out of the jar, announce the name of the person selected and the basic topic of the story, and ask the person to stand up and tell the full story. Remind the class that at the end of the day, there will be prizes for the most entertaining story, the funniest story, the most unusual story, etc. As each person tells a story, write the person's name and a short title for the story on the flip chart.

5. Throughout the day, when orientation information overload starts to wear the class down, energize the class by picking a few stories from the jar, following the directions in step 4 each time.

6. At the end of the day, ask the class to applaud *every* story as you read the names and story titles from the flip chart, but ask them to clap the loudest for the story they liked best. Award prizes accordingly.

With 14 years of experience in training and development, Doris Sims was a contributor to Mel Silberman's 1999, 2000, 2001, and 2002 *Training and Performance Sourcebooks*, as well as *The Consultant's Toolkit*. Her ideas have also been published in *Creative Training Techniques* newsletters, *Training Magazine*, and *Training Directors Forum* newsletter. Doris served as a presenter at the Training Director's Forum Conference, Training '99, IQPC Employee Orientation Program Conferences, and the 1999 ASTD International Conference. Doris is a human resource development director at Alcatel. Doris earned an MS in Human Resource Development from Indiana State University in 2001.

Contact Information   *2301 Bennington Avenue*
Flower Mound, TX 75028
972-539-1649
dmsims@home.com

STORY STRIPS

Make copies as needed of these story strips and cut them out. Place several story strips on each classroom table so participants will have plenty of story idea choices.

Tell the story behind an interesting scar that you have.

Name: _____ Story Summary: _____

_____

Describe the most eccentric teacher or professor you had in school.

Name: _____ Story Summary: _____

_____

Tell us the story of something you did as a child or as a teenager that your parents don't know about, even to this day.

Name: _____ Story Summary: _____

_____

What do you hear yourself saying that your parents used to say?

Name: _____ Story Summary: _____

_____

Tell us about your pet peeve.

Name: _____ Story Summary: _____

_____

Describe an item in your refrigerator (or freezer) that is no longer edible, and tell us why it is still in your refrigerator.

Name: _____ Story Summary: _____

_____

What was the most unusual gift you ever received?

Name: _____ Story Summary: _____

_____

Describe your "15 minutes of fame" or a "brush with the famous" moment you have experienced.

Name: _____ Story Summary: _____

_____

Describe the best or the worst customer service experience you've had.

Name: _____ Story Summary: _____

_____

Describe your earliest memory from childhood.

Name: _____ Story Summary: _____

_____

Describe the worst date you've ever had.

Name: _____ Story Summary: _____

_____

Chapter 45

Orange You Going to Ask Me?

An Orientation Game Focused on Consumer Insight and Brand Perspective

 This activity focuses on the consumer and how to connect with the consumer, the purchaser of the Ford Motor products. The company wants to reinforce why this is important to every single employee, whatever their function, whatever their job. This activity is used on the "brand and consumer insight" day of the Ford orientation program.

Appropriate Group Size for the Activity: This activity works well with groups of any size.

Approximate Length of Time: 30 minutes

YOU'LL NEED

- An orange

- A flip chart at the front of the room

- Paper for participants to take notes about key points, either plain pieces of paper or a matrix included in the participant package

- Two volunteers from the orientation audience

- A subject matter expert on the topic of consumer insight or "the voice of the customer"

PREPARATION

Prepare for the activity by asking for two volunteers.

CONDUCTING THE ACTIVITY

1. Tell the participants that they are now going to learn what it means to be a consumer company and how consumer insight will help create products that delight and connect with the customer.

2. Ask the two volunteers to come to the front of the room. One is asked to be the "seller" and the other is asked to be the "potential buyer." Other participants will be observers. Ask them to take notes on the seller's approach.

3. Instruct the seller to sell the orange to the potential buyer, without asking the buyer any questions.

4. Tell the potential buyer that he or she cannot answer questions or give any indications of interest in the orange.

5. Give the seller several minutes (about 3 to 5 minutes, depending on how it is progressing).

6. At the end of the selling period, ask the seller what key selling points he or she focused on. Write these selling points on a flip chart so they can be referred to later.

7. Ask the buyer if the selling points were relevant to him or her and if the seller connected with him or her as a consumer. If so, how? If not, why not?

8. A subject matter expert (SME) on consumer insight then provides concepts and information on consumers and how to connect with them. The SME should emphasize understanding customer needs by asking questions and working to create solutions that fit the lifestyle and situation of the customer.

9. The orange selling exercise is then repeated. The same two volunteers are asked to come to the front of the room. This time, however, the other participants are allowed to help the seller develop a list of questions that might help him or her focus more on the consumer during the sales call. These questions are typically lifestyle questions that focus on how the product could fit into the buyer's lifestyle.

10. The selling portion of the exercise is repeated. This time, however, the seller is equipped with a list of questions, and the buyer is allowed to answer questions.

11. Key selling points are again listed on a flip chart.

DEBRIEFING THE ACTIVITY

Ask the question, "What changed between the first selling experience and the second one?" While debriefing the session, reinforce the importance of understanding our consumers and gathering information from them so we can design products or services to fit their lifestyles.

Listen for suggestions such as:

- How to find insight into consumer needs and desires

- What type of mind-set must exist in companies that wish to be consumer-focused

- How employees can have a passion for applying customer insight in the decisions they make every day

Make reference to other industries and how they have implemented this concept successfully. Also mention some companies that have not done this, and what has happened to them. Ask for stories from the participants regarding experiences they have had as consumers, especially regarding salespeople who have not listened to their needs or tried to understand their lifestyle and situation.

Christine R. Day is a human resource business solutions partner at Ford Motor Company's Fairlane Training and Development Center in Dearborn, Michigan. As a manager, she supports global learning and performance deployment initiatives, performance management, transformation and growth, benchmarking, and new employee assimilation strategy.

Christine has traveled extensively, taught classes, and managed programs internationally. She served as a project leader for the team that was awarded the American Society for Training and Development Automotive Industries Program of the Year. She also teaches part-time in the MBA program at Eastern Michigan University. Author of *Discovering Connections,* Christine holds a Ph.D. in organizational communications.

Contact Information   *19000 Hubbard Drive*
Dearborn, Michigan 48121
313-390-5052
Fax 313-390-4666
cday4@ford.com

Chapter 46

Customizable Bingo Review Game

A Spirited Board Game to Review Company Benefits, Policies, and More!

 This Bingo board game provides an excellent way to review information given in a new employee orientation. The dynamics of game play require new employees to recall and apply newly learned information in a timed question-and-answer sequence.

CASE SCENARIO

The two groups eyed each other suspiciously across the table. The mood was tense.

"W-e-l-l, what's your answer?" asked the Group One member who was holding a question card.

"We need more time," members of Group Two pleaded.

"You've had more than enough time," was the reply. "Now, what is your answer?"

After a quick consultation, one member of Group Two said: "It's located in the South Wing?"

There was a short pause, then a member of Team One said: "That's correct."

"Yes-s-s-!!!" chorused Group Two, followed by a refrain of cheers and high fives.

Group Two placed its chip on the game board. Now it was Group One's turn to roll the die and answer a question.

This scene was part of a three-hour new employee orientation that culminated in playing of the board game, Orientation Bingo. After two hours of presentation, the group of new hires was divided into two teams, each team seated at its own game board. The teams took turns rolling the dice and responding to questions about the orientation presentation. The first team to cover five spaces in a row was declared the winner. Each player received a baseball cap sporting the company logo. Many employees wore their prizes, their "badges of excellence," long into their tenure at the company.

To prepare for the game, the lead trainer teamed with a human resources specialist to develop 60 short-answer questions. These questions were then reproduced on cards for the game. The lead trainer noted that preparation usually took twice as long, to set up the game for play. "But, it's so-o worth it!" beamed the lead trainer. "Feel the excitement and look how absorbed they are with our information!"

Appropriate Group Size for the Activity: Four or more players. Each game board has two teams of players, 2 to 5 players per team. Larger classes may require multiple game boards, each with two sets of teams. Because of the team size and team number flexibility, this game works well for both small and large orientation groups.

Approximate Length of Time: 25 to 50 minutes

YOU'LL NEED

- One game board for each set of two teams (See the sample game board.)

- One stack of question cards for each set of two teams (See the sample question cards.)

- 20 chips for each team (Each team uses a different color set of chips.)

- One die for each team (Use a die that matches the color of the team's chips, or rotate one die between the two teams.)

- One timer (optional)

- One card reader, to cover the answer when shown to the responding team (optional)

PREPARATION

1. Prepare a series of questions concerning your company's benefits, facilities, policies, and procedures. Place these questions onto question sheets, and then cut the sheets into question cards. (If possible, laminate the question cards for durability.) Prepare one stack of question cards for each game board.

2. Make a copy of the game board provided. Laminate the game board, if possible. Prepare one game board for each set of two teams.

3. Purchase poker-style chips and 16 mm dice from your local toy store. If possible, use matching sets of chips and dice for each team, such as red chips and die for one team and white chips and die for the other team. This will simplify play.

CONDUCTING THE GAME

Game Objective: To win by covering five board spaces in a row, horizontally, vertically, or diagonally from corner to corner.

1. Form sets of two teams, with 2 to 5 new employees on each team.

2. Have each set of teams meet at its own game board.

3. Have each team select a stack of chips and matching die (optional).

4. Place a stack of cards alongside the playing board for each set of teams.

5. Instruct each team to select a team captain. The captain is responsible for stating the team's final response.

6. Select one team to go first, or have teams roll their die to select the team that will go first. (It is a competitive advantage to go first in this game.)

Game Play—Round 1

■ The first team rolls the die.

■ The first team places the die on the space that matches the number of the die. This temporarily marks the space.

■ The first team responds to a question from the card stack. The timer may be used for each team if you would like to limit the response time.

— If the team gives the *correct* answer, they cover the space by removing the die and replacing it with a chip.

— If the team gives the *incorrect* answer, they remove the die from the game board.

■ This concludes Round 1. Play now alternates to the opposing team.

Game Play—Round 2

■ The game is played the same way for all rounds.

End of Game

■ The first team(s) to complete five spaces in a row wins. Distribute prizes and congratulations!

DEBRIEFING THE GAME

Following the game play, take a few minutes to transform the players back into class participants. Most facilitators have their own method of debriefing, but you may wish to follow a debriefing process of "What?" "So what?" and "Now what?" after completing the game.

What?   This portion allows players to express their feelings about the play of the game.

What happened?

How do you feel?

So what?   This portion allows you to discuss the "moments of learning" that happened during play.

What one major idea or concept did you learn?

What critical incidents lead to insights or learning?

Now what?   This portion helps the players reflect on how the information covered in the game relates to the company.

How does this relate to our company?

What can you take back to the work site?

Steve Sugar, president of The Game Group, is a writer and teacher of learning games. Steve is the author of *Games That Teach* (Jossey-Bass/Pfeiffer), coauthor of *Primary Games* (Jossey-Bass), and coauthor of *Games That Teach Teams* (Jossey-Bass/Pfeiffer). He has written game systems used worldwide, including QUIZO, X-O Cise, Management 2000, and LearnIt! (HRD Press). *Personnel Journal, Training & Development Journal,* and *Training Magazine* have interviewed Steve about learning games.

Steve contributed chapters on game design to *The ASTD Handbook of Training Design and Delivery* and *The ASTD Handbook of Instructional Technology,* has written several ASTD Info-Line publications, serves on the Editorial Advisory Board of the *Thiagi Game Letter,* and is a frequent contributor to the Jossey-Bass/Pfeiffer *Annuals.* Steve is a faculty member at the University of Maryland Baltimore County (UMBC) and a frequent presenter at international ASTD, TRAINING, and ISPI conferences.

Contact Information   *The Game Group*
10320 Kettledrum Court
Ellicott City, MD 21042
410-418-4930
info@thegamegroup.com

ORIENTATION BINGO GAME BOARD

1	4	5	3	2
2	5	3	1	4
3	2	4	5	1
4	3	1	2	5
5	1	2	4	3

SAMPLE QUESTION CARDS:
ORIENTATION BINGO

What is the name of our Chief Executive Officer?	Name all of the company's holidays.	The company's stock is traded on the NYSE under what symbol?
How many countries are we located in?	Name one of our main competitors.	Name two of our company's products or services.
What is the name of our dental care provider?	The company began service in what year?	Who would you contact if you need help with benefits?
How many hours of sick time do you earn in your first year of employment?	On what date will you receive your first paycheck?	Where do you find information about the company's sexual harassment reporting procedure?
What is the name of our Chief Financial Officer?	If you select medical insurance, when does your coverage begin?	How many people work at our company?
Where is the facility's ATM machine located?	How many speakers gave presentations in this orientation program?	What is the company's Web site address?

Chapter 47

The Hunt for Company Policies!

Teach Basic Company Policies and Benefits Using a Scavenger Hunt Method

 While it is important for new employees to learn basic company policies, procedures, and benefits, it can be tedious and time-consuming to present all of this information in a lengthy lecture format. Some basic and easily understandable policies can be "discovered" by employees using a scavenger hunt method, in which employees receive a list of items to "find" and a time limit in which to find them. This activity will particularly appeal to the kinesthetic learner in all of us, and it can actually reduce the time needed to teach company policies, rather than lengthen it.

Appropriate Group Size for the Activity: This activity works best for a group ranging from 3 to 50 employees. However, the activity could work for a larger group if the employees work in teams, to keep the activity more manageable.

Approximate Length of Time: The length of time needed for this activity depends upon the number of policies, procedures, or benefits the employees are to find. Factor approximately 1 minute per item: If you have 20 items for the employees to find, plan 20 minutes for the activity.

YOU'LL NEED:

- One or more sources of company information for employees to "find" policies, benefits, procedures, and company products or services. There are two ways to provide this:

  1. If you want the employees to stay in the classroom, have sources in the room such as orientation workbooks, employee handbooks, brochures, pamphlets, company policy manuals, or other hard-copy materials.

2. If the employees can leave the classroom, and if your company managers support this approach, the new employees can go on an actual scavenger hunt by asking questions of current employees to see how many answers they can obtain within the time limit. This approach is ideal: It is more fun and energetic (and it keeps your current employees up to date!). But it could also be impractical, depending on the company's size and flexibility about distracting current employees from their jobs.

- Copies of the Company Policy Scavenger Hunt! handout for each employee

- Pens or pencils for the employees

- A watch or clock with a second hand

- Prizes

PREPARATION

If the employees will be walking through the facility gathering answers on their scavenger hunt, then the facilitator needs to ensure that managers and employees of each department support this plan, and that they are prepared for it. Also, the instructor needs to create an answer sheet for the handout that matches your own company policies and benefits.

CONDUCTING THE GAME

1. Refresh the employees' memories on the concept of the scavenger hunt: Participants have a list of items to find, and they normally obtain these items by going from house to house to see how many items they can gather. The participants are scheduled to meet back at the starting location at a specified time to determine who gathered the most items from the list.

2. Explain to the class that they will be participating in a Company Policy Scavenger Hunt. Then pass out a copy of the handout to each employee.

   If they are staying in the classroom, they will find the items in their orientation workbooks and employee handbooks and whatever other sources you have provided for them. If they will be leaving the classroom, they are to move through the facility (no running, of course), asking current employees to provide the "items" on the list by answering a question. Each current employee in the facility can answer only **one** question, so the new employees must move on to another current employee once they have received one answer.

3. Write the time when the game will be over on the flip chart. (Allow approximately 1 minute per item for an in-classroom scavenger hunt, and slightly more time for an out-of-the-classroom scavenger hunt, depending on the size of your facility and how much walking they will need to do.) Instruct the class that only scavenger collections that arrive at or before the time listed on the flip chart will be accepted. Explain that the employee(s) who have the most correct items within the time limit will win a prize. Then, dismiss the class (ring a bell or honk a horn if you have any sort of sound effect).

4. When the employees return, review each item on the handout to announce the correct answer. Tell the employees they are on the honor system to mark all correct answers, and that they should write in any missing information or make corrections if needed. If you promised prizes for the winner(s), identify at that point the participants who obtained the most correct answers within the time limit.

DEBRIEFING THE GAME

After the activity is complete, you can present any additional information regarding company policies that was not covered during the activity.

With 14 years of experience in training and development, Doris Sims was a contributor to Mel Silberman's 1999, 2000, 2001, and 2002 *Training and Performance Sourcebooks*, as well as *The Consultant's Toolkit*. Her ideas have also been published in *Creative Training Techniques* newsletters, *Training Magazine*, and *Training Directors Forum* newsletter. Doris served as a presenter at the Training Director's Forum Conference, Training '99, IQPC Employee Orientation Program Conferences, and the 1999 ASTD International Conference. Doris is a human resource development director at Alcatel. Doris earned an MS in Human Resource Development from Indiana State University in 2001.

Contact Information   *2301 Bennington Ave.*
Flower Mound, TX 75028
972-539-1649
doris.sims@usa.alcatel.com

COMPANY POLICY SCAVENGER HUNT!

The object of this activity is to collect the answers to the 20 questions below, within the time limit provided by the instructor. The individual or team that obtains the most answers in the shortest time period wins!

I need to return to the room by this time: _____:_____

Item #	Item Description	Answer or Items Collected
1	Name or collect three items that can be recycled in the company. (One extra point is granted if the items are actually collected).	
2	How many vacation days would a nonexempt employee receive in the first year if employment started on May 1?	
3	What is the company's dress code policy on Fridays?	
4	In an emergency situation within the company facility, what number should an employee call to get help?	
5	What is the company's intranet (internal) Web site URL address?	
6	What number should an employee call to obtain information in the event of inclement weather?	
7	How many floating holidays would an employee have if he or she began employment on February 1?	
8	Who should an employee contact to reserve a conference room?	

Item #	Item Description	Answer or Items Collected
9	What is the name of the top Human Resources manager in the company?	
10	What are the names of the medical insurance carriers employees can select from?	
11	What is the company's policy on smoking?	
12	Give one example of an inappropriate use of the company's e-mail system.	
13	Who should an employee contact to schedule business travel?	
14	Provide one example of "gross misconduct" behavior.	
15	What are the names of the dental insurance carriers employees can select from?	
16	When will you receive your first paycheck?	
17	Give an example of an employee "conflict of interest" situation.	
18	What is the name of the corporate newsletter?	
19	In what month will you receive your first annual performance review?	
20	What is the name of the life insurance carrier for company employees?	

Chapter 48

Celebrating New Talent

A Networking Activity That Celebrates the Talents of Each New Employee

One of the company values that Ford Motor Company likes to communicate through the new employee orientation is the idea that everyone in the company has valuable or unique talents. This activity, used early in the orientation program (usually on the morning of the first day), reinforces that concept. It also allows participants to meet each other and to hold short, informal discussions.

Appropriate Group Size for the Activity: This activity works well with groups of any size.

Approximate Length of Time: 20 to 25 minutes, depending on the size of the group

YOU'LL NEED

- A pen or pencil and a blank sheet of paper for each participant

PREPARATION

One of the important aspects of this activity is its simplicity. No instructor preparation is needed. It can be used as a planned activity, or as a filler while the group waits for a speaker to arrive or to begin another activity.

CONDUCTING THE ACTIVITY

1. Give the participants the following instructions:
   - For the next 15 minutes, you are asked to circulate around the room and meet five people from job functions other than your own. For example, if you work in Accounting, then you want to meet people who do not work in Accounting.

- When you meet these people, ask them their names and the following two questions:

  - "Why did Ford hire you?"

  - "What special or unique talents do you have?"

- As you are talking with each person, record his or her name and special talents on your paper.

- After you are done, we will share any interesting information you discovered about your new coworkers.

2. Now, give the word for the participants to network the room, allowing about 15 minutes. *Note:* It is strongly recommended that you also participate in the activity. This will allow you to learn about the participants personally and to connect with multiple participants as individuals.

DEBRIEFING THE ACTIVITY

Ask the question, "What special or unique talents did you discover that your new coworkers have?" Ask participants to call out answers, and celebrate each talent as it is discussed. Reinforce the concept of the value of diversity to the company, and point out how diversity can appear in many different forms.

Christine R. Day is a human resource business solutions partner at Ford Motor Company's Fairlane Training and Development Center in Dearborn, Michigan. As a manager, she supports global learning and performance deployment initiatives, performance management, transformation and growth, benchmarking, and new employee assimilation strategy.

Christine has traveled extensively, taught classes, and managed programs internationally. She served as a project leader for the team that was awarded the American Society for Training and Development Automotive Industries Program of the Year. She also teaches part-time in the MBA program at Eastern Michigan University. Author of *Discovering Connections,* Christine holds a Ph.D. in organizational communications.

Contact Information   *19000 Hubbard Drive*
Dearborn, MI 48121
313-390-5052
cday4@ford.com

Chapter 49

3-D Bingo: A Walking Tour

Turn Your Company Facility Tour into an Interactive Game!

The NASS Orientation Bingo activity is used to present factual information in a semistructured way while fostering networking and reducing any preconceived barriers between field and headquarters staff. The new employees are the "Bingo players," and receive directions and materials in a large group setting, such as in the orientation classroom, from the instructor.

The Bingo players quickly disperse to visit the organizational units and individuals—the "Bingo presenters"—who can answer the factual Bingo questions. As they enjoy refreshments provided for them, the Bingo players spend a bit of time meeting and getting to know the Bingo presenters.

The NEO Bingo activity's purpose is evident in its goals, which are:

1. To learn a maximum number of key facts related to specific headquarters organizational units, thus covering all game board squares.

2. To meet as many specified headquarters staff members as possible.

3. To become familiar with the physical office locations of specific headquarters organizational units.

4. To informally network with headquarters staff in their offices.

5. To reduce any preconceived psychological barriers between field and headquarters staff by enjoying snacks provided for participants.

Appropriate Group Size for the Activity: This activity is suitable for any manageable number of participants: minimum 10, maximum 50, ideal group size 25.

Approximate Length of Time: The activity can be conducted in as little as one hour, or expanded comfortably to two hours. The size of your facility and organization affect the time requirement.

YOU'LL NEED

- A current, updated organizational chart for each player

- A list of headquarters staff telephone numbers and office locations for each player

- A map of the headquarters office area for each player

- Prepared Bingo boards for each player

- Prizes for the players

PREPARATION

1. Review the goals outlined earlier, namely the acquisition of factual information and networking.

2. Gain the support of several organizational units and employees who are willing to spend time preparing for, meeting, and discussing basic factual information with the NEO participants.

3. In conjunction with the staff whose organizational units are involved, prepare sufficient factually based questions to have one question per Bingo square. For example, if the Bingo Board is 5 by 5, then 25 questions are needed; if the board is 5 by 6, then 30 questions are needed. Care should be taken to ensure that the questions have specific right and wrong answers, so that the debriefing will quickly identify who won by having all the correct answers. Type the questions in the boxes in small print, including the name of the person who submitted the question or from whom the answer can be obtained, along with the organizational unit designation, such as a Branch or Section or room number.

4. Because the organizational employees, called Bingo presenters, actually present the factual information in an informal casual manner, they need to be involved and motivated to play the Bingo game. Involving them early in the preparation process is a way to get them interested and excited. They can develop questions and prepare the snack menu and food. Some of our organizational units have "progressive snacking," ranging from appetizers to finger foods to desserts. Finger food or snacks are provided so the NEO Bingo players are inclined to linger longer and get to know the Bingo presenters better than they would if they simply asked a question and left immediately.

CONDUCTING THE ACTIVITY

1. Assemble the new employee participants in a large room.

2. Give them each a Bingo board, a current organizational chart, a list of headquarters staff telephone numbers and office locations, and a map of the headquarters site.

3. Describe the goal or game objective: to visit the appropriate organizational units in order to obtain the correct answer to each question.

4. Give time limits: "You have [be specific] minutes to complete this activity and return to this room."

5. Give them directions by stating or posting, the following:

"Each of you must obtain answers to all the questions on the Bingo board. You will get the answers by visiting the appropriate individuals or organizational units. Use your organizational chart and map to find the Bingo presenters and their offices and ask them the questions. Write a short form of the answer in the square below the question on the Bingo board. Spend some time discussing the questions and answers with the Bingo presenters, and get to know them as you enjoy the snacks they have prepared for you. By [give time] return to this room, having obtained answers to as many questions as possible. Your goal is to obtain answers to all Bingo board questions."

6. Release the new employees to start the activity.

DEBRIEFING THE ACTIVITY

After the NEO Bingo players return to the large classroom, the instructor has three tasks to complete:

1. REVIEW THE ANSWERS TO THE FACTUAL QUESTIONS.

Have the participants give the answers to the questions. This can be easily and quickly accomplished in a round-robin fashion by going around the table or up and down the rows. If any NEO participants are confused or have questions, clarify as needed.

2. DETERMINE AND REWARD THE WINNERS.

After the review, ask who completed all the Bingo board squares and has all the correct answers. Also, find who is missing answers and how many of them are missing. If there are a few winners and most people have some but not all of the answers, then reward the winners and give small token prizes to the non-winners. Such a result might indicate that there was insufficient time allotted to the activity, because the goal is for all Bingo players to win.

However, if most of the people have all of the answers, and just a few have missed some, reward the losers and give the small token prizes to the winners. Such a result might indicate that just the right amount of time was allotted to the activity.

3. SUMMARIZE THE LEARNING GOALS AND BENEFITS OF THE BINGO GAME.

Review the learning goals and benefits of the Bingo game, and answer any final questions.

Linda M. Raudenbush holds a BA in Mathematics and Secondary Education from St. Joseph College, an MS in Applied Behavioral Science from Johns Hopkins University, and an Ed.D. in Human Resource Development from George Washington University. Linda has more than 25 years of marketing, managing, training, and consulting experience in both private and public sectors.

Linda has been an adjunct professor at National-Louis University and Strayer University in the Washington, D.C. area, and is in her twelfth year of part-time teaching at the University of Maryland, Baltimore County. She authored a chapter of the 1996 Sage Publication, *The Adjunct Faculty Handbook;* and an article in a 2000 issue of *Human Resource Development Quarterly,* a journal published by Jossey-Bass; and coauthored an article in *The 2001 Annual: Volume 2–Consulting,* published by Jossey-Bass/Pfeiffer.

Linda has been a regular session presenter at the annual University System of Maryland Women's Conference for the last six years, and has presented sessions at other human resource development and organizational development conferences. She also consults in the HRD/OD field, and is currently and HRD/OD specialist at the U.S. Department of Agriculture in the National Agricultural Statistics Service.

Contact Information   *USDA NASS DAFO TCDO - Room 4133*
1400 Independence Ave., S.W.
Washington, D.C. 20250
202-720-6016
lraudenbush@nass.usda.gov
www.usda.gov/nass/

2000 NASS SURVEY AND CENSUS DIVISION—BINGO

1. What is the rotational scheme for Fruit and Veg Chem Use Surveys? SAB/EESS	2. Place a question pertaining to your organization here	3. Place a question pertaining to your organization here	4. Place a question pertaining to your organization here	5. Place a question pertaining to your organization here
6. Place a question pertaining to your organization here	7. What new survey will be conducted in 17 states in Jan. 2001? Brenda M.	8. Place a question pertaining to your organization here	9. Place a question pertaining to your organization here	10. Place a question pertaining to your organization here
11. Place a question pertaining to your organization here	12. Place a question pertaining to your organization here	13. Which is the leading agricultural state? CPB/CSS	14. Place a question pertaining to your organization here	15. Place a question pertaining to your organization here
16. Place a question pertaining to your organization here	17. Place a question pertaining to your organization here	18. **FREE SPACE!***	19. What does A.E.L.O.S. stand for? David H.	20. Place a question pertaining to your organization here
21. True or False: Census data collection will cost $5 million. S. Vaughn	22. Place a question pertaining to your organization here	23. Place a question pertaining to your organization here	24. Place a question pertaining to your organization here	25. Name the 3 screening surveys that were integrated in 2000. SAB/EESS

*More or fewer "Free Space" squares can be used on the game board, depending on the number of departments in the organization and the number of corresponding questions needed.

Chapter 50
Employees Meet the Values

New Employees Learn the Company Values in an Interactive Way

Many organizations list their values in their orientation program. But how many employees remember them after the program? More important, do employees understand the behaviors that are associated with each value? New employees want to know how to behave appropriately within their new culture, and a behavior that is appropriate at one company can be inappropriate at another.

The activity described in this chapter provides the time and structure for employees to really think about the company values by identifying appropriate behaviors associated with each one. It presents the company values in a fun and participatory way.

This game requires that an organization have a publicly stated (and practiced) set of (core) values. The best use of this activity is early in an orientation program, because organization values are foundational.

Appropriate Group Size for the Activity: This activity works best for a group of 10 to 40 participants, with the ideal size about 20 participants.

Approximate Length of Time: 45 minutes

YOU'LL NEED

- Overhead projector and screen
- Flip chart paper and masking tape
- Felt-tipped markers
- Post-It notes (10–12 notes per participant)
- Pens for participants
- Overhead transparency slide that lists the company values

PREPARATION

1. Arrange comfortable seating with tables, preferably in an arrangement that promotes interaction and allows easy access to walls for hanging flip chart pages.

2. Prepare an overhead transparency listing the values of the organization. (Include accompanying statements or definitions.)

3. Prepare a handout that resembles the list on the transparency, except that the list should be word processed flush left on the left half of an 8 1/2- by 11-inch sheet of paper, leaving the right half of the page blank.

4. Make copies of the handout for each participant.

5. Write each value at the top of a sheet of flip chart paper, and hang those flip chart pages around the room.

CONDUCTING THE ACTIVITY

1. Introduce the concept of organization (core) values, as well as the organization's specific values, giving a behavioral example of each.

2. Give each participant a copy of the handout that lists the company values. Ask them to fill in a behavioral example next to each value on the handout. (See the sample handout provided.)

3. Ask participants to share examples from their lists.

4. Assign each participant two or more values to work on.

5. Give each participant five to seven Post-It notes. Have participants write one specific behavior on each note that exemplifies the values that were assigned to them in step 4. Tell the participants to place the notes on the appropriate flip chart page.

6. Make more Post-It notes available to the participants and ask them to review what the rest of the participants have posted on the flip chart pages. Invite them to add other specific behavioral examples to the sheets, using the extra notes. During this time, play suitable learning music.

7. Conduct an overall review or discussion of the behaviors assigned to each value. Thank participants for their input and answer any questions.

DEBRIEFING THE ACTIVITY

Conclude the activity by making the following points to the participants:

■ They have just generated behavioral expectations for each other that aligned with the values.

■ Explain that talking about values is not just an activity held during orientation. Ongoing discussion helps perpetuate the values in the organization's culture.

■ Tell participants that their lists will be put online in a file that includes similar lists generated by other groups of new employees.

Robert Preziosi is professor of management at the Wayne Huizenga Graduate School of Business and Entrepreneurship, Nova Southeastern University. He has been training trainers since the 1970s. Robert teaches a capstone MBA course in Leadership and Values and a course in HRD to HRM students. He is a former vice president of management development and training for a Fortune 50 company. In 2000, he was named Professor of the Decade, and he has received two Torch awards from ASTD for Leadership. Robert is a frequent contributor to the Jossey-Bass/Pfeiffer *Annuals* and the McGraw-Hill *Sourcebooks*. He is also a frequent presenter at national and international conferences.

Contact Information   *Nova Southeastern University*
3100 S.W. 9th Avenue
Ft. Lauderdale, FL 33315
954-262-5111
preziosi@huizenga.nova.edu

Sample   Sample

Corporate Values Sheet

Corporate Values	Examples of Excellence (Demonstrating the Values)
1. Integrity	Consistently uphold company policies
2. Focus on Customers	Provide accurate information quickly
3. Lifelong Learning	Learn something new every day
4. Teamwork	Always be willing to lend a hand
5. Diversity	Learn more about other cultures
6. Community Service	Volunteer for Junior Achievement

Part 6

Orientation Checklists and Surveys

INTRODUCTION

Many tasks are involved in preparing for, orienting, and training a new employee. Many companies use checklists to ensure that all tasks are completed and all information is conveyed to the new employees.

In addition, many companies conduct surveys to ensure that new employees have received all the information, equipment, and introductions required to integrate them into the new company and to begin their new jobs at the highest level of productivity possible.

Part 6 contains checklists and surveys to track and measure the task completion and initial job satisfaction level of new employees. The checklists and surveys included are:

- A Manager's Checklist—Helping New Employees Succeed

- Before the Employee's First Day

- I'm New Here—What Should I Learn?

- New Employee Workstation Survey

- A 90-Day New Employee Survey

- New Employee Checklists—Before, During, and After!

- Selecting On-the-Job Trainers

Chapter 51

A Manager's Checklist: Helping New Employees Succeed

A Checklist to Help Managers Orient and Prepare New Employees

In my consulting practice, I have observed a common mistake made by organizations, which led to the creation of this checklist. Although organizations dedicate many resources toward recruiting, interviewing, and hiring the right candidate, once the new employee is on board, they don't furnish him or her with critical information quickly.

Of course, the company's HR professionals conduct an orientation or at least guide new employees through the myriad forms that must be completed. But what new employees are really hungry for is comprehensive and realistic information about what's required to perform the job. They also need a great deal of training, coaching, and other forms of assistance that can only come from the people they report to.

Therefore, I designed a checklist for use by supervisors and managers. I often conduct public seminars, revealing innovative ways to recruit and retain great employees. Because I provide this checklist at every seminar, it has received close examination and extensive discussion. As a result, I know it's a helpful tool!

Jeanne Baer is president of Creative Training Solutions

Contact Information   *1649 South 21st Street*
Lincoln, NE 68502
800-410-3178
402-475-1127
jbaer@cts-online.net
www.cts-online.net

A MANAGER'S CHECKLIST—
HELPING NEW EMPLOYEES SUCCEED

You may think that it's up to your human resource people to provide a good orientation. You're partly right—the HR staff should lead new employees through the labyrinth of company policies and benefits paperwork. They may also share the foundational information about your company—its history, mission, and contribution to the community.

But the way *you* treat these impressionable new employees is even more important. If you can't create the conditions that make them feel like a welcome part of your team immediately, you won't keep them long.

Here are ten powerful things you can do in the first few weeks of a new employee's service, to help him or her succeed.

❑ 1. **Define the job accurately and completely,** and be sure the employee understands. Although the employee saw a job description during the hiring process, it's time to go over it in detail. What does it *really* mean?

❑ 2. **Explain the new employee's role** in your department and in the company at large. Why is her work so important? What special contribution will he be making?

❑ 3. **Explain the ISO procedures** and how the employee's work will fit in with the completed product or service, if you're working on or have qualified for various ISO certifications.

❑ 4. **Explain what training and development will be available** to help him or her master skills. (Then be sure the new hire *gets* that training, as soon as possible, and be prepared to do some coaching afterward, to confirm correct performance and correct what needs to be improved.)

❑ 5. **Make sure the new employee understands emergency procedures,** what to do in case of an accident, and other safety issues.

❑ 6. **Introduce the new hire** to the people he or she will be working with—up, down, and across. Make sure you point out a "model" (a coworker who has mastered important skills) and a "buddy." The buddy can take him to lunch the first day, give her a guided tour, help train him, help her get to know others, and answer questions on all sorts of little things that come up.

❑ 7. **Help the new employee understand your unique culture.** What's the dress code? When and how do people take lunch and other breaks? When and how do they get together to meet or solve problems? How strict are policies? How involved are employees in company-sponsored athletic teams and events? Do people go out together after work?

❑ 8. **Make the job as manageable as possible,** and make conditions as predictable and controllable as you can, until the new employee gets the rhythm of his or her work in your company. Be prepared to help the new hire sort priorities, at first.

❑ 9. **Make performance standards clear,** and let the employee know how he or she is doing: Better or faster than you expected? Good enough for now? When will the quantity or quality need to match that of other employees? Be observant, so you can "catch" the new employee doing something right and comment on it, specifically! Positive feedback is a very powerful tool to motivate and reinforce; it trains the employee to give you *more* of the behavior you're looking for.

❑ 10. **If a personal crisis occurs** within these first critical weeks, don't cast the new hire out on his or her own to handle it. Be a good listener, and refer the employee to professional sources of help such as an employee assistance program.

If you do these ten things to help your new employees succeed, you'll not only create top performers more quickly, but you'll *keep* them longer, too!

Chapter 52

Before the Employee's First Day

Use This Checklist to Prepare for the New Employee's Arrival

Have you ever started a new job only to find that your computer hasn't been ordered, you have no office supplies, and the phone on your desk is still tied to a former employee in the workplace? How did that make you feel, and how productive were you until these things were resolved?

The new employee's mentor, manager, or department administrative assistant can use this checklist before the new employee's first day, to ensure that everything is ready. This increases the initial productivity of the new employee. It also helps new employees feel welcomed, because you took the time and the forethought to prepare their work space.

With 14 years of experience in training and development, Doris Sims was a contributor to Mel Silberman's 1999, 2000, 2001, and 2002 *Training and Performance Sourcebooks,* as well as *The Consultant's Toolkit.* Her ideas have also been published in *Creative Training Techniques* newsletters, *Training Magazine,* and *Training Directors Forum* newsletter. Doris served as a presenter at the Training Director's Forum Conference, Training '99, IQPC Employee Orientation Program Conferences, and the 1999 ASTD International Conference. Doris is a human resource development director at Alcatel. Doris earned an MS in Human Resource Development from Indiana State University in 2001.

Contact Information   *2301 Bennington Ave.*
Flower Mound, TX 75028
972-539-1649
dmsims@home.com

CHECKLIST—BEFORE
THE NEW EMPLOYEE STARTS

Our mission is to introduce new employees into a welcoming, caring atmosphere, by helping them to feel included in the workgroup, preparing their work area, and demonstrating that we value them as team members in our company.

❑ Distribute a memo (via e-mail or hard copy) to notify others of the new employee's start date, background, and position title.

❑ Order any new furniture or keys needed for the new employee's work space.

❑ Make sure the new employee's work space is clean.

❑ Purchase basic office supplies and place these on the new employee's desk.

❑ Place applicable reading materials—policy and procedure guides, a guide to the telephone and voice mail system—on the employee's desk.

❑ Prepare a banner or sign and place it in the employee's new work space to welcome him or her.

❑ Order computer equipment and computer supplies, if needed. If choices are available (such as desktop, laptop, or docking station computer), contact the employee before the first day to determine preferences.

❑ Order a new phone, if needed. Work with communications personnel to ensure the new phone and voice mail are tied to the new employee.

❑ Request all computer software to be purchased and loaded on the computer.

❑ Order new user IDs and passwords as needed.

❑ Prepare a "First Week" schedule of meetings, orientation classes, and tasks that the employee can refer to during the first week of employment.

❑ Communicate with building security personnel to obtain the appropriate security access for the new employee, and to ensure that security personnel are aware of the new employee's starting date.

❑ Order a corporate credit card (if applicable) for the new employee.

❑ Assign a mentor or a buddy coworker to the employee.

❑ Register the new employee for the new employee orientation program and for any other classes he or she will need to attend within the first month.

Chapter 53

I'm New Here— What Should I Learn?

Determine the New Employee's Training Needs Using Competency Charts

A new employee's orientation needs don't end after the initial orientation class. After the new employee completes the general orientation, the manager and the employee should meet to discuss additional new employee training needs, based on specific competencies for the position and the employee's current competencies.

Using a competency analysis and a personalized training plan approach for new employees creates the following positive results:

- The employee becomes more productive in a shorter amount of time.

- Training needs and solutions are identified using a planned, systematic approach, rather than a haphazard, hit-or-miss approach.

- The new employees' job satisfaction and morale increase because they feel more comfortable and confident earlier in the position, and they feel valued because their development needs are being addressed.

- Once the personalized training plans are identified for new employees, the manager's time is reduced, because new employees have plans to follow on their own; the manager should review the employees' progress toward completing the training plans at periodic intervals.

- Areas of training development needs are identified (rather than falling through the cracks), because the charts are developed for each position; the department will likely identify competencies for which there currently are no training materials available.

■ Accuracy of the transfer of information to new employees increases; without a systematic approach to training new employees on the job, the risk that they will be trained incorrectly or that they will receive misinformation is higher.

A STEP-BY-STEP APPROACH: USING COMPETENCY CHARTS TO IDENTIFY NEEDS

Use the competency charts in this chapter to identify the job functional competencies. Compare these charts to the employee's current competency set, and then develop a personalized training plan for the employee, following the steps outlined here.

STEP 1: IDENTIFY THE COMPETENCIES NEEDED FOR EACH JOB IN THE DEPARTMENT.

Before new employees arrive, the manager (working with members of the team and with the assistance of training or human resource personnel, if desired) needs to determine the Knowledge, Technical/Computer Skills, and Nontechnical Skills and Behaviors for each position in the department. This will become the "model competency chart" for each position, so it is important to include the competencies of the most highly competent employees in the department. But it is also important to include the ideas the newer, less experienced employees will have regarding "What I wish someone had taught me" when they first arrived on the job.

Ideally, a competency identification team composed of the department manager or supervisor, one or two experienced, highly competent employees, and one or two new employees should meet face-to-face to brainstorm, discuss, and finalize the competencies needed for each job function within the department.

STEP 2: COMPLETE THE COMPETENCY CHARTS TO RECORD THE DATA FROM STEP 1.

To complete the Job Functional Competency Chart provided with the information identified by the competency identification team, enter the job title, date the competency chart was prepared, and name or title of the person (or group) who prepared the chart. Then enter the description of each competency needed for the position, using the categories Knowledge, Technical/Computer Skills, and Nontechnical Skills and Behaviors to guide you.

Next, use the rating scale in the second column to determine the level of knowledge or skill needed in the position, referring to the scale definitions at the top of the chart. For example, retail employees need to have an awareness of the company's organizational structure (a level-1 training need), but they need to know the products they will be selling at a highly accurate level on a daily basis (a level-3 training need).

Then, identify the training resources that are currently available for each item. Training resources may be formal (instructor-led classes, online classes, a procedure guide, a job aid) or informal (for example, meet with Justin to obtain a demonstration, or sit with Carol while she answers customer calls). If no training resource is available and the item is a mid- to high-level priority, a training resource needs to be developed.

STEP 3: MEET WITH THE NEW EMPLOYEE TO IDENTIFY INDIVIDUAL TRAINING NEEDS.

Once the charts are complete for each job function in the department, copies can be made to use as worksheets during meetings between new employees and the manager. The manager should enter the new employee's name on each chart. Then, the manager and employee discuss each competency and the knowledge or skill level needed for the new employee's job function, and then compare that to the employee's current knowledge or skill level for that item. The manager then circles **Yes** or **No** on the chart to indicate if training is needed for that item.

After completing this exercise, the manager can summarize the training the employee needs to obtain on the Individual Training Plan Summary chart provided.

Then, with the employee's personalized training plan developed, the information can be entered into the form online. The employee receives a copy to use as a checklist as he or she completes the training plan, and the manager retains a copy. The employee can now use this customized training plan to schedule training courses, to determine coworkers to meet with to obtain specific information or skills, and to determine what to read on the job to learn policies and procedures.

STEP 4: MEET WITH THE EMPLOYEE PERIODICALLY TO REVIEW TRAINING PROGRESS.

The manager and the employee should meet at periodic intervals to discuss the new employee's progress in obtaining the training and competencies that have been identified for him or her on the chart.

STEP 5: UPDATE THE CHARTS REGULARLY.

Review and update the charts on a periodic basis, to ensure that competencies reflect the current job requirements for each position and the organization's current strategic goals.

With 14 years of experience in training and development, Doris Sims was a contributor to Mel Silberman's 1999, 2000, 2001, and 2002 *Training and Performance Sourcebooks,* as well as *The Consultant's Toolkit.* Her ideas have also been published in *Creative Training Techniques* newsletters, *Training Magazine,* and *Training Directors Forum* newsletter. Doris served as a presenter at the Training Director's Forum Conference, Training '99, IQPC Employee Orientation Program Conferences, and the 1999 ASTD International Conference. Doris is a human resource development director at Alcatel. Doris earned an MS in Human Resource Development from Indiana State University in 2001.

Contact Information   *2301 Bennington Avenue*
Flower Mound, TX 75028
972-539-1649
dmsims@home.com

JOB FUNCTIONAL COMPETENCY CHART—KNOWLEDGE

1) Enter a description for each concept an employee in this position will need to know. 2) Identify the knowledge level needed for each item to be successful in the position. 3) List the training resources available for each item. 4) Then circle the employee's current knowledge level for each item, and identify whether the employee needs training for the item. Complete this form for each job title in the department.

Department Name/Job Title: _____

Date: _____ Prepared By: _____

Employee Name: _____

Starting Date: _____

Knowledge Level Rating Descriptions:

1 = Has/needs an awareness   2 = Has/needs to use this knowledge occasionally   3 = Has/needs to use this knowledge on a daily basis

Describe the concepts an employee will need to know to perform this job	Knowledge Level Needed	List Training Resources Available	Employee's Current Level	Is Training Needed?
	1 2 3		1 2 3	Yes No
	1 2 3		1 2 3	Yes No
	1 2 3		1 2 3	Yes No
	1 2 3		1 2 3	Yes No
	1 2 3		1 2 3	Yes No
	1 2 3		1 2 3	Yes No
	1 2 3		1 2 3	Yes No
	1 2 3		1 2 3	Yes No

JOB FUNCTIONAL COMPETENCY CHART— COMPUTER SYSTEMS AND TECHNICAL SKILLS

1) Enter a description for each technical skill an employee in this position will need to have. 2) Identify the skill level needed for each item to be successful in the position. 3) List the training resources available for each item. 4) Then circle the employee's current skill level for each item, and identify whether the employee needs training for the item. Complete this form for each job title in the department.

Department Name/Job Title: _____

Employee Name: _____ Date: _____ Prepared By: _____

Starting Date: _____

Skill Level Rating Descriptions:

1 = Has/needs basic skill level 2 = Has/needs an intermediate skill level 3 = Has/needs an advanced skill level

Describe the skills an employee will need to know to perform this job	Knowledge Level Needed	List Training Resources Available	Employee's Current Level	Is Training Needed?
	1 2 3		1 2 3	Yes No
	1 2 3		1 2 3	Yes No
	1 2 3		1 2 3	Yes No
	1 2 3		1 2 3	Yes No
	1 2 3		1 2 3	Yes No
	1 2 3		1 2 3	Yes No
	1 2 3		1 2 3	Yes No
	1 2 3		1 2 3	Yes No

JOB FUNCTIONAL COMPETENCY CHART—
BEHAVIORS AND NONTECHNICAL SKILLS

1) Enter a description for each behavior an employee in this position will need to demonstrate. 2) Identify the behavioral skill level needed for each item to be successful in the position. 3) List the training resources available for each item. 4) Circle the employee's current behavioral skill level for each item, and identify whether the employee needs training for the item. Complete this form for each job title in the department.

Department Name/Job Title: _____ Date: _____ Prepared By: _____

Employee Name: _____ Starting Date: _____

Behavioral Skill Level Rating Descriptions:

1 = Has/needs basic skill level   2 = Has/needs an intermediate skill level   3 = Has/needs an advanced skill level

Describe the behavioral skills an employee will need to know to perform this job	Knowledge Level Needed	List Training Resources Available	Employee's Current Level	Is Training Needed?
	1 2 3		1 2 3	Yes No
	1 2 3		1 2 3	Yes No
	1 2 3		1 2 3	Yes No
	1 2 3		1 2 3	Yes No
	1 2 3		1 2 3	Yes No
	1 2 3		1 2 3	Yes No
	1 2 3		1 2 3	Yes No
	1 2 3		1 2 3	Yes No

INDIVIDUAL TRAINING PLAN SUMMARY

This training plan is designed for: _____

Employee's start date _____ Today's date _____ Prepared by _____

After the manager and employee have discussed and recorded the competency needs and the employee's current competency levels on each competency chart, this page can be used to summarize the information to create a customized training plan for the employee.

Description of the training to obtain	Who to contact for this training	Date and location	Knowledge/Skill level to attain	Complete training within . . .	✓
			1 2 3	First month First 90 days First Year	
			1 2 3	First month First 90 days First Year	
			1 2 3	First month First 90 days First Year	
			1 2 3	First month First 90 days First Year	
			1 2 3	First month First 90 days First Year	

If needed, make multiple copies of this form to record all applicable training needs for each employee.

313

SAMPLE: JOB FUNCTIONAL COMPETENCY CHART— BEHAVIORS AND NONTECHNICAL SKILLS

1) Enter a description for each behavior an employee in this position will need to demonstrate. 2) Identify the behavioral skill level needed for each item to be successful in the position. 3) List the training resources available for each item. 4) Circle the employee's current behavioral skill level for each item, and identify whether the employee needs training for the item. Complete this form for each job title in the department.

Department Name/Job Title: <u>Customer Service Representative</u>   Date: <u>01/01/2001</u>   Prepared By: <u>Customer Service Supervisor</u>

Employee Name: <u>Newy Newton</u>   Starting Date: <u>6/1/2001</u>

Behavioral Skill Level Rating Descriptions:

1 = Has/needs basic skill level   2 = Has/needs an intermediate skill level   3 = Has/needs an advanced skill level

Describe the behavioral skills an employee will need to know to perform this job	Knowledge Level Needed	List Training Resources Available	Employee's Current Level	Is Training Needed?
Sample Items	1 2 3		1 2 3	Yes No
The ability to listen to the customer's need or concern, and reflect it back to the customer accurately.	1 2 [3]	1. Attend the Customer Skills Program. 2. Sit with Megan and listen in on her calls.	[1] 2 3	[Yes] No
The ability to calm an angry customer and bring the conversation back to business to resolve the issue.	1 2 [3]	1. Handling Difficult Customers video. 2. Sit with Charles and listen in on his calls.	[1] 2 3	[Yes] No
The ability to predict or identify customer needs, begin the sales process, and connect the customer with the appropriate salesperson.	1 [2] 3	1. Attend the Company Products Course. 2. Read the department guide to learn the policies for handing off a potential sale.	1 2 [3]	Yes [No]

Chapter 54

New Employee Workstation Survey

This Follow-Up Survey Ensures the New Employee's Work Area Is Set Up

This survey is designed to ensure employees receive all their necessary equipment (office, phone, computer, system identification codes and passwords) on time. Idle time spent by new employees is a large liability and speaks poorly of the company. This survey attempts to track the source of the problem to identify any trends, weaknesses in the system, gaps, and flaws—so they can be corrected.

New employees complete this survey when they have returned to their office or workstation and have met with their managers. If there is a problem with obtaining their equipment, they are instructed to fill out the form and send it in. If no problems are experienced, they do not need to complete the form. Once the form is turned in, the new employee's manager is contacted to find out what the problem is, and what the anticipated time frame will be to repair it. Surveys are analyzed and plotted on a regular basis to identify any changes in trends.

SURVEY RESULTS

If employees don't receive their equipment in a timely fashion, there may be a variety of causes, and Alcatel wants to identify these so they can be corrected. For example, office space may be unavailable because a department plans to move soon. Computers can be delivered too soon before an employee begins work, be taken back, and not returned on time. An employee's paperwork can be lost in the system. Whatever the problem, this survey attempts to resolve it by pinpointing and identifying any weaknesses in the system.

From these surveys, it has been determined that equipment and workstation delays that arise are not attributable to any one cause. What could have been a blind attempt to fix a problem has become a more focused approach. A few strategy teams have sprung up to attack these problems that were so well hidden in the past.

The "New Employee Workstation Survey" was written by Adam Haddad.

Contact Information   *Joicelyn Fields*
Alcatel USA
1000 Coit Road, M/S HRD7
Plano, TX 75075
972-477-4366
Joicelyn.Fields@alcatel.com

NEW EMPLOYEE
POST-ORIENTATION SURVEY

▼
A L C▲T E L

Please complete this form no later than one week after completion of New Employee Orientation, and send it to your HR Representative in the envelope provided. Please answer "YES," "NO," or "NOT APPLICABLE (N/A)" to each question below.

Employee Name: _____

Name of Manager: _____

Name of Administrative Assistant:_____

RS 2000 Case Number: _____

Office Number: _____

Date of Hire: (mm/dd/yy)_____

(1) Division: (select one)

❑ Operations

❑ Terrestrial Network Division

❑ Wireline Switching

❑ Network Systems Group

❑ Sales/Legal/Contracts

❑ Customer Service

❑ HR/Facilities/Information Technology/Finance

❑ Wireline Access/Fixed Wireless

(2)   Building: (select one)

❑ PB1	❑ Jupiter 1	❑ 402A	❑ 414
❑ PB2	❑ Jupiter 2	❑ 405	❑ 446
❑ PB3	❑ Jupiter 3	❑ 406	❑ 2201
❑ CHB	❑ Jupiter 4	❑ 407	❑ 3905
❑ PB6	❑ Jupiter 5	❑ 408	
❑ PB7	❑ Jupiter 6	❑ 410	
❑ PB10	❑ 401	❑ 412	
❑ PB11	❑ 402	❑ 413	

	Yes	No	N/A
(3) Does your position require that you have an office?	❏	❏	❏
(4) Did you have an office when you arrived at your building?	❏	❏	❏
(5) Does your position require that you have a PC?	❏	❏	❏
(6) Did you have a PC upon completion of the orientation?	❏	❏	❏

(7) If no, were you told when you would receive it?

❏ 1 week   ❏ 2 weeks   ❏ 3 weeks   ❏ 4 weeks

	Yes	No	N/A
(8) Did you have access and passwords to the necessary profiles and accounts needed to perform your job?	❏	❏	❏

(9) If no, were you told when you would receive your profiles and accounts?

❏ 1 week   ❏ 2 weeks   ❏ 3 weeks   ❏ 4 weeks

	Yes	No	N/A
(10) Does your position require that you have a workstation?	❏	❏	❏
(11) Did you have the proper workstation upon completion of the orientation?	❏	❏	❏
(12) If no, were you told when you would receive a workstation?	❏	❏	❏

❏ 1 week   ❏ 2 weeks   ❏ 3 weeks   ❏ 4 weeks

	Yes	No	N/A
(13) Does your position require that you have a telephone?	❏	❏	❏
(14) Did you have a telephone upon completion of the orientation?	❏	❏	❏

(15) If no, were you told when you would receive a telephone?

❏ 1 week   ❏ 2 weeks   ❏ 3 weeks   ❏ 4 weeks

	Yes	No	N/A
(16) Were your e-mail and voice mail passwords provided to you?	❏	❏	❏
(17) Did you meet your supervisor immediately following the orientation?	❏	❏	❏
(18) Were you introduced to your department Administrative Assistant?	❏	❏	❏
(19) Were you given a tour of your immediate work area (the restrooms, break room, copier and fax machines, fire extinguishers, and mail room)?	❏	❏	❏
(20) Was your office clean?	❏	❏	❏
(21) Did you receive any office supplies?	❏	❏	❏

(22) What else would you like to see included in the New Employee
　　　Orientation?

_____

_____

_____

_____

(23) Additional Comments:

_____

_____

_____

_____

_____Thank You!_____

Chapter 55

A 90-Day New Employee Survey

Determine a New Employee's Satisfaction Level during the First 90 Days

The primary reason DeRoyal, a provider of over 25,000 medical supplies and services, decided to implement 90-day new employee surveys was to determine how well the orientation program was working. Did the orientation provide the information and connections new employees needed on the job? DeRoyal felt it was a basic follow-up action to evaluate the time and effort expended on the employees. Orientation does not stop after the first three days of our specific program. In a sense, all employees continue to be oriented with DeRoyal as both long-term and new employees. This survey helps us to pinpoint retention strategies.

Retaining employees is a major cost reduction area for companies today, and finding out if the employees have had a pleasant experience in their first 90 days can help the company build on that progress going forward. The Human Resources department didn't want to throw our new employees to the wolves, so to speak. We want to remain a constant resource for employees throughout their careers by continuously evaluating our services to ensure we are meeting their needs. (As a side note, the employees also complete a one-page survey after our three-day orientation program to evaluate specifics about the orientation program.)

SURVEY LOGISTICS

Every new employee who has been employed with us for 90 days completes this survey. The Human Resources department distributes the survey and collects all responses. We ask that the surveys remain anonymous to help obtain candid feedback.

Once the data is collected, it allows everyone involved in the new hire orientation process to review what our positive influences are and what improvements may need to be made. As a result, we have obtained many new ideas and improvement suggestions for our orientation program.

As an example, based on feedback from the survey, we have restructured the manager's role as part of the new employee's orientation. These changes include holding the manager responsible for preparing the employee's basic tools needed to perform the job (computer, phone, voice mail, paper, pens, etc.). We now have the managers begin this process a week prior to the employee arriving, rather than waiting until the employee arrives.

Another example relates to our benefits presentation and enrollment process. At DeRoyal, we have a 90-day benefits enrollment waiting period. Benefits are explained during the first three days of the program, but the employees requested a more in-depth explanation of our company benefits, as well as an additional enrollment meeting conducted closer to their specific benefit eligibility date. In response, we created a new in-depth explanation that is now conducted at the three-day orientation, and update meetings are being considered for employees to attend closer to their eligibility dates for the benefits program.

Employees are told in the three-day orientation program that they will receive this survey during their first 90 days, so they are aware of the company's expectation that they complete this survey. This is a great way to be connected to the employees and to keep in touch with their needs.

SURVEY RESULTS

As already mentioned, we have made several improvements to the employee's first 90 days of employment based on survey results. The first 90 days of a new job are stressful enough; we don't want to create any additional stress for employees because they don't have the tools and information necessary to do their jobs.

The first 90 days are pivotal to new employees who are still questioning whether they made the right job move or career decision. Creating an open-door policy with candid feedback and a comfort level with our employees is a main goal of the company and of the HR department. These surveys give us a window to what is happening in individual departments, and they help ensure that our new employees feel welcome and a part of the team.

Rebecca Harmon is director of corporate human resources at DeRoyal. Rebecca received her bachelor's degree in Psychology with an emphasis in Industrial Organizational Psychology from the University of Tennessee. Rebecca joined DeRoyal in 1997, where she is responsible for all hiring practices, for ensuring compliance with all federal contract guidelines, and for facilitating employee relations. Rebecca served as a presenter at the 2000 International ASTD Conference.

Contact Information   *200 DeBusk Lane*
Powell, TN 37849
865-362-2341
rharmon@deroyal.com

CONFIDENTIAL
90-DAY NEW EMPLOYEE SURVEY

Please take a few minutes to complete this survey with regard to your first few months of employment. Please be constructive in your feedback, whether it is positive or negative. We strive to make continuous improvements in our orientation process! Your information will be very valuable in achieving this goal.

Please rate the following questions from 1 to 5,
with 1 being the *least* effective and 5 being the *most* effective.

Prior to your first day of employment, did you receive all the
information needed for a successful first day?   1   2   3   4   5

Please explain what was most helpful and if any information was missing.

_____

_____

_____

_____

Do you feel you received a proper explanation of our benefits
to help you make educated benefit selection decisions?   1   2   3   4   5

If not, please explain.

_____

_____

_____

_____

In your department, did your supervisor or team leader
introduce you to your coworkers, discuss your job responsibilities
and the department policies, and make you feel comfortable?   1   2   3   4   5

If no, please explain and list ideas for change.

_____

_____

_____

_____

After the orientation program, was your workstation set up at
least within 5 working days?   1   2   3   4   5

Phone   1   2   3   4   5

Computer, ID, Passwords   1   2   3   4   5

Workstation Furniture   1   2   3   4   5

List any suggestions to enhance this process:

_____

_____

_____

_____

In your opinion, have you received adequate training and
resources to do your job effectively?   1   2   3   4   5

If no, please give suggestions on improving this.

_____

_____

_____

_____

Did your new team members welcome you, and were they
a good resource for you?   1   2   3   4   5

Please explain.

_____

_____

_____

Now that you have been with the company for 90 days,
how do you feel about your career decision?   1   2   3   4   5

Please explain.

_____

_____

_____

_____

How did you feel about the hiring process?

Overall	1	2	3	4	5
Interview with Human Resources	1	2	3	4	5
Interview with Department Manager	1	2	3	4	5
Compensation Package	1	2	3	4	5

What attracted you to our company?

_____

_____

_____

_____

What attracted you to your new position?

_____

_____

_____

_____

Please use this space to make any other comments or suggestions regarding your hiring process, new hire orientation, job-specific training, and your overall company experience.

_____

_____

_____

_____

_____

_____

Thank you for your time and assistance with this survey. Your input is greatly appreciated and will help us to continuously improve our employment and orientation process.

Please return your completed survey to Human Resources.

Chapter 56

New Employee Checklists— Before, During, and After!

Use These Checklists at Multiple Sites to Ensure a Consistent Orientation

Wyndham International has developed a new employee orientation program called Beginnings. Beginnings is designed to be facilitated by each hotel for its newly hired employees. To make the process an easy one and to improve consistency across all hotels, the design team felt the need to create a series of checklists to be used prior to, during, and after the actual orientation day. Once a signed copy of the required checklist is placed in the employee's file, it becomes a mechanism by which files can be audited by regional HR staff.

The checklists in this chapter can be used to 1) ensure that everything is prepared before the employee arrives, 2) ensure that all topics are covered during orientation, and 3) assess the employee's understanding and evaluation of the topics covered after orientation.

The Human Resources director or the Beginnings facilitator typically uses these forms. However, the checklists were also designed to be used by the department head at the employee's site, if the property has no on-site Human Resources department. The forms tie into the three phases of Beginnings: 1) upon hire, 2) during the orientation program, and 3) post-orientation day.

SURVEY RESULTS

The feedback on the forms has been overwhelmingly positive. Users cite the ease with which they can use the forms. Of particular note is the ability they have to customize them for a specific hotel. From a consistency standpoint, our regional Human Resource Development personnel have seen a marked increase in the consistency of employee files—that is, all required forms are now being included in the employees' files, whereas prior to Beginnings, it was hit-or-miss.

THE "BEFORE" WYNDHAM ORIENTATION SURVEY

The Pre-Orientation Checklist is designed to help prepare for the employee before his or her arrival. When preparation is completed by the employee's first day, productivity is increased and the employee feels valued and welcomed into the company.

This survey may be completed by the new employee's manager, the department administrative assistant, or the person who will be the new employee's buddy, whoever is most appropriate in your company and situation.

PRE-ORIENTATION CHECKLIST

"The more we are prepared . . . the more favorably impressed the new employee will be . . . first impressions are lasting ones!"

Here is a checklist of things that need to happen **after** the new employee accepts the job offer, but **before** the first day of work.

Employee _____   Date of Hire _____

TASK TO BE COMPLETED	ASSIGNED TO	INITIALS	DATE COMPLETED
Name tag is made			
Uniform is fitted (if possible/applicable)			
Parking card or parking pass arranged			
Passcards, keys made			
Employee is set up in the system (if applicable)			
Office/desk/work area is set up with supplies			
Schedule for first week/pay period is prepared by immediate supervisor welcoming employee to include:			
Letter/phone call			
Welcome			
What to wear on first day			

TASK TO BE COMPLETED	ASSIGNED TO	INITIALS	DATE COMPLETED
What to bring with them (identification, tools, or equipment)			
Who will meet with them			
What the Orientation Day will include			
What their start and finish times will be on the first day			
An offer to answer any questions			
Letter/memo is sent to manager scheduling employee for Orientation Day			
Letter is sent inviting employee to Orientation Day			
CONDUCT THE FOLLOWING IF ORIENTATION IS NOT ON THE FIRST DAY OF WORK			
New Hire paperwork is completed (complete new hire checklist)			
Uniform is provided			
Mini-tour of property is conducted			
Standards of appearance are reviewed			
House rules are reviewed			

Completed by _____ Date _____

THE "DURING" NEW EMPLOYEE ORIENTATION CHECKLIST

The Right Way Checklist is to be completed during a meeting between the new employee and his or her manager, on the employee's first day. At properties where human resource or training personnel are available, some or all of these topics may be covered in a group session.

The purpose of this checklist is to ensure that all legal, safety, benefits, and company procedure information is covered, without an item being forgotten. This process also helps to ensure a consistent delivery of information across a large number of remote locations. In addition, completing all items on the checklist will ensure that the employee's file contains all the necessary forms and paperwork.

THE RIGHT WAY, THE WYNDHAM WAY
NEW HIRE ORIENTATION CHECKLIST

To be completed by the Department Manager
and the New Employee on the first day of employment

Employee's Name _____   Starting Date __/__/____

Pre-Employment Procedures	Mgr. Initials	Pre-Employment Procedures	Mgr. Initials
Applicant Evaluation Form		Driver's Record Check	
Driver's Application		Employment Application	
Drivers Drug Test Policy (CDL)		Reference Checks—two minimum	

New Hire Paperwork	Mgr. Initials	New Hire Paperwork	Mgr. Initials
Blank Performance Appraisal		Job Description(s)	
Cash Handling Policy*		Personnel Action form (PAF)	
Drug-Free Workplace Policy		Safety Rules—Departmental	
Driver's Responsibility form*		State Tax Withholding form*	
Employee Resource Guide (House Rules, Employee Guide, Standards of Appearance)		State Disability (California Only)*	
EEO and Emergency Contact Sheet		Tip Declaration*	
Harassment-Free Policy		Uniform Issuance	
House Bank Contract		Vesting Service form	
I-9 form with supporting documentation		W-4 Federal Tax Withholding form	
Insider Trading Policy (2)		Workers' Compensation Facts (California only)*	

* If applicable

Review of Policies/ Procedures/Benefits	New Hire Initials	Review of Policies/ Procedures/Benefits	New Hire Initials
Attendance/Call-in procedures		Locker: Assignments/Packages/ Inspections	
Bloodborne Pathogens		Pay cycle (days, time)	
Bulletins/Announcements		Personal phone calls/beepers	
Comp./Discounted Room Nights		Performance Reviews	
Coaching, Counseling & Discipline		Problem Solving/Open Door	
EAP Brochure (attending future benefits & 401(k) meetings)		Quality of Service Incentive	
Employee of the Month		Reporting to Work/Scheduling	
Employee Bonus Referral		Review Standard Operating Procedures/Standards of the Week	
Employee Meal Sign-up/ Cost/Payment		Safety Bingo/Poker	
Employee Break Periods/Room		Safety/Accident Reporting	
Employee Entrance/Parking		Use of Time Clock	
Emergency Procedures		Vacation/Holiday/Sick Time	
Haz Com—Department Specific		Wyndham Way/WynStar	
Hotel tour/Introductions			

_____   _____

Employee Signature   Date

_____   _____

Department Manager Signature   Date

Remember: The employee's and manager's initials indicate that these topics have been reviewed *prior to* the formal orientation class.

THE "AFTER" NEW EMPLOYEE ORIENTATION CHECKLIST

The Post-Orientation Checklist is to be completed during a meeting between the new employee and the human resource representative (or the employee's manager, department mentor, or buddy), to evaluate the employee's knowledge of the orientation performance objectives.

This provides a checkpoint to identify any information that the employee is not completely familiar with, and it provides another opportunity to impart information and fill any gaps that may be discovered during the meeting. It is also another checkpoint to ensure the employee either has attended or has registered for other required initial training courses.

POST-ORIENTATION CHECKLIST

Employee Name: _____   Hire Date: _____

Department: _____

#	Item	Employee Initials	HR Initials
1.	ERG: Review the employee's Employee Resource Guide to verify all appropriate materials were added, i.e., the RightStart Training Check List, Training Workbooks, Job Description and Performance Appraisal.		
2.	The employee understands and can explain the basic components of "The Wyndham Way."		
3.	The employee understands and can explain the performance review process.		
4.	The employee understands and can explain the process for problem resolution.		
5.	The employee has successfully completed applicable RightStart Training.		
6.	The employee has reread and understands the rules and regulations and standards of appearance.		
7.	The employee has been trained and understands emergency procedures, accident procedures, MSDS, and Bloodborne Pathogens procedures.		
8.	The employee is currently scheduled for or has attended Benefits Training.		
9.	The employee is aware of the current incentive programs that apply to his or her position.		
10.	The employee is scheduled for 90-day performance review and is aware of the appointment.		
11.	The employee understands and can explain rate of pay, pay date, and how to resolve questions about pay.		
12.	The employee completed Customer Service Module I.		
13.	The employee completed Customer Service Module II.		
14.	The employee completed Empowerment Training.		
15.	The employee has completed or is scheduled for Be the Brand training.		

Document the required follow-up actions in the spaces below:

Description of Follow-Up Action	Target Completion Date

Completed by:_____   Date Completed:_____

THE "AFTER" NEW EMPLOYEE EVALUATION

The Post-Orientation Interview is to be completed during a meeting between the new employee and the human resource representative. This process should *not* take place between the new employee and his or her manager, because the employee may not feel comfortable providing candid feedback in that situation.

The purpose of this evaluation is to take a reading regarding how the employee feels about his or her integration into the company, and to measure the level of satisfaction with the new position, department, manager, and initial training. This provides both positive and constructive feedback to those who are responsible for the orientation process, to reinforce what the company is doing well to orient new employees and to identify where opportunities for improvement may lie.

POST-ORIENTATION INTERVIEW

Dear Human Resources Representative: To obtain feedback regarding the new employee's overall work experience, discuss the following topics verbally with the new employee. Ask the employee to rate each topic from 1 to 5, with 5 being the highest rating.

Employee Name:_____ Hire Date: _____

Department: _____

Topic	Rating	Comments
Overall rating of supervisor	1 2 3 4 5	
Quality of tools and supplies to properly complete your job duties	1 2 3 4 5	
Job expectations met	1 2 3 4 5	
Effectiveness of initial training and orientation (departmental, customer service, etc.)	1 2 3 4 5	
Effectiveness of initial job training	1 2 3 4 5	
Communication within your department	1 2 3 4 5	
Communication within the hotel	1 2 3 4 5	
Overall work environment	1 2 3 4 5	

Do you have any suggestions or comments regarding how we can improve as an employer, and/or how our initial training program can be improved?

_____

_____

_____

_____

Completed By: _____ **Date:** _____
                  Human Resources Representative

Steve Schuller is director of training for Dallas-based Wyndham International, one of the largest hotel management companies in the world. A recognized leader in the company's human resources department, Steve is responsible for the development and administration of training programs for Wyndham International's 300-plus hotels and 32,000 employees. Steve received his bachelor of arts degree from Cornell University's School of Hotel Administration in Ithaca, N.Y.

Current initiatives include the implementation of an advanced customer service training program as well as a leadership development program for all Wyndham-branded hotels. Steve is also involved in the development of global training programs for all Wyndham International employees, including a new employee orientation program, a supervisory development class, and a series of management development modules.

Contact Information   *1950 Stemmons Freeway, Suite 6001*
Dallas, TX 75207
214-863-1616
Sschuller@Wyndham.com

Chapter 57
Selecting On-the-Job Trainers

Use This Checklist to Identify Department On-the-Job Trainers

Training will continue for new employees after the general orientation program, whether formal training exists or not. If planned training programs do not exist for a job function, department managers can either 1) train all employees themselves, 2) select an experienced employee to serve formally in a training role in the department, or 3) allow training to take place in a random and possibly inaccurate or incomplete manner.

If the manager chooses to select an experienced employee in the department to serve as an On-the-Job Trainer (OJT), the selection process should be considered carefully. If the OJT trainer is not successful in this role, the OJT trainer's job satisfaction could plummet and a valuable employee could be lost. Also, the employees the OJT trains may have low morale, inaccurate training, or incomplete training.

The checklist in this chapter can be used to assist in the selection process of an OJT trainer. The ideal candidate will have most, if not all, of the competencies and attributes listed.

With 14 years of experience in training and development, Doris Sims was a contributor to Mel Silberman's 1999, 2000, 2001, and 2002 *Training and Performance Sourcebooks,* as well as *The Consultant's Toolkit.* Her ideas have also been published in *Creative Training Techniques* newsletters, *Training Magazine,* and *Training Directors Forum* newsletter. Doris served as a presenter at the Training Director's Forum Conference, Training '99, IQPC Employee Orientation Program Conferences, and the 1999 ASTD International Conference. Doris is a human resource development director at Alcatel. Doris earned an MS in Human Resource Development from Indiana State University in 2001.

Contact Information *2301 Bennington Ave.*
Flower Mound, TX 75028
972-539-1649
dmsims@home.com

ON-THE-JOB (OJT)
TRAINER SELECTION CHECKLIST

Check each item that applies to the On-the-Job Trainer candidate you are considering or interviewing. The more "yes" answers you have for a candidate, the more likely the candidate will be a successful on-the-job trainer.

The OJT Candidate's Name: _____

❏ Is the candidate enthusiastic about becoming an on-the-job trainer within the department?

❏ Does the candidate demonstrate a high level of job function competence and knowledge within the department?

❏ Does the candidate enjoy working with and talking with people?

❏ Has the candidate's manager clearly defined and communicated the role and responsibilities of the on-the-job trainer in the department?

❏ Has the candidate's manager demonstrated support of the on-the-job trainer function, by reducing the candidate's normal job responsibilities and by providing a realistic amount of time for the candidate to spend developing training materials and training new employees?

❏ Has the candidate's manager added the on-the-job trainer responsibilities of the candidate as a job performance objective, to be measured on the candidate's annual performance review?

❏ Does the candidate have at least intermediate word processing software skills?

❏ Can the candidate type at least 35–40 words per minute?

❏ Does the candidate have any previous training experience?

❏ Does the candidate have previous experience writing procedures or training materials? (Review writing samples, if available.)

❏ Has the candidate demonstrated a high level of accountability and follow-through on other assigned projects?

❏ Does the candidate understand the importance of the role of the on-the-job trainer, including the role he or she will play in reducing errors and turnover in the department? Will the candidate be able to measure results of the training in these terms?

❏ Is the candidate already seen as a leader or a knowledgeable and respected mentor in the department?

The Orientation Oracle Answers Your Questions

Part 7 is designed to answer the most frequently asked questions about new employee orientation.

PREVENTING ORIENTATION INSTRUCTOR BURNOUT

Dear Orientation Oracle,

We hold new employee orientation frequently. What can we do to keep the instructors from becoming bored and burned out from teaching the same things over and over?

Signed,

Burdened with Burnout

Dear Burdened,

First, orientation instructors should continuously try new ideas and methods of teaching the orientation program to keep themselves interested. Try alternating different games and activities weekly or monthly to keep it exciting for both the instructor and the students.

Also, it is ideal to have at least two people who can conduct the orientation program, so they can alternate and back each other up in case of instructor illness or a scheduling conflict, and to avoid a situation in which one person is conducting orientation frequently.

Troy Van Houten of Micron Technology, Inc. says, "We have a rotational schedule for our team of instructors, which helps prevent burnout. We also have two people in orientation—one acting as a lead, and one acting as a helper. Throughout any given month, you could be in any one of three roles during orientation: You may not teach it at all, you may be leading the orientation, or you may be helping in orientation."

Instructors can also take heart by remembering that even though the material may seem redundant to them, it is new to the employees. Even though you have presented the company's benefits hundreds of times, new employees are interested in making the most of their benefits and making good benefit choices. New employee orientation instructors should never apologize for a topic or section of the orientation they think is boring. Doing so is a sure way to set expectations of boredom!

Christine Day of Ford Motor Company adds, "Get people who love to teach. Those people don't worry about burnout because they already understand that it is a new audience each time."

Also, try bringing in different speakers to present various sections of the program (although there should always be one main facilitator who is the "glue" and the leader of the program at all times). This provides variety for the students and a break for the orientation instructor.

PREVENTING ORIENTATION PARTICIPANT BOREDOM

Dear Orientation Oracle,

Some of the employees seem to be bored in my orientation program—some of the information I have to provide is so tedious. What I can do to avoid participant boredom?

Signed,

Tired of Employees Nodding Off

Dear Tired,

Review three main components of the orientation program to alleviate the boredom problem.

The first component is the methodology used to deliver information. Review the ideas in this book, especially the orientation games and activities, to increase the interactive nature of your program. No one likes to sit and listen to presentations all the time. Participation is key to reducing or eliminating boredom, and it also increases retention of information and skills learned. Change the methodology as frequently as possible: Use table exercises and discussions, videos and games to vary the delivery method frequently.

The second component to review is the presentation skills of the orientation instructor and the subject matter experts. Of course, if basic presentation skills need some improvement, such as making eye contact, voice volume, voice inflection, and appropriate gestures, this is the first area to concentrate on. The orientation presenters should all receive training on delivering effective presentations. An ideal method is for presenters to join a local Toastmasters group, which is inexpensive and highly effective.

Beyond ensuring that presentation skills are top-notch, consider these issues as well:

- **Smile and project positive enthusiasm** about the company and the topics you are covering. If you do not project how much you enjoy working for the company yourself, your presentation will be flat. Remember, one of the purposes of orientation is to alleviate any new job remorse and to help the employees feel good about the choice they made. Your job is not just to impart information, but also to continue to sell the merits of the company to the new employees.

- **Work to build rapport with the new employees** as you are presenting information. This cannot be achieved from behind a podium, so I recommend eliminating a podium from the room. Ask the employees questions; learn their names and use their names when you talk with them; share something about yourself. It's your job to make employees feel special and valued as they enter the company.

  Building rapport with employees and getting to know them also makes every class interesting to you, because each class will have its own personality, and each person in the class has a different style, talents, and personality. Also, you will be seen as a role model in the company: When employees see you, they will remember you from the orientation program. You are lucky to be able to meet every new employee in the company!

- **Don't appear to be bored yourself.** Remember that even though you have presented your information many, many times, this is the first time each group is hearing it. Disney employees present the same show multiple times each day; how would it be if they started becoming robotic in their shows? Guest satisfaction would drop. Every time I've been to Disney World, I've felt that the Cast Members are excited about what they are doing. They never project boredom with doing the same show again. This is a model to use as we present orientations week after week and month after month!

Never indicate that any part of the orientation program is boring, and never apologize for anything being boring. If it is boring, change it instead of apologizing.

The final component to consider is the new employees' own responsibility for participation in the program. They bear responsibility to engage their minds in the program, and to start their new jobs with a positive attitude. Christine Day of Ford Motor Company advises orientation program leaders introducing the program on the first day to tell the participants, "This program is an interactive learning experience. If you are bored, then you need to think harder about what the speaker is saying—how it relates to serving the customer, how it relates to your job, and how it relates to your department's issues. Ask the speaker questions and engage *yourself*."

EVALUATING AND DEMONSTRATING THE IMPORTANCE OF ORIENTATION

Dear Orientation Oracle,

How can I evaluate my orientation program and demonstrate the importance and return-on-investment of our orientation program to our senior managers?

Signed,

Searching for Proof

Dear Searching,

Of course, obtaining and reviewing the ratings and comments from course evaluation sheets is an excellent way to review the thoughts of your customer base—the new employees—and to continuously improve your program. Here are additional ways to obtain evaluations and return-on-investment documentation:

1. Christine Day of Ford Motor Company shares a method: "Keep in constant touch with the supervisors receiving the new employees from your orientation program. What differences do they see? How would they value that? Can they quantify it? For example, a supervisor providing comments about Ford's REV orientation program felt an employee who completed the program was two years ahead of employees who did not attend the training, in terms of understanding the company, the ability to get things done, and knowing company processes and how they were integrated."

2. If you have not already implemented an orientation program, take a baseline measurement now to determine how much time, effort, and cost is associated with getting employees to sign up for their benefits on an individual basis. You may find that the company is even covering the employees' premiums until they complete their paperwork. Benefits paperwork is handled much more efficiently and quickly if an orientation program is in place, so the company will likely save money in terms of both time spent by benefits personnel and fewer premiums that the company picks up until the registration process is complete.

3. Try using pre- and post-assessments to conduct a level-two evaluation of the learning that takes place in the classroom. This is especially a good idea for required training such as safety procedures, or to test product knowledge, industry knowledge, and employment law knowledge (in management orientation). If you are concerned about adding more stress to a new employee's life, use an anonymous approach. Using this approach, employees don't put their names on their assessments, and you simply measure the average score of the total group on the pre-test, compared to the average score of the total group on the post-test.

4. Have the employees demonstrate what they learned in the orientation program by having them complete actual tasks. For example, have them correctly set a table according to a restaurant's specifications, or balance a cash drawer against receipts, or complete a task on a computer.

5. Compare the first year turnover rate for new employees who complete orientation to the rate for those who don't. Or, if you have not yet implemented an orientation program, take a baseline measurement now to record the turnover rate of new employees in the company, and take another measurement in a year of the same population. Talk to your Human Resources manager to determine the cost of hiring and training new employees, and multiply that figure by the fewer numbers of employees who left the company in the first year after your program was implemented, in order to determine a return-on-investment for the company.

6. Conduct an "It's a Wonderful Life" evaluation of your orientation program: If you weren't there to facilitate orientation, how would the orientation process take place? How many people would need to be involved in the process of benefits administration, teaching new employees about company policies and processes, and so on? A cost savings can be associated with the number of personnel hours saved due to the efficiency of orienting new employees as a group.

7. Use a 90-day survey process to further evaluate your program (a sample is included in Part 6, Orientation Checklists and Surveys). The information you will receive from this survey will be different from what you learned in the evaluation conducted immediately after the class. Employees will report any areas of confusion that they still experienced on the job after the orientation, which the orientation facilitator can review to determine how this information should be added to the orientation process. You will receive comments and ratings that show the value the employee received from the orientation, and what he or she was able to apply on the job.

KEEPING ORIENTATION MATERIALS UP TO DATE

Dear Orientation Oracle,

How can I keep my orientation training materials up to date with current executive names, key business statistics, and phone numbers without hours of maintenance work each month?

Signed,

Fed Up with Updating

Dear Fed Up,

Consider using blanks in your orientation training materials for employees to fill in the current information. Rather than giving out an organizational chart with all the names filled in, consider providing an organizational chart that is the correct size and structure, and having the employees fill in the boxes on the chart as you display their names on your PowerPoint slide and discuss their positions in more detail.

Instead of saying the company has 1,500 clients and trying to keep that figure updated in the book, enter a sentence that says, "XYZ Corporation has _____ clients in the U.S. and Canada." The employees can fill in the blank as the facilitator discusses this information. (The facilitator should also show the information on a PowerPoint slide to ensure that accurate information is copied into the new employees' books.)

This approach will not only save you time maintaining the book, it will increase retention of information for the employees. They will follow along more closely with the discussion, and writing the information themselves will help them to remember it.

Christine Day of Ford Motor Company says, "We change our material (update, revise, add, delete, tweak) every single session. That is why we use PowerPoint slides and not huge participant manuals. This fresh material also keeps the teachers fresh."

ORIENTING A SMALL NUMBER OF EMPLOYEES

Dear Orientation Oracle,

We have only a few new employees every month, at the most. How can I use the ideas in this book to make my program more interactive, when there are only a few people to interact with in the classroom?

Signed,

Orienting Small Numbers

Dear Orienting,

First, many of the games and activities in this book can be used for fewer than 10 people. The group size is indicated on the first page of each activity, so look for the ones that will fit your group size.

In addition, it may be appropriate for you to have a fairly brief orientation for new employees as they join the company in order to sign up for benefits and handle payroll tasks and then have a more comprehensive program monthly or quarterly (or every six months or even annually) to cover company strategy, culture, values, products, services, and customers. Then the group will be large enough for you to integrate many interactive exercises and games into the program.

This approach also may be more beneficial to employees, because it will allow them to meet more people, and it may be a more efficient use of the orientation facilitator's time. The U.S. Department of Agriculture uses this approach (see Chapter 23). They have an annual residential program that brings together all the new employees hired that year (in their case, the program is for professional-level employees only) for an interactive and comprehensive program.

ORIENTING EMPLOYEES IN REMOTE LOCATIONS

Dear Orientation Oracle,

We have employees in remote locations, and we can't afford the travel cost associated with having them come to the corporate orientation program. What can we do to provide an orientation program for them and to help them feel part of the company?

Signed,

Reviewing Remote Possibilities

Dear Reviewing,

There are many ways to provide orientation for remote employees without incurring travel expenses:

1. Prepare training materials, a leader's guide, and videos for managers of the remote locations to conduct orientation programs. (Read about Red Lobster's "Take the Plunge!" program in Chapter 21, which follows this format.)

2. Prepare online orientation information that employees in remote locations can access through your company's intranet site or other electronic means, combined with meetings with local personnel. (See the Champion Laboratories Case Study in Chapter 17 for a description of this format.)

3. Use a self-study approach using hard copy materials, combined with coaching by the new employee's manager right at the site. Both the employee and the manager use a workbook to walk them through the orientation material. (See Chapter 22, Self-Directed Orientation Modules, for a description of this format.)

4. Use a train-the-trainer approach to select personnel at the local site to learn to be trainers for that location, using materials prepared by the corporate office. (See Chapter 16 on Kahunaville's POW! Program, which follows this format.)

Other companies also use distance learning videoconferencing or live training through a Web site as additional options to provide orientation training for their new employees at remote sites.

INTERPRETING COMPANY CULTURE IN THE ORIENTATION PROGRAM

Dear Orientation Oracle,

How can we integrate a sense of (and a commitment to) our company's culture and values in the program?

Signed,

Committed to Company Culture

Dear Committed,

Many of the contributors to this book have shared their methods of not only including company culture and values in their orientation programs, but focusing on them in the program. Review Kahunaville's and Red Lobster's programs (Chapters 16 and 21) to see how they focus on these topics in orientation.

Also, try using the Mission or Vision Telephone Game in Chapter 33. This is an activity that helps your new employees learn the mission or vision statement in a highly interactive and fun way.

Many companies have a video of the president, chairman, or CEO of the company, presenting his or her thoughts on the focus, strategy, values, and core competencies of the company.

Other companies have top executives appear on a rotating basis to give a live presentation to the new employees, to ensure one of them can always be there to present as a top leader of the company.

Some companies have executives attend an orientation luncheon, to meet and talk with the new employees on a more informal basis.

If it is important to you to include a strong sense of the company's culture and values in your orientation program, it is critical to have this presentation delivered by your top leader(s) in some format. People have a need to make a connection with the leaders of the organization in order to form a stronger commitment to the organization.

ORGANIZING ORIENTATION MATERIALS

Dear Orientation Oracle,

We give so much "stuff" to our employees during orientation—forms to fill out, brochures and booklets from insurance carriers, internal marketing materials, and newsletters. How can we organize the material so it is easier for the employee to handle and refer to after the orientation program?

Signed,

Saturated with Stuff

Dear Saturated,

There are many ways to organize all the materials given to new employees, and with new technology available to us, some of the material can be available to employees through electronic means, rather than through paper means.

First, organize your paper materials. Here are ideas that can be used to make sense of the materials employees refer to during class and when making benefit decisions:

■ Order canvas bags with your company's mission statement printed on them. Employees can use these bags to carry their brochures and orientation materials around.

■ Create a checklist of the forms each employee will need to turn in by the end of the orientation program, if applicable. This will help the employee to stay organized and to keep track of the forms.

■ Some companies send the benefit forms, the brochures, and the physician directories directly to the employee's residence before employment with the company begins. Many of these companies include a video to explain the benefit choices, and the employee is requested to make benefit selections before starting work or soon after the first day.

This approach eliminates both large amounts of materials and paperwork from the orientation classroom and the time that would normally be spent in the orientation program on benefits. Of course, if this approach is used, there needs to be some forum for employees to ask questions about their benefits.

■ Place all of the materials and the orientation workbook pages into a binder, rather than passing out loose information throughout the class. The binder can serve as a reference book when the employee returns to the job.

Some companies prepare the binder of materials and information prior to the orientation program, and others provide an empty binder at the beginning of the program (preferably with preprinted tabs to identify major topics, and with a pocket at the front of the binder for brochures). Then, materials that are passed out during orientation are three-hole punched, so employees are always placing current materials in their binders.

Second, think about transferring some of the material that is distributed in orientation to the company's intranet site, or to a CD-ROM if an intranet site is not available. As Christine Day of Ford Motor Company says, "Put it on the Web! This way, you can update it frequently, and the 'stuff' they got in orientation is not outdated in a month or so. Then, it is critical to keep the Web site current!"

ADDRESSING ORIENTATION ATTENDANCE

Dear Orientation Oracle,

We have an excellent orientation program and the majority of our employees attend it and benefit from it. However, some of our managers don't send their employees to the program. What ideas do you have for ensuring that all employees attend?

Signed,

Anxious about Attendance

Dear Anxious,

There are many ways to reduce or eliminate this problem. Use one of the ideas listed here or a combination of them to alleviate this problem.

1. Structure the registration process directly through the human resource recruiter—not through the department managers. If possible, schedule employee starting dates in conjunction with orientation dates, so that all employees, through the direction of their recruiter, attend orientation on their first day.

2. Meet with the manager(s) who are not sending their employees to orientation. Listen to their concerns and reasons for not sending employees to orientation, and work to address these issues. Sometimes managers are not aware of what is covered in the program, or they may have misconceptions about the program that can be clarified, or you may receive helpful feedback and ideas to make it easier for all managers to send their employees to orientation.

3. Obtain testimonials from managers who support your orientation program, and post an article in the company newsletter or on the company's intranet discussing the program and including the testimonials, so other managers can learn about the benefits of the program from their peers.

4. If applicable, ask the managers who are not supporting the program well to serve as subject matter experts in the orientation program. Sometimes, getting people involved resolves this issue.

5. Appeal to the bottom-line reasons for sending employees to orientation:

   • If employees are prohibited from attending a program to learn about and sign up for benefits in a time frame that is consistent with company policy and with the rest of the employees, this could potentially lead to a litigation risk. There is a business risk whenever compensation or benefits are discussed with employees in a manner that is inconsistent with company policy and procedure for the organization.

   • Prohibiting or ignoring orientation sends a very negative message to new employees. It lowers initial motivation and productivity, and increases turnover statistics of employees within the first year of employment.

   • Employees need to attend orientation to learn about other company policies to protect the company from security breaches, potential sexual harassment issues, safety issues, and other legal and ethical issues. Again, business risk is increased when employees are uninformed, especially when the employer cannot show that the employee received training on these topics.

6. If none of the previous ideas work, and if top management supports your orientation program, track the attendance of employees in the orientation program by department, and send a report of non-attendance by name and sorted by department manager categories to top management.

THE LENGTH OF YOUR ORIENTATION PROGRAM

Dear Orientation Oracle,

What is the ideal length for an orientation program?

Signed,

Thinking about Time

Dear Thinking,

There is no one ideal length for an orientation program, and the length of existing programs within U.S. corporations varies widely—from companies with no program at all to companies that provide weeks of orientation and initial job functional training. A common scenario is for an organization to have a general orientation program for all employees to attend that lasts from one to two days. Then, the employee is trained for a specific job function. Some companies require safety training for employees as part of their orientation programs, due to the products they produce and OSHA requirements associated with them.

Ideally, the length of an orientation program is determined by the content that needs to be covered. The program designer determines the topics and objectives of the program, which will be different for each company. (See Chapter 13, The New Employee Orientation Shopping List, to assist you with your needs assessment and topic selection process.) The program designer then determines the specific content needed for each objective, and decides on the presentations, activities, table discussions, and videos that will be used to cover each objective. A time is associated with each piece of the program, and an overall length is determined from the addition of each piece. The time frame is fine-tuned after a pilot program is delivered.

PREVENTING NEW EMPLOYEE INFORMATION OVERLOAD

Dear Orientation Oracle,

We need to cover a lot of information in our orientation program. How can we prevent new employees from experiencing information overload?

Signed,

Worried about Weary New Employees

Dear Worried,

First, employees will be able to retain more information if they are not sitting still and listening to lecture after lecture. Include a variety of teaching methods, and try to switch to a different method every 20 to 30 minutes, but at least every hour. There are so many teaching methods to use in addition to presentations—consider small group discussions, videos, games, role plays, and scenario exercises.

Try to vary the classroom environment for the new employees. Include a tour of the facility (ideas for creative tours and a scavenger hunt are included in Part 5). Troy Van Houten at Micron Technology, Inc. moves the group to different rooms with different instructors as often as every 2 to 3 hours, if classroom resources are available. If possible, have the group move to a different location for lunch.

Consider topics that can simply be provided in the form of reference materials for the employee, rather than covering them in detail in the orientation program. For example, the instructor can simply tell the class that information about the company's inclement weather policy and hotline phone number are on the company's Web site or in the employee handbook, without going into detail.

Consider dividing the orientation into two parts. Benefits and other immediate information can be covered weekly in a brief session for a small number of new employees, and a larger session can be held monthly to cover company culture, values, products, and services. In this way, the employee is not bombarded with all the information on the first day, and it may prove to be a more efficient use of the orientation facilitator's time.

Finally, make sure you are providing enough breaks for the new employees, and that the breaks are long enough for the employees to refresh and regroup.

SEPARATE ORIENTATIONS FOR EMPLOYEES AND MANAGERS

Dear Orientation Oracle,

We are designing an orientation program for the first time, and we are wondering if we should have separate orientation programs for employees and for managers or one program for both.

Signed,

In a Quandary

Dear Quandary,

The answer to this question will ultimately depend on the purpose and content of your orientation program. However, the majority of companies have an orientation program for employees of all levels to attend together, and some companies also have an additional orientation program for managers to attend in addition to (but not in place of) the general program. Normally, the management orientation program contains information that managers will need to know to conduct their job functions, such as how to process an employee status change, the company's performance appraisal process, and merit increase procedures.

See Part 4 of this book for Management Orientation information and ideas.

Having a foundational orientation program for all levels of employees to attend together has the following advantages:

- Managers have the same need to learn about their benefits, company culture, and policies as any other employee.

- Managers need to see the orientation that employees are receiving.

- Having a combined program to deliver information that is common to all levels of employees is the most efficient use of time for the orientation facilitator and for any subject matter experts involved in the program.

- A common program promotes teamwork and communication between managers and employees.

Executives may have unique orientation needs. See Chapter 27 to learn how a major hospital transitions its executives into the workplace.

Index